JUSTIFYING VIOLENCE

New Approaches to Conflict Analysis

Series editor: Peter Lawler, Senior Lecturer in International Relations, Department of Government, University of Manchester

Until recently, the study of conflict and conflict resolution remained comparatively immune to broad developments in social and political theory. When the changing nature and locus of large-scale conflict in the post-Cold War era is also taken into account, the case for a reconsideration of the fundamentals of conflict analysis and conflict resolution becomes all the more stark.

New Approaches to Conflict Analysis promotes the development of new theoretical insights and their application to concrete cases of large-scale conflict, broadly defined. The series intends not to ignore established approaches to conflict analysis and conflict resolution, but to contribute to the reconstruction of the field through a dialogue between orthodoxy and its contemporary critics. Equally, the series reflects the contemporary porosity of intellectual borderlines rather than simply perpetuating rigid boundaries around the study of conflict and peace. *New Approaches to Conflict Analysis* seeks to uphold the normative commitment of the field's founders yet also recognises that the moral impulse to research is properly part of its subject matter. To these ends, the series is comprised of the highest quality work of scholars drawn from throughout the international academic community, and from a wide range of disciplines within the social sciences.

PUBLISHED

Christine Agius
Neutrality, sovereignty and identity: the social construction of Swedish neutrality

Eşref Aksu
The United Nations, intra-state peacekeeping and normative change

M. Anne Brown
Human rights and the borders of suffering: the promotion of human rights in international politics

Anthony Burke and Matt McDonald (eds)
Critical security in the Asia-Pacific

Lorraine Elliott and
Graeme Cheeseman (eds)
Forces for good: cosmopolitan militaries in the twenty-first century

Greg Fry and Tarcisius Kabutaulaka (eds)
Intervention and state-building in the Pacific: the legitimacy of 'cooperative intervention'

Richard Jackson
Writing the war on terrorism: language, politics and counter-terrorism

Tami Amanda Jacoby and
Brent Sasley (eds)
Redefining security in the Middle East

Jan Koehler and Christoph Zürcher (eds)
Potentials of disorder

David Bruce MacDonald
Balkan holocausts? Serbian and Croatian victim-centred propaganda and the war in Yugoslavia

Adrian Millar
Socio-ideological fantasy and the Northern Ireland conflict: the other side

Jennifer Milliken
The social construction of the Korean War

Ami Pedahzur
The Israeli response to Jewish extremism and violence: defending democracy

Maria Stern
Naming insecurity – constructing identity: 'Mayan-women' in Guatemala on the eve of 'peace'

Virginia Tilley
The one state solution: a breakthrough for peace in the Israeli–Palestinian deadlock

Justifying violence

Communicative ethics and the use of force in Kosovo

NAOMI HEAD

Manchester University Press

Copyright © Naomi Head 2012

The right of Naomi Head to be identified as the author of this work has been asserted by her in accordance with the Copyright, Designs and Patents Act 1988.

Published by Manchester University Press
Altrincham Street, Manchester M1 7JA, UK
www.manchesteruniversitypress.co.uk

British Library Cataloguing-in-Publication Data is available

ISBN 978 1 5261 1698 7 *paperback*
ISBN 978 0 7190 8307 5 *hardback*

First published by Manchester University Press in hardback 2012

This edition first published 2017

The publisher has no responsibility for the persistence or accuracy of URLs for any external or third-party internet websites referred to in this book, and does not guarantee that any content on such websites is, or will remain, accurate or appropriate.

Printed by Lightning Source

CONTENTS

Preface — vii
Acknowledgements — ix
Abbreviations — xi
A note on terminology — xii

Introduction — 1

I READING KOSOVO: LEGITIMACY AND JUSTIFICATION

1 Locating Kosovo and legitimacy   21

2 Putting out the fire while the coals still burn: Kosovo prior to 1999   44

3 Communicative action in International Relations   77

II COMMUNICATIVE ETHICS AND THE USE OF FORCE

4 The Habermasian project: dialogue as normative grounds and object of critique   105

5 The communicative imperatives   133

6 Applying the communicative imperatives: debating Kosovo   157

7 Conclusion   190

Bibliography — 202
Index — 231

PREFACE

One of the most fundamental concerns in contemporary international politics remains the justification for the use of force. The conditions regulating the use of force have been the subject of much historical investigation in the disciplines of Law, Theology, Philosophy, and International Relations (IR). This work has examined the moral and legal bases of the use of force and the manner in which it should and has been applied. The aim of this book is not to develop further substantive restraints for the use of force but to investigate the manner in which claims to the legitimacy of force are voiced and articulated by those who wield instruments of violence. This project initially began as a much more substantive exploration of criteria for the use of force for humanitarian purposes in what was both a personal and academic concern over the moral dilemmas posed by genocide and ethnic cleansing in the 1990s. My realisation that this did not address the problem of the ultimately political nature of the interpretation of such criteria led to a shift in focus to the type of justifications offered by actors who claimed legitimacy for the use of force, and specifically to a study of those justifications in the context of NATO's controversial military intervention in Kosovo in March 1999.

Given that NATO acted without an explicit mandate from the UN Security Council, what is at stake in the debates over the rights and wrongs of intervention in Kosovo remains in large part an issue of legitimacy. Recognised as a crucial discursive battlefield, legitimacy emerges at the heart of the debate surrounding justifications for the use of force in international politics. This book makes the case that legitimacy cannot be conflated with either the moral or legal positions normally called upon to justify actions and persuade others of their rightness. Indeed, legitimacy embraces not only moral, legal, and constitutional justifications, but, at its core, has a communicative dimension. *How* we make and evaluate arguments – an ethics of communication – bears heavily on the degree of legitimacy secured for particular justifications for the use of force.

Nowhere has such a procedural focus on communication and justification been articulated more comprehensively than in the critical theory of Jürgen Habermas and his theory of communicative action and discourse ethics. Habermas's influence contributes a critical and normative orientation to this study in that it seeks both understanding and emancipation. The subject of considerable debate in social and political theory, communicative ethics has more recently been drawn on in IR. Retaining the notion of a 'regulative idea', adhered to by its leading proponents, Habermas and Karl-Otto Apel, I build on existing conceptions of communicative ethics as a way to interrogate the justifications for the legitimate use of force. This secures a critical communicative dimension to legitimacy which calls for reflection on and the transformation of communicative practices in international politics.

Having interpreted Habermas's model of discourse as a principle of legitimacy rather than a concrete institutional design, it is clear that practical political dialogues and debates take place under a variety of conditions and constraints. Consequently, the ability to identify different forms of constraints on practical discourse, such as exclusion or coercion, offers access to a powerful account of legitimacy. An application of communicative ethics to the justifications for the use of force which enabled the decision to intervene in Kosovo reveals a narrative which runs counter to and unsettles conventional interpretations of the 'illegal but legitimate' nature of NATO's intervention. Communicative ethics offers criteria for deciding which constraints are legitimate in international politics and which are not. Such a theoretical perspective seeks to foster real spaces for dialogue which offers political alternatives to coercive or military action in situations of conflict which are precluded by the traditional paradigms of International Relations.

In a study oriented to a critical evaluation of communication, it would be surprising if reflections on my own use of language had not emerged and I would like to add a final word to readers. The research for this project has been undertaken within the fields of International Relations and Critical Theory during which time I have encountered multiple audiences and varied vocabularies. Despite the conceptual discomfort which has occurred at times, these encounters have greatly enriched my thinking and have been woven together in my conceptualisation of communicative ethics. While similar language often appears in both disciplines, it is at times the case that it means different things. In this instance, readers will know that many terms and concepts which form the bread and butter of one discipline may be perceived somewhat more hazily by others. I have tried, as much as possible, to alleviate such problems of interpretation but, where necessary, I would invite readers to engage with both sides of the disciplinary coin.

ACKNOWLEDGEMENTS

I would like to voice my thanks to those friends and colleagues who, in various ways, have accompanied me along this journey. Thanks must go to those in the School of Politics and International Studies at the University of Leeds, where this book took its first shape during my PhD. I would like to thank Jason Ralph both for his constructive interventions as a supervisor which made me think harder, and for his later support as a colleague. I would also like to thank my friends and fellow PhD students at Leeds who provided lasting friendship, frequent entertainment, and much support throughout.

I would like to thank the Department of International Politics at Aberystwyth University which provided a second and hugely influential institutional and intellectual home during the period of my ESRC Postdoctoral Fellowship. Thanks must also go to the ESRC for their financial support (Grant PTA-026-27-1979) and the opportunity this provided to focus on developing my research. I would also like to thank the Department of Politics at the University of Glasgow where this book was finished, during my first year there. The very warm welcome of my colleagues and the space granted to complete the project made a difficult task much easier. I would also thank the editorial team at Manchester University Press whose patience and support saw this project through to completion.

One other institution has contributed importantly to the development of this book. Nansen Dialogue Network made it possible for me to visit Kosovo in 2006 and the generosity and warmth of their staff in Pristina and Mitrovica was hugely appreciated. Moreover, Nansen's own dialogic methodology has been a source of theoretical reassurance and practical inspiration to me. The work they and others do in the field of conflict transformation has fuelled my own belief in the intimate and inescapable relationship between critical theory and practice.

I would like to thank Vivienne Matthies-Boon whose fortuitous and timely intervention at a conference in 2004 has led to a lasting friendship and intellectual partnership. Viv has been a source of reassurance and a dialogical partner as I endeavoured to find my way along the complex path of Habermasian discourse ethics. I am indebted to Viv, Robert Fine, Karin Fierke, and Cian O'Driscoll for their willingness to read and comment on various draft chapters along the way, as well as many others who have wittingly or otherwise contributed through discussions at conferences where ideas contained in the book have been presented.

The influence of two friends and colleagues in particular permeates every

Acknowledgements

page of this book and has produced intellectual partnerships which have substantially enriched and shaped my thinking. It is no exaggeration to say that, while any mistakes or flaws remain my responsibility, without the frequent and provoking discussions with Ricardo Blaug and Nicholas Wheeler, this would not be the same book.

Ricardo has been supervisor, mentor, friend and colleague throughout the evolution and transformation of this book, and his personal and professional input has invariably gone above and beyond the call of duty. In the spirit of critical theory, he has been invaluable in providing a critical, reflective and, at times, inspirational interlocutor. I am greatly indebted to his unwavering faith both in the PhD project and in me as an academic and I am extraordinarily grateful to him for his support and encouragement over a number of years.

Entering the process somewhat later when I arrived at Aberystwyth, Nick offered a stimulating and challenging counterpoint from International Relations. His knowledge of the discipline and willingness both to listen and to question has shaped the conceptual and structural development of the book and opened intellectual doors. I am grateful for his support and belief in the book, his willingness to read and comment on the whole draft and his contribution to the title, *Justifying Violence*.

Finally, thanks must above all go to my family who have been unstinting believers in my ability to start and finish this book. Their belief in the value of education shaped the path which led me to first consider doing a PhD and the financial support provided by my parents and grandparents during the PhD permitted me to begin this journey. It is to my parents, without whom none of this would have been possible, that I dedicate this book.

ABBREVIATIONS

CDHRF	Council for the Defence of Human Rights and Freedoms
EC	European Community
ECCY	European Community Conference on Yugoslavia
EU	European Union
FRY	Federal Republic of Yugoslavia
ICG	International Crisis Group
ICISS	International Commission on Intervention and State Sovereignty
IICK	Independent International Commission on Kosovo
IR	International Relations
KLA/UÇK	Kosovo Liberation Army/Ushtria Çlirimtare e Kosovës
LBD	United Democratic Movement
LDK	Democratic League of Kosovo
LPK	People's Movement of Kosovo
NAC	North Atlantic Council
NATO	North Atlantic Treaty Organization
NGO	Non-governmental organisation
OSCE	Organization for Security and Cooperation in Europe
SFRY	Socialist Federal Republic of Yugoslavia
UN	United Nations
UNICEF	United Nations Children's Fund
UNTANS	United Nations Temporary Authority for a Negotiated Settlement
WHO	World Health Organization

A NOTE ON TERMINOLOGY

It is necessary to explain the terminology used due to the plurality and political nature of language in Kosovo. When referring to inhabitants of Kosovo I refer to 'Kosovo Serbs' or 'Kosovo Albanians' to distinguish between ethnicities. From time to time I also employ the term 'Kosovar' which means 'Kosovo Albanian'. Personal names are given in the relevant language or as published. Kosovo, as the name of the geographical territory during the conflict, is also contested. Serbs refer to it as 'Kosovo-Metohija', whilst Albanians refer to it as 'Kosova'. For uniformity I will refer to it throughout as 'Kosovo'. This does not indicate a position on the issue of Kosovo's political status either during the conflict or since its declaration of independence in 2008. Serbian is used for place names although, once again, this does not indicate a position on language policy in Kosovo.

Introduction

> By narrowing the space for dialogue you create a boxing ring.
>
> Alexsander Baljak[1]

The dilemma of humanitarian intervention

THE MORAL DILEMMA posed by humanitarian intervention[2] and represented by the need to 'avert a humanitarian catastrophe' in Kosovo in 1999,[3] is frequently translated into a binary dichotomy for action: either we intervene militarily in cases of supreme humanitarian emergency[4] or we do nothing. When justifying their actions or inactions in such cases, states cannot avoid the need to legitimate their positions in the public sphere, a process undertaken through offering justifications which draw on legal and moral reasoning. Despite the moral imperative to act, framing the situation in terms of military action or inaction 'limits the capacity of international law to develop adequate responses to post-Cold War security and humanitarian crises'.[5] While the dominant justification invoked by NATO that the recourse to force in Kosovo was a 'last resort' was unquestionably powerful in the face of the humanitarian crisis which existed on the ground, it also served to make it significantly harder to contest the terms of the public debate.

The criterion of 'last resort' forms part of the just war tradition's *jus ad bellum* and played an important role in justifying the shift to the use of force in 1999.[6] In the context of non-consensual use of force for humanitarian purposes, the International Commission on Intervention and State Sovereignty (ICISS) defined last resort as follows:

> Every diplomatic and non-military avenue for the prevention or peaceful resolution of the humanitarian crisis must have been explored ... This does not necessarily mean that every such option must literally have been tried and failed: often there will simply not be the time for that process to work itself out. But it does mean that there must be reasonable grounds for believing that, in all the circumstances, if the measure had been attempted it would not have succeeded.[7]

'Last resort' should not be mistaken for an objective standard. Indeed, as will be argued, it is precisely the intersubjective nature of such a criterion which requires the further consideration of communicative ethics and political judgement when there remains disagreement over whether last resort has in fact been reached. The argument made here is not that last resort *cannot* be reached, but that in the case of Kosovo, an interrogation of the decision-making process through the lens of communicative ethics reveals missed opportunities for productive dialogue and illegitimate 'communicative practices' which challenge the contention that it had been reached.[8] Thus, legitimacy and its relationship with communicative practices integral to processes of justification reach to the heart of our concern.

Re-reading Kosovo: legitimacy and justification

Investigating the quality of the justificatory process and the character of the communicative practices which shape the decision-making process enables an evaluation of the claims to legitimacy for the use of force articulated by actors in the public sphere. It is argued that much of the IR literature which addresses the relationship between legitimacy and the use of force makes the category error of conflating legitimacy criteria with particular substantive moral and legal principles. Taking its inspiration from the 'communicative turn' in social and political theory and applications of these ideas to the field of IR, the book argues for the need to develop the communicative dimension of legitimacy beyond existing accounts which are predominantly found in relevant strands of the constructivist literature.[9] First, it will be argued that the validation of claims to legitimacy can only be established through intersubjective processes of argumentation; a proposition accepted by constructivists and Habermasians alike.[10] Second, this process requires that a communicative dimension to legitimacy be grounded in a critical theoretical account of communicative ethics which offers a procedural lens through which to interrogate *and evaluate* such claims to legitimacy.

The 'communicative turn' counters dominant perceptions in IR that it is material power which governs the international realm. Language, from this perspective, is constitutive of our social and political world. As Inis Claude wrote, the 'obverse of the legitimacy of power is the *power of legitimacy*'.[11] Those scholars who seek to conceptualise a communicative dimension to legitimacy with reference to a critical theoretical account largely do so through the lens of Jürgen Habermas's theory of communicative action. Drawing on the critical and emancipatory nature of Habermasian critical theory, I argue for a *critical communicative dimension* to legitimacy which moves beyond existing constructivist and critical approaches and is secured through the theoretical framework of communicative ethics. The latter refers to a critical-normative theoretical approach which is informed by but not synonymous with Habermas's theory of communicative action and discourse

Introduction

ethics. Building on the debates over communicative ethics in critical and social theory, it advances a critical and normative framework relevant to questions concerning the legitimate use of force in international politics.[12]

Communicative ethics is the methodological and conceptual backbone of a critical communicative dimension to legitimacy. It secures critical leverage for both spectators and political actors/participants which stems from the theoretical premises underpinning communicative ethics and the recognition of the implication of immanent claims to legitimacy voiced by actors in the public sphere. At the heart of communicative ethics is what I call the 'communicative imperatives'. The latter provide a set of criteria enabling us to operationalise the insights derived from the wider theoretical position. The empirical target of the communicative imperatives are communicative practices: specific moments of communicative interactions (notably the offering of justifications) between various actors in the public sphere which can be held up to the ethical lens established by the communicative imperatives. Hence, the communicative imperatives enable a critical evaluation of claims to legitimacy through a focus on particular communicative practices. While 'communicative' retains specific meaning when applied to the terms indicated above, 'dialogue' is used in the book as a broader term to allude to those interactions which take place when people talk to each other in negotiations, Security Council meetings, private meetings, and so on. Recognising the complexities of empirical reality, dialogue encompasses practices which represent varying degrees of strategic and/or communicative action.

Chapter 1 sets out the nature of the problem which was posed by the armed conflict in Kosovo and identifies the strengths and, crucially, the limitations of the way in which English school theorists of international society have responded to issues raised by the use of force for humanitarian purposes.[13] Within international society theorising, the question of humanitarian intervention has been extensively debated between the so-called pluralist and solidarist camps.[14] These approaches are focused on because they are concerned with order and justice, legality and morality in international politics; these were key discourses drawn upon by actors to justify or oppose intervention in Kosovo in March 1999. Two concepts in particular are examined which speak to pluralist and solidarist concerns: 'good international citizenship', and the 'responsibility to protect' doctrine developed by the International Commission on Intervention and State Sovereignty (ICISS).[15] Common to both concepts is a concern over the implications for legitimacy of the inclusionary and exclusionary practices established by the construction of moral and political boundaries. Although good international citizenship and the responsibility to protect doctrine recognise the necessity for the public offering of justifications in order to legitimate action, these justifications are generally framed in moral and legal terms. Thus, while advocates of these concepts acknowledge a communicative dimension to legitimacy – the dynamics and legitimating functions of communication and language – this is not usually located in critical theoretical accounts of communicative ethics which are sensitive to the (de)legitimating functions of practices of inclusion and exclusion.

Chapter 2 draws attention to the broader temporal and historical context surrounding the decision to use force for humanitarian purposes in Kosovo. Intervention never takes place on a blank canvas. Yet all too often, the moral imperative to 'do something' erases our ability to reflect upon how we arrived at this position. It serves to shift the focus from a consideration of the degree to which states may be held accountable for their prior actions or inaction and shifts the consideration of responsibility solely to the moment of crisis and the immediate need to protect human rights.[16] By and large, writing on the Kosovo intervention has focused on the period 1998–99, with less consideration of the international dimension to the conflict prior to 1998. The period prior to 1998 is usually only considered in order to provide a particular interpretation of the political history of Kosovo.[17] As Alex Bellamy observes, this suggests that there was no international dimension prior to 1998. Despite the fact that 'this proposition itself presupposes a decision (made by influential states and international organisations) that the conflict should not be seen as an international one prior to 1998, it is also factually inaccurate'.[18] Consequently, by failing to consider the debates and key issues before 1998, it might appear that the conflict which broke out took the West by surprise. A closer look at the preceding period indicates that this is far from the truth and that the refusal – in and of itself a form of action – to place the simmering and predictable conflict in Kosovo on the international agenda earlier, paved the way for the situation which broke out in 1998.

In addition to limited engagement by the international community prior to 1998 and a history of varied engagement throughout the earlier wars in the former Yugoslavia, there was a series of missed opportunities for creative political engagement particular to Kosovo which will be examined in more detail. Furthermore, while attention is frequently paid to significant international events like the 1995 Dayton Accord, more often ignored is the non-violent political action by citizens within Kosovo and Serbia which, if supported, might have yielded political alternatives. Certainly, the existence of these political activities and the international reaction to them casts doubts upon the essentialised, pre-given ethnic identities attached to those involved by the international community and, significantly, the language of last resort used to justify the strategic shift to military intervention in a situation cast in oversimplified, black and white terms. Anne Orford has remarked in relation to economic and development policies that 'surprisingly little attention has been paid to the presence and activity of international institutions and agencies in countries prior to the outbreak of violence, ethnic cleansing or genocide'.[19] In other words, humanitarian crises do not emerge out of nowhere – they have a history which often involves both engagement by and exclusion from the international community. Intervention in these crises must be understood to take place from the context of this history, rather than allowing the language of emergency and exception to enable the moral arguments for humanitarian intervention to be separated from our, at times, egregious involvement with these countries, their leaders, and elites. Communicative ethics sensitises us to the kind of practices which enable particular discourses to become dominant and to the practices of exclusion which serve to marginalise actors or discourses.

The missing piece of the jigsaw: communicative ethics

The problem outlined thus far requires us to equip ourselves with theoretical and conceptual tools capable of both explaining and evaluating the relationship between legitimacy and justification in the context of particular decision-making processes or negotiations. Thus, the communicative ethics framework at the heart of this book seeks to reveal ways in which communicative practices impact upon legitimacy in the international sphere. Although embedded in a rich theoretical tradition, communicative ethics is not a purely theoretical construct but one intended to exercise practical and critical purchase on empirical cases.[20] Our attention in the case of Kosovo thus turns to real communicative practices. This focus seeks to avoid being blinkered by the moments of crisis with which we are presented and which tend to restrict our responses to more strategic-moral calculations.

Despite the influence of Habermas's theory of communicative action, his reflections on NATO's use of force in Kosovo in 1999 are a helpful starting point as they, paradoxically, illustrate the limitations of many considerations of the use of force in IR. Habermas was in favour of the intervention in Kosovo, and he articulated his views most clearly in an article published in *Die Zeit* in April 1999, later translated and published in English. Although the article is written in the context of contemporary German politics, Habermas's cosmopolitan world perspective is clear. The intervention in Kosovo offered an opportunity to move away from the classical conception of international law for sovereign states towards the development of cosmopolitan law and a world civil society: 'Direct membership in an association of global citizens would protect the citizens of an individual state against the arbitrariness of his or her own government.'[21] Advocating a 'legal pacifist' approach, he identifies the absence of a 'proper institutionalisation of cosmopolitan law' as responsible for the gap between 'the legitimacy and the effectiveness of peacekeeping and peacemaking interventions'.[22] The legal ambiguity of the situation in Kosovo, aided by the weak global institutionalisation of human rights, is where Habermas locates the concerns over legitimacy and morality provoked by NATO's intervention. He argues that the moral legitimacy on which NATO had no choice but to base its actions – he accepts the assumption that the Security Council was blocked by the threat of Russia's veto – is problematic because it relied on norms for which 'no effective and universally recognized instances assure their application and enforcement'.[23]

By emphasising the need to strengthen international institutions and move to cosmopolitan law and world citizenship, an alternative, more interventionist and human rights-oriented tone emerges in his writings. This begs the question of whether there really is sufficient common understanding and communication within a world 'public sphere' to support such a move. Where does the necessary authority come from? This shift is clearest when he argues that only if human rights become part of a 'global democratic legal order, as have basic human rights in our national constitutions, will we be able to work from the assumption that on the global level the addressees of these rights can simultaneously understand themselves as their authors'.[24] He does not ask, or answer, the question of which sources we might address ourselves to in order to find such a world-wide consensus, nor reflect upon the communicative practices by which such a consensus might legitimately be formed.[25]

Habermas succinctly analyses the flaws within the current system and is worth quoting at length:

> When they authorize themselves to act militarily, even nineteen indisputably democratic states remain partisan. They are making use of interpretative and decision-making powers to which only independent institutions would be entitled if things were already properly in order today; to that extent their actions are paternalistic. There are good moral grounds for this. Whoever acts with an awareness of the inevitability of a transitory paternalism, however, is also aware that the force he exercises still lacks the quality of a compulsory legal action legitimated by a democratic civil society of global citizens. Moral norms appealing to our better judgement may not be enforced in the same fashion as established legal norms.[26]

Despite the advocacy of an approach which has less critical purchase than we are accustomed to, Habermas has perhaps rightly suggested that we need to institutionalise these (moral) normative claims to rightness in order for intervention to be legitimate and so remove sources of 'disquiet'. If we do so, then the notion of humanitarian intervention is defunct in current structural and legal circumstances because we are caught between the promise (if that is what it is) of a cosmopolitan legal order, and the critical realism of classical international law. The statist bias and foundation of the United Nations, particularly the Security Council, serves to keep this paradox static, as it is hard to envisage member states concurring with the transition from Westphalian international law to a new 'cosmopolitan law'.

Introduction

One of the reasons for disquiet that Habermas rightly raises in regard to Kosovo is that it represents 'a strategy of negotiations that left no alternative to armed attack'.[27] Among the most important and disquieting complications of armed intervention in Kosovo in the name of humanitarianism that he notes are doubts about the appropriateness of the military means in use:

> Every incident of 'collateral damage', every train that goes down with a bombed Danube bridge, every tractor laden with Kosovo Albanian refugees, every Serbian settlement, every civil target that is unintentionally hit by a stray bomb, does not highlight just another contingency of war, but a suffering, which 'our' intervention has on its conscience.[28]

When considering the validity of justifications offered to legitimate intervention in Kosovo, Habermas argues that 'universalist justifications do not by necessity always function as a veil for the particularity of undeclared interests'.[29] He argues that '[w]hat a hermeneutics of suspicion levels against the attack on Yugoslavia is pretty lightweight', thereby dismissing suggestions that strategic interests sheltered behind the justifications of NATO states. He rejects the argument that politicians resort to external wars to bolster domestic support; he also rejects the various suggestions that intervention could be attributed to the desire to secure a role for NATO in the twenty-first century, to extend the United States' sphere of influence, or to protect against the influx of refugees and asylum seekers into European Union countries.[30]

While I concur with his dismissal of these particular arguments as *primary* drivers for the intervention, I disagree with his refutation of 'hermeneutics of suspicion' more broadly. Habermas makes too big a claim for universal justifications. This is, at least in part, a reflection of his rather ambitious opinions of the normative foundations for states' actions. As Danilo Zolo suggests, Habermas does not 'balk at lending NATO's political and military leadership the motivations and ends of his own personal cosmopolitan philosophy and theory of the moral universality of human rights'.[31] Habermas's support for NATO's adoption of the role of human rights protector in the absence of more established legal mechanisms,[32] runs the risk of conflating legitimacy with particular moral norms. In his acknowledgement, however, that self-legitimation and self-empowerment by NATO member states should not become the rule, there is significant room for a critical examination – 'a 'hermeneutics of suspicion' – of the legitimating process and decisions made concerning justifications for the use of force without necessarily subscribing to Habermas's broader perspective of the global condition. Before accepting his conclusion concerning the overall legitimacy of the intervention, it is fair to suggest that missing from his reflections on Kosovo is a critique of the communicative practices of NATO states and other actors driven by the procedural preoccupations embedded in his own theory of communicative action and, in particular, discourse ethics. The strategic move he suggests instead in order to enact the institutionalisation of cosmopolitan law breaches the limit to theory which he was careful to establish and defend in his earlier work.

The aim, therefore, is to challenge the dominant interpretations of the conflict in Kosovo, in turn permitting a different set of rules to be drawn on in constituting practices concerning the use of force, legitimacy and justification.[33] Habermas's theory of communicative action and discourse ethics serves as the starting point for a consideration of the relationship between legitimacy and justification. In this vein, Chapter 3 addresses the 'linguistic' or 'communicative turn' in critical and social theory of which Habermas is a central proponent and which has spilled over into the work of IR scholars. The epistemological challenge issued by critical theory to positivism was reflected in a corresponding shift in IR theory from which emerged a range of critiques of positivist approaches to the social sciences.[34] Consequently, critical theorists in IR began to ask questions concerning the nature of knowledge claims and how meaning and truth were constituted. Approaches to IR which favoured a neutral and objective understanding of reality were rejected and alternative epistemological positions quickly emerged. These articulated an awareness of the relationship between knowledge, power and interests, and undermined any claim to an 'objective reality', instead presupposing an intersubjective and, at times, a radically subjective approach to knowledge and meaning. The predominant target of these critical approaches was the realist/neorealist orthodoxy which identified material power as an endemic feature of international politics and one that structured state interactions. While there is a diverse array of critical perspectives in IR, many of which do not draw their inspiration from critical theory narrowly understood as deriving from the Frankfurt School, they nonetheless share a common vision of world politics as one which is not dominated by considerations of material power and interests.[35]

Poststructuralists share a desire to expose the way in which particular uses of language can shape agendas and marginalise alternative voices. But while they advocate the creation of alternative spaces and articulation of different voices, they rarely offer more concrete insight into how such alternatives might be manifested.[36] In this vein, David Campbell argues that 'no political theorisation, prior to its materialisation, can legislate for politics (at least while retaining a sense of the paradox of politics rather than effecting an authoritarian position)'.[37] The problem of institutionalisation he alludes to remains the dilemma faced by critical theory when we seek to transpose it into practice. The Derridean approach is to avoid the offering of concrete solutions, but to wait for the opportunity to 'change things, to think differently, to invent' 'in the moment'. This approach means that it is not possible to demonstrate how this kind of negotiation might occur, or even if it will.[38]

Introduction

However, this places those in the 'here and now' in a somewhat difficult position.[39] Stephen K. White articulated the difficulty of negotiating the ethical-political implications of poststructuralism as 'a perpetual withholding gesture'; an unwillingness to judge action in the world in normative terms of 'better' or 'worse' and a principled opposition to generating consensus.[40] For these reasons, while the conception of communicative ethics articulated here remains sensitive to the concerns of marginalisation, 'otherness' and discursive power also central for poststructualists, it is nevertheless not primarily situated in the poststructuralist literature.

Adopted by both constructivists and critical IR theorists, the paradigm shift represented by the communicative turn served to illustrate the limitations of realist preoccupations with material power and strategic action. Realist approaches fail to capture the character of moral deliberation and argument or the manner in which this shapes and constitutes interests, identities and international law.[41] Reflecting the intellectual leanings of the two branches in IR which have adopted a Habermasian lens, Habermas articulates the dual purpose of his work in his discussion of theory and practice: 'In the one case, we have a social praxis, which as societal synthesis, makes insight possible; in the other case, a political praxis which consciously aims at overthrowing the existing system of institutions'.[42] As Habermas conceived of two forms of normativity intrinsic to critical theory – diagnostic and remedial – so is this mirrored in the multiple meanings ascribed to 'normative' in IR. On the one hand, it refers to the role of norms and rules in the intersubjective understanding of actors in international politics and therefore retains a primarily explanatory or sociological role. On the other hand, it refers to a critical and emancipatory orientation which seeks to reveal the marginalisation of subaltern voices in IR.

Seeking to establish and deploy a communicative ethics framework in IR, we must recognise the importance of Habermas's work for the problem of legitimacy and justification surrounding the use of force in international politics, whilst at the same time acknowledging its limitations and seeking conceptual and theoretical resources from critical theory more widely. As Habermasian critical theory seeks to retain a practical intent, discourse ethics is an appropriate resource to draw on because Habermas recognises the centrality of communication and dialogue to questions of justification, and offers normatively grounded regulative criteria for a communicative ethics. By exploring the work of scholars in both critical and constructivist camps who bring together the tripartite themes of the legitimacy of the use of force, a communicative-theoretic approach, and the intervention in Kosovo, we can see that the underlying purposes of the critical and constructivist projects remain somewhat different and neither, as they have been articulated to date, fully captures the potential offered by a Habermasian-informed analysis of the role of justifications for the use of force. In this vein, Robyn Eckersley writes, 'Habermas offers both a sociological understanding of the legitimacy of treaty negotiations, including the tensions between ideals and practices and the requirements of public justification, as well as a critical framework that enables an evaluation of the *degree* of legitimacy of particular negotiations and outcomes from the perspective of both state *and* non-state actors.'[43] The latter half of this statement has received less attention in IR and this has undermined the empirical uses to which Habermas's project has been applied. This critique has been acknowledged by Andrew Linklater, whose work has incorporated a sophisticated exposition of Habermasian ideas into a critical theory of IR. He writes:

> For the most part, critical theorists have failed to develop empirical investigations of the constraining role of micro- and macro-social and political structures. Inquiries into methodology and the philosophy of the social sciences and more recently, in Habermas's work, studies of communicative action and communicative rationality have outpaced empirical analyses of the contexts in which human beings confront (to use the language of the Frankfurt School) unnecessary social constraints and distorted forms of culture and communication.[44]

This is a challenge taken up in Part II of the book through an elaboration of a particular approach to communicative ethics, embodied in the criteria established by the 'communicative imperatives' developed therein, and brought to bear on an empirical analysis of the decision-making process surrounding the decision to use force in Kosovo in 1999. The intersection of critical theory and IR has led to an increased focus on the ways in which images of ethnic identity, national interests, states and global values aid in the constitution of power relations which favour some but disadvantage many others. Thus, it addresses the ways in which structures and beliefs function to exclude or marginalise specific groups.[45] In keeping with this critical orientation, the aim is to problematise current practices of exclusion and coercion, locating specific examples in the international deliberations surrounding the intervention in Kosovo and revealing how these communicative and structural distortions impacted upon the communicative process and the legitimacy of the intervention.

Communicative ethics: from theory to practice

The notion of communicative ethics originally emerged from the Frankfurt School of critical theory and, in particular, Habermas's work on communicative action. Based on his theory of universal pragmatics, communicative ethics has been considered in IR as an '*ethical* theory of norm formation'.[46] More specifically, for Habermas, it is underpinned by two key propositions.

Introduction

First, that '"normative validity claims have a cognitive sense" and can therefore be "treated *like* truth claims". Second, the validation of a claim that a norm is just requires "a real discourse and is not possible in the form of a monological argumentation carried through in a hypothetical manner"'.[47] At its core, Habermasian communicative ethics is a procedural and intersubjective approach to knowledge, and a formal, cognitive approach to the 'problem of the rational validation or justification of (metaethical) principles'.[48] Chapter 4 sets out the relevant debates surrounding his theory of communicative action and discourse ethics and, in doing so, identifies a number of limitations which, to varying degrees, are remedied through engagement with other critical theoretical approaches.

Building on existing theories of communicative ethics and the limitations to Habermas's project identified in Chapter 4, Chapter 5 articulates a series of communicative imperatives and the ensuing concerns over the relationship between theory and practice which strike at the heart of the emancipatory and evaluative orientation of critical theory. It strives to establish a framework which embraces both the sociological and critical orientation intrinsic to constructivist and critical theorising. Cognisant of the complex relationship between theory and practice, the communicative imperatives seek to avoid falling foul of the charge levelled at Habermas that his theory is too abstract to retain any leverage over empirical practice, whilst at the same time retaining a sufficient awareness of the limitations to theory envisaged by Habermas to prevent its totalising tendencies. Given the dual purpose of the communicative imperatives as an instrument of critique and of normative development, we can identify their relevance for two key sets of actors: participants and observers. Sensitivity to the complex relationship between theory and practice, between any form of criteria and their application, raises the need for a corresponding understanding of political judgement by actors in the face of indeterminate moral and legal criteria and the problem posed by contrary interpretations of particular situations. This translates into a question of reflective judgement and Hannah Arendt's belief in the capacity of individuals to make political and moral judgements in the public realm. The capacity for reflective judgement belongs, for Arendt, to both actor and spectator. The focus on actors embraces the critical theoretical understanding central to communicative ethics whereby the potential for emancipatory political change and action resides in the participant. The critique of real communicative practices in the case of Kosovo undertaken in Chapter 6 derives, however, from the perspective of the spectator and constitutes an *ex post* evaluation of existing communicative practices.

Central to Habermas's theory of communicative action is a recognition of different orientations to language use, communicative and strategic, and it is germane to briefly clarify references to the 'strategic use of language' in order to consider their parallel usage in IR. First, there is the strong distinction which Habermas draws between strategic action (oriented towards success based on the rules of rational choice) and communicative action (oriented towards understanding). Strategic action, in this context, is instrumental. It is a means–ends relationship whereby the actor seeks to exert effective influence (through threats or rewards) over the decisions of a rational opponent.[49] Communicative action is oriented towards reaching understanding and consensus through a dialogical process. This, for Habermas, is not simply intended to remain an analytical distinction, but to map on to the orientations of social actors.[50] A number of critiques have been levelled at this distinction, notably, the presence of both orientations in the complex reality of politics, the difficulty in identifying pure examples of either, and the intersubjective nature of both forms of communication. This suggests that while Habermas's distinction serves an important purpose in analytical terms, in practice we must also explore the relationship *between* strategic and communicative rationalities. This is a theme which will be pursued through the book and responds to the realist criticism that the world of international politics is too messy and dominated by material concerns to leave much room for normative concepts of deliberation.

There are similarities between strategic action as defined above and the notion of strategic language use in IR. In this context, language is frequently used as a cover for strategic interests.[51] Habermas refers to this as 'concealed strategic action' whereby 'at least one of the parties behaves with an orientation to success, but leaves others to believe that all the presuppositions of communicative action are satisfied'.[52] Using language strategically, however – the 'language of manoeuvre'[53] – leads to eventual entanglement in this language.[54] Karin Fierke has claimed that this language both 'constrains and enables actors. A policy will fail, regardless of one's purpose in pursuing it, if it cannot be presented as legitimate and plausible.'[55] The acknowledgement that public utterances, no matter how strategic their purpose, may constrain or enable actors, runs through the work of those constructivists who have explored the role of language in constituting the possibilities of political action.

Sketching out the Habermasian and IR positions on strategic action is important because the book engages with both, and the consequent tension which emerges has implications for the relationship between theory and practice which is addressed throughout. The tension derives from the recognition, on the one hand, that an important limitation to Habermas's theory is identified, whilst, on the other, that the retention of the critical leverage offered by such an analytical distinction is desirable. Habermas's understanding of the distinction between strategic and communicative action extends beyond the constructivist approach to language in that it is embedded in a

Introduction

rich and complex theory of communicative action which encompasses a capacity to perceive and critique 'the manifestation of communication pathologies'[56] through a formal-pragmatic reconstruction of language. This tension complicates matters empirically given that strategic action encompasses both overt and concealed action. The difficulty in identifying either communicative action or the correct form of strategic action empirically – as will be seen in the case of Kosovo – emerges from the challenge posed by knowing the real intention or motivation of another actor. Whilst it is perhaps the case that this tension remains unresolvable, an imperfect sense of the distinction derived from Habermas is integral to the critical capacity of a communicative ethics because it offers us insights into the internal and external conditions of speech which may distort communication.[57]

The intention of communicative ethics is not to pass moral judgement on particular outcomes. It does not decisively indict or praise NATO's intervention in Kosovo. It seeks, instead, to shed light on the legitimacy of the processes surrounding the decision to intervene. The implications of reading the decision to intervene in Kosovo through a communicative ethics lens are twofold. First, a normative grounding is secured for the argument that legitimacy as it is currently conceived in IR lacks a sufficiently critical communicative dimension. Second, by focusing on the relationship between legitimacy and justification, we can challenge the general consensus that the intervention was 'illegal but legitimate'. In other words, the focus on legal and moral aspects of legitimacy, however important, risks obscuring the role of language in the construction of legitimacy: *how* we arrive at decisions is as important as the substantive content of those decisions.

In making this claim, Chapter 6 revisits a number of moments in the narrative set out in Chapter 2 and reveals a number of previously unconsidered or under-theorised elements of the deliberations on Kosovo in the Security Council, during the Holbrooke negotiations in 1998 and at the negotiations in Rambouillet in 1999. As claims to legitimacy are articulated through language, so they may be evaluated on the basis of the communicative practices they enact. The interpretive power of the communicative imperatives is such that we can understand the dynamics of the communicative practices surrounding Kosovo to demonstrate the presence of, *inter alia*, coercion, exclusion, a lack of reflexivity and recognition. In so doing, we acknowledge the (de)legitimating functions of language. Furthermore, the broader temporal context encompassed by communicative ethics reveals a series of missed opportunities for constructive dialogic engagement by the international community over the conflict in Kosovo throughout the 1990s. These factors at the very least raise questions over the construction of the justification of last resort for the use of force and ask whether all diplomatic alternatives had been exhausted. Such conclusions call for the recognition

Introduction

of alternative, communicative, and non-violent practices in conflict transformation.

NOTES

1. H. S. Røhr (ed.), *Dialog – Mer Enn Ord* (Lillehammer: Nansenskolen, 2005), 95.
2. I use 'humanitarian intervention' to refer to 'the threat or use of force across state borders by a state (or group of states) aimed at preventing or ending widespread and grave violations of the fundamental human rights of individuals other than its own citizens, without the permission of the state within whose territory force is applied'. J. L. Holzgrefe and R. Keohane (eds), *Humanitarian Intervention: Ethical, Legal and Political Dilemmas* (Cambridge: Cambridge University Press, 2003), 18.
3. Tony Blair's statement to the House of Commons, 23 March 1999.
4. N. J. Wheeler, *Saving Strangers: Humanitarian Intervention in International Society* (Oxford: Oxford University Press, 2000), 34. Wheeler prefers this term over the just war criterion of just cause because it captures the exceptional nature of these cases.
5. A. Orford, *Reading Humanitarian Intervention* (Cambridge: Cambridge University Press, 2003), 17.
6. A. J. Coates, *The Ethics of War* (Manchester: Manchester University Press, 1997), Chapter 8; J. T. Johnson, *Morality and Contemporary Warfare* (New Haven: Yale University Press, 1999), 22–36; H. Grotius, *The Rights of War and Peace*, Book III (ed. by Richard Tuck) (Indiana: Liberty Fund, 2005), 1133–48.
7. International Commission on Intervention and State Sovereignty, *The Responsibility to Protect* (Canada: International Development Research Centre, 2001), 36.
8. Communicative practices refer in the context of the case of Kosovo to the offering of justifications and reasoned arguments in the public sphere. Justifications are a form of communicative practices, but the latter are not reducible to justifications. There is also a distinction between the theoretical framework of communicative ethics and the empirical object of study which are communicative practices.
9. Exceptions include D. Lloyd Jones, *Cosmopolitan Mediation? Conflict Resolution and the Oslo Accords* (Manchester: Manchester University Press, 1999); C. Bjola, *Legitimising the Use of Force in International Politics: Kosovo, Iraq and the Ethics of Intervention* (Abingdon: Routledge, 2009); S. Chilton and M. Cuzzo, 'Habermas's Theory of Communicative Action as a Theoretical Framework for Mediation Practice', *Conflict Resolution Quarterly*, 22:3 (2005).
10. C. Reus-Smit, 'International Crises of Legitimacy', *International Politics*, 44:2/3 (2007), 159–60.
11. I. Claude, 'Collective Legitimation as a Political Function of the United Nations', *International Organization*, 20:3 (1966), 368. Emphasis added.
12. For example see: J. Habermas, *Moral Consciousness and Communicative Action* (Cambridge: Polity Press, 1990), hereafter *MCCA*; S. Benhabib and F. Dallmayr (eds), *The Communicative Ethics Controversy* (Cambridge, MA: MIT Press, 1990); K.-O. Apel, 'On the Relationship Between Ethics, International Law and Politico-Military Strategy in Our Time: A Philosophical Retrospective on the Kosovo Conflict', *European Journal of Social Theory*, 4:1 (2001).
13. I use 'international community' to refer to various actors from the Security Council, Contact Group, Rambouillet negotiations, Holbrooke proceedings, NATO, and the G-8. I follow Hedley Bull in defining international society: 'a group of states, conscious of certain common interests and common values, form a society in the sense that they conceive themselves to be bound by a common set of rules in their relations with one

another, and share in the working of common institutions'. *The Anarchical Society* (Basingstoke: Palgrave, 2002), 13.
14 See N. J. Wheeler, 'Pluralist or Solidarist Conceptions of International Society: Bull and Vincent on Humanitarian Intervention', *Millennium Journal of International Studies*, 21:3 (1992); A. Linklater, 'The Good International Citizen and the Crisis in Kosovo', in A. Schnabel and R. Thakur (eds), *Kosovo and the Challenge of Humanitarian Intervention: Selective Indignation, Collective Action, and International Citizenship* (Tokyo: United Nations University Press, 2000); Wheeler, *Saving Strangers*; A. Linklater and H. Suganami, *The English School of International Relations: A Contemporary Reassessment* (Cambridge: Cambridge University Press, 2006).
15 ICISS, *The Responsibility to Protect*.
16 Orford argues that international law, like the discourse of humanitarian intervention, focuses on moments of crisis: the 'focus is always on the moment when military intervention is the only remaining credible foreign policy option. The question that is produced by law's focus on the moment of crisis is always "What would you suggest we do if we are in that situation again?" The assertion that this is the only moment which can be considered renders it impossible to analyse any other involvement of the international community or to think reflexively about law's role in producing the meaning of intervention.' Orford, *Reading Humanitarian Intervention*, 18.
17 For excellent historical accounts see M. Vickers, *Between Serb and Albanian: A History of Kosovo* (London: C. Hurst & Co., 1998); J. Mertus, *Kosovo: How Myths and Truths Started a War* (London: University of California Press, 1999); N. Malcolm, *Kosovo: A Short History* (London: Pan Books, 2002).
18 A. Bellamy, 'Kosovo: After the War, the War of Words', *The International Journal of Human Rights*, 5:3 (2001), 99. For evidence of information about the situation in Kosovo, see the reports produced by the Mission of Long Duration established by the Conference on Security and Cooperation in Europe in September 1992–June 1993, the resolutions adopted by the UN General Assembly regarding human rights violations, and the reports of the UN Commission on Human Rights, in M. Weller, *The Crisis in Kosovo 1989–1999: From Dissolution of Yugoslavia to Rambouillet and the Outbreak of Hostilities*, vol. 1 (Cambridge: Documents & Analysis Publishing Ltd, 1999), Chapters 5 and 6.
19 Orford, *Reading Humanitarian Intervention*, 85.
20 For examples of applications of Habermas's work in other spheres see J. Forester 'Critical Theory and Planning Practice', in J. Forester (ed.), *Critical Theory and Public Life* (Cambridge, MA: MIT Press, 1985); R. Kemp, 'Planning, Public Hearings, and the Politics of Discourse', in Forester (ed.), *Critical Theory and Public Life*; M. Mclean, *Pedagogy and the University: Critical Theory and Practice* (London: Continuum, 2006); R. Blaug, 'The Distortion of the Face to Face: Communicative Reason and Social Work Practice', *British Journal of Social Work*, 25:4 (1995), 423–39; J. S. Dryzek, 'Critical Theory as a Research Program', in S. K. White (ed.), *The Cambridge Companion to Habermas* (Cambridge: Cambridge University Press, 1995).
21 J. Habermas, 'Bestiality and Humanity: A War on the Border Between Law and Morality', *Constellations*, 6:3 (1999), 264.
22 Ibid., 269. By legal pacifism, Habermas refers to the construction of peace through the strengthening of international institutions and the universalisation of law along Kantian lines.
23 Ibid.
24 Ibid., 270. For a critical perspective on the institutionalisation of international or cosmopolitan law see R. Fine, 'Political Argument and the Legitimacy of International Law: A

Case of Distorted Modernization', in C. Thornhill and C. Ashenden (eds), *Legality and Legitimacy: Normative and Sociological Approaches* (Baden-Baden: Nomos, 2010).

25 J. Habermas, 'The Constitutionalization of International Law and the Legitimation Problems of a Constitution for World Society', in J. Habermas, *Europe: The Faltering Project* (trans. Ciaran Cronin) (Cambridge: Polity Press, 2009). Habermas repeats this strategic shift here, omitting consideration as to how we might arrive at the normative positions he advocates which, as he acknowledges, are far from current realities. For a critique of Habermas's normative position, see D. Zolo, 'A Cosmopolitan Philosophy of International Law? A Realist Approach', *Ratio Juris*, 12:4 (1999); O. Payrow Shabani, *Democracy, Power, and Legitimacy: The Critical Theory of Jürgen Habermas* (Toronto: University of Toronto Press, 2003).

26 Habermas, 'Bestiality and Humanity', 270.

27 Ibid., 265.

28 Ibid., 266.

29 Ibid., 268.

30 Ibid: 'For politicians who have little scope in domestic affairs, due to the globalisation of economies, a noisy show of strength in foreign affairs might offer some chance to improve their profile. But neither the motive of extending and securing the sphere of influence attributed to the United States, nor the motivation of finding a role attributed to NATO, nor even the motive attributed to "fortress Europe", of a precautionary defence against immigration movements, explain the decision to engage in such a weighty, risky and costly operation.'

31 D. Zolo, *Invoking Humanity: War, Law and Global Order* (London: Continuum, 2002), 80.

32 W. Smith, 'Anticipating a Cosmopolitan Future: The Case of Humanitarian Military Intervention', *International Politics*, 44:1 (2007), 79.

33 K. M. Fierke, *Changing Games, Changing Strategies: Critical Investigations in Security* (Manchester: Manchester University Press, 1998), Chapter 1.

34 V. Boon and N. Head, 'Critical Theory and the Language of Violence: Exploring the Issues', *Journal of Global Ethics*, 6:2 (2010), 79–87; T. Diez and J. Steans, 'A Useful Dialogue? Habermas and International Relations', *Review of International Studies*, 31:1 (2005), 127–40.

35 S. Smith, K. Booth and M. Zalewski (eds), *International Theory: Positivism and Beyond* (Cambridge: Cambridge University Press, 1996); J. George, *Discourses of Global Politics: A Critical (Re)Introduction to International Relations* (Boulder, CO: Lynne Rienner, 1994); M. Hoffman, 'Critical Theory and the Inter-Paradigm Debate', *Millennium: Journal of International Studies*, 16:2 (1987), 231–49; N. J. Rengger, 'Going Critical? A Response to Hoffman', *Millennium*, 17:1 (1988), 81–9; N. J. Rengger, 'The Fearful Sphere of International Relations', *Review of International Studies*, 16:4 (1990), 361–8.

36 Fierke, *Changing Games*, 6.

37 D. Campbell, 'Why Fight: Humanitarianism, Principles and Post-Structuralism', *Millennium: Journal of International Studies*, 27:3 (1998), 513.

38 D. Bulley, 'Negotiating Ethics: Campbell, Ontopology and Hospitality', *Review of International Studies*, 32:4 (2006), 658. Bulley is not using negotiation simply in terms of dialogue, but in the Derridean sense of resisting closure, of shuttling between different positions; it is not dialectic in the sense that there is any easy resolution of two positions in a third, but a negotiation between two incompatible imperatives which retain something of their normative purity.

39 For a helpful description of this tension see S. K. White, *Political Theory and Postmodernsim* (Cambridge: Cambridge University Press, 1991), 21, 28.

40 Ibid., 18. This is not to suggest that poststructuralists do not address ethics; the

commitment of poststructuralists to a 'world-disclosing' orientation and a 'responsibility to otherness' is highly ethical. It is an 'ethics of resistance to totalisation rather than an ethics oriented towards the creation of substantive agreement on normative principles'. R. Shapcott, *Justice, Community and Dialogue in International Relations?* (Cambridge: Cambridge University Press, 2001), 73.
41 A. Linklater, *Men and Citizens in International Relations* (London: Macmillan, 1990), 2nd edn, 216–17.
42 J. Habermas, *Theory and Practice* (London: Heinemann Educational Books, 1974), 2.
43 R. Eckersley, 'Soft Law, Hard Politics, and the Climate Change Treaty', in C. Reus-Smit (ed.), *The Politics of International Law* (Cambridge: Cambridge University Press, 2004), 98.
44 Linklater, cited in Lloyd Jones, *Cosmopolitan Mediation?*, 92. A notable exception is Bjola, *Legitimising the Use of Force in International Politics*.
45 White, *Political Theory and Postmodernism*.
46 C. Reus-Smit, 'Society, Power, and Ethics', in Reus-Smit (ed.), *The Politics of International Law*, 286.
47 S. K. White, *The Recent Work of Jürgen Habermas: Reason, Justice and Modernity* (Cambridge: Cambridge University Press, 1988), 48.
48 F. Dallymayr, 'Introduction', in S. Benhabib and F. Dallmayr, *The Communicative Ethics Controversy* (Cambridge, MA: MIT Press, 1990), 3.
49 J. Habermas, *The Theory of Communicative Action: Reason and the Rationalization of Society*, vol. 1 (Cambridge: Polity Press, 1984) 285, 329 (hereafter *TCA*); Fierke, *Changing Games*, 171.
50 Habermas, *TCA*, vol. 1, 286.
51 Ibid., 332–3.
52 Ibid., 332.
53 M. Hollis and S. Smith, *Explaining and Understanding International Relations* (Oxford: Clarendon, 1990).
54 Fierke, *Changing Games*, 171; Wheeler, *Saving Strangers*, 4.
55 Fierke, *Changing Games*, 171.
56 Habermas, *TCA*, vol. 1, 331.
57 For an excellent discussion on communicative distortion along these lines, see J. Bohman, 'Formal Pragmatics as a Critical Theory', in L. E. Hahn (ed.), *Perspectives on Habermas* (Illinois: Open Court Publishing Company, 2000), 10–117.

I

Reading Kosovo: legitimacy and justification

1

Locating Kosovo and legitimacy

Illegal but legitimate.
Independent International Commission on Kosovo[1]

Introduction

THE INTERVENTION IN Kosovo and the preceding years of conflict represent a tangled knot of morality and legality. Declared 'illegal but legitimate' by the Independent International Commission on Kosovo (IICK) in 2000, serious questions emerge over the nature of legitimacy in IR. As once remarked upon by Martin Wight, international legitimacy is both 'elusive and nebulous'.[2] Nowhere was this clearer than over NATO's intervention in Kosovo in March 1999 which was not explicitly authorised by the Security Council. Whilst acknowledging the importance of moral and legal discourses to address the dilemma which Kosovo posed for international society, this chapter draws attention to the limitations posed by conflating the concept of legitimacy with questions of legality and morality.[3] All conceptions of legitimacy make implicit or explicit reference to insiders and outsiders, whether it is through acknowledging adherence to substantive values of international society, or through discussion of right process. As such, a communicative dimension of legitimacy should make explicit a focus on the practices of inclusion and exclusion which shape and influence decision-making processes and accompany the claims to legitimacy regarding the use of force. Communicative ethics does not seek to replace legal and moral discourses of legitimation. Instead, it focuses on the communicative practices which constitute the claims to legitimacy.

This chapter explores two concepts popular within a broadly normative school of thought, 'good international citizenship' and the 'responsibility to protect', for several reasons. Both concepts actively consider the problem of the use of force for humanitarian purposes in international society, and they have both, in different ways, acknowledged the problem posed by practices of inclusion and exclusion. Crucially, however, they demonstrate the limits to conceptualisations of legitimacy when it is conflated with morality and/or legality.[4] The following sections draw our attention to the thematic problem of practices of inclusion and exclusion more explicitly, before setting out the parameters of the debate concerning legitimacy in IR.

While both the responsibility to protect doctrine and good international citizenship recognise the importance of justifications in debating the use of force, thus according some degree of recognition to a communicative dimension of legitimacy, this study highlights the need for such a dimension to be rooted in critical theoretical conceptions of communicative ethics. Despite the recourse to moral and legal languages of justification, the critical and reflective character of communicative ethics was absent from much of the negotiations and dialogue preceding NATO's intervention in Kosovo. Rather than paint a counter-factual picture of the negotiations process and intervention, it is the contribution of communicative ethics to a communicative dimension of legitimacy that the book will explore with a view to revealing alternative interpretations of the legitimacy of the decision-making process.[5]

Kosovo: the tangle of morality and legality

The advent of military humanitarianism in the case of NATO's intervention in Kosovo in 1999 illustrated the degree to which post-Cold War international politics had shifted. To many, Kosovo represented the dilemma characterising contemporary humanitarian interventions which opposes the normative power of human rights against the legal power of the principles of state sovereignty and non-intervention.[6] The re-emergence of legal and moral discourses reflected in part the revival of the Security Council following the end of the Cold War, during which time its powers had effectively been paralysed by the reciprocal use of the veto by the permanent members. The change in circumstances saw an expansion of the Security Council's ability and willingness to interpret 'threats to international peace and security' under Chapter VII of the UN Charter. This enabled, for the first time, a conflict like that in Kosovo to be declared a 'threat to international peace and security' by the Security Council[7] and permitted the exercise of measures under Chapter VII up to and including the use of military force.[8]

Those in favour of the use of force in Kosovo maintained that since all diplomatic remedies had been exhausted and given both the imminent risk of humanitarian catastrophe and the threat of Russia's veto within the Security Council, the only prospect for an effective humanitarian intervention seemed to depend on acting outside the Council. Anti-interventionists declared NATO's actions illegal without explicit authorisation from the Council and perceived them to fundamentally challenge the prohibition on recourse to force within existing international law. They did not accept the argument that diplomatic means were properly used or exhausted.

Legal and moral concerns were merged in the key question of whether humanitarian intervention could be legitimate or legal in the absence of explicit Security Council authorisation, highlighting concerns over who has the authority to intervene and on what grounds. Whilst international law states that only the UN Security Council can authorise external intervention in the absence of the host state's consent, the UN Charter only permits the use of force in cases of self-defence against armed attack under Article 51 or collective security.[9] Article 2(4) of the Charter prohibits the threat or use of force by states against the political independence and territorial integrity of any other state.[10] While the Security Council is empowered to authorise the use of force on the basis of its responsibility towards maintaining international peace and security, the Charter also grants foundational importance to human rights. On this basis, some advocates suggest a responsibility to intervene in order to protect civilians against massive human rights violations.[11] The well-known verdict of the IICK that NATO's actions were 'illegal but legitimate' serves to highlight the moral and legal issues intertwined at the heart of the paradox within the UN Charter between sovereignty and non-intervention on the one hand, and the protection afforded human rights on the other.[12] Consensus about the relationship between legitimacy, morality and legality as regards the use of force for humanitarian purposes arguably remains as elusive now as it was in 1999.

Good international citizenship: pluralism, solidarism and cosmopolitan harm

The contemporary debates over good international citizenship represent an awareness of this tension between conflicting interpretations of the Charter. Recognised within these debates are potential forms of exclusion, notably through boundaries established between citizenship and humanity, between order and justice and, by implication, between the universal and the particular. The most observable forms of exclusion remain constituted along the boundaries of sovereignty and territory in delimiting the extent of moral community. However, in more recent constructions of good international citizenship advocated by Andrew Linklater, a focus on the principles of harm enables a closer examination of how exclusionary practices resonate more closely with the concerns of a critical theoretical nature. Whilst good international citizenship is, ultimately, accepting of the state as a key actor, most advocates recognise that it should challenge existing practices of inclusion and exclusion.[13]

The concept that originated with Gareth Evans, former Australian Foreign Minister, was intended as a prescription for Australian foreign policy, but has since been adopted by contemporary IR scholars as offering potential models for state behaviour within the international community.[14] Evans proposed that foreign policy should concern itself with and be motivated by issues such as preserving world order, encouraging global reform and honouring responsibilities and duties to aid the flourishing of mankind.[15] This view is premised on the fundamental principle, originating with Vattel, that the state is required to place the 'welfare of international society ahead of the relentless pursuit of its own national interests'.[16] Reflecting the 'reality of international interdependence' and emerging global problems, good international citizenship is an 'exercise in enlightened self-interest' and requires a careful mix of realism and idealism.[17]

The concept of good international citizenship has been given most attention within the parameters of the English School of International Relations wherein pluralism and solidarism reflect different normative positions as to how international society should be ordered and the relative weight granted to notions of order and justice.[18] Both, in other words, articulate a vision of ethics and foreign policy.[19] Pluralism demonstrates a preference for international order and for the preservation of the principles of non-intervention and sovereignty. Pluralists remain deeply sceptical of the potential for progress in world affairs, and the limit might, for them, be the international equivalent of 'police action', 'where states exhibit solidarity in their response to law-breaking states which violate the cardinal rules and norms of the society of states'.[20] They warn of the dangers inherent in unilateral humanitarian intervention, arguing that the absence of a consensus on what moral principles should justify such interventions means that to sanction the use of force by particular states would erode the foundations of international order, built as it is on the rules that establish tolerable rules of coexistence between states sharing different conceptions of justice. Advocates of pluralism remind us of the difficulties in constructing an agreed set of conditions, the violation of which might permit humanitarian intervention, suggesting that what constitutes sufficiently serious human rights violations is still uncertain. They argue that there is no consensus over where the boundary between humanitarian war and military aggression lies.[21] More importantly, in the absence of consensus on the rules governing unilateral humanitarian intervention, pluralists highlight the fact that such intervention sets dangerous precedents for those states who might wish to act on their own moral principles, thereby weakening the international order as defined by sovereignty, non-intervention, and the non-use of force.[22] Pluralists like Robert Jackson value prudence and highlight the need for states to balance national, international and humanitarian responsibilities when acting in the international sphere.[23] While states may recognise they have humanitarian responsibilities, these do not trump their primary responsibility to protect the security of their citizens. This places significantly stronger constraints on the possibility of legitimate humanitarian intervention than is apparent in other normative arguments.

The alternative normative position which emerges out of the writings of the English School is solidarism, which concerns a deeper level of responsibility and greater demands upon the collective will. Solidarism emerged following increased focus on human rights from the 1960s onwards among those who wondered whether states could be expected to reconceptualise the humanitarian responsibilities within international society, rather than privileging their national and international responsibilities. Hedley Bull, a founding figure of the English School, recognised that solidarism 'might require a challenge to the non-intervention principle. On this reading of solidarism, state leaders are "burdened with the guardianship of human rights everywhere."'[24] This type of solidarism places the rights and duties of individuals at its heart as opposed to the pluralist preference for the limited rights and duties of states alone.[25] Nicholas Wheeler and Tim Dunne have defined good international citizenship as a viewpoint which 'argues for a mutual interdependence between the provision of national security, the strengthening of international order and the promotion of human rights'.[26] Those who adopt positions along the solidarist continuum rebuke pluralist international society theory for its potential to reify a particular set of relations and practices (both theoretically and empirically) in ways which offer the means to perpetuate the interests of the most powerful states.

Linklater has re-formulated the principle of good international citizenship (both pluralist and solidarist versions) around the notion of harm. Tracing the obligation not to act in ways which harm others back to Kant's *Perpetual Peace*, Linklater identifies the harm principle as central to both domestic and international politics. He distinguishes between the duty of non-maleficence – a negative duty not to harm – and the positive duty of beneficence.[27] This distinction has some bearing on the various convictions held by pluralists and solidarists. Accordingly, Linklater distinguishes between international and cosmopolitan harm conventions to capture the arrangements states have made to reduce the harm they do to each other. Whereas the former may first look to the interests of co-nationals, the latter challenges the notion that the state's primary duty is to protect the welfare and interests of co-nationals and seeks to break down the barrier between insiders and outsiders.

Central to the debate within good international citizenship between pluralism and solidarism is the question which rears its head in times of crisis: to what extent should states and individuals act to relieve the suffering of others? While pluralism and solidarism offer different answers to this question, both draw on different practices of inclusion and exclusion. Linklater and Hidemi Suganami have clarified the principles for good international citizenship in a pluralist international society,[28] arguing that they are concerned 'with creating and preserving international harm conventions which work to the advantage of the great powers'.[29] These do not, therefore, protect non-sovereign communities such as indigenous peoples, protect individuals from harm in the case of human rights abuses which do not become a matter for international society as a whole, nor protect smaller states from the vagaries of the balance of power aimed at preventing harm to the great powers. In this sense, they may be linked to Cox's definition of problem-solving, whereby the focus is on the smooth functioning of international society rather than challenging and transforming unequal power relations.[30]

The principles of good international citizenship for a solidarist differ significantly in their normative scope.[31] Solidarists claim that states have an obligation to protect the rights and interests of individuals who are seen as members of international society in their own right. While this challenges the traditional notion of state sovereignty, there appears to be increasingly less resistance to the idea that states are answerable to the international community for the treatment of individuals. Both interpretations of good international citizenship were articulated in the dialogue surrounding the conflict in Kosovo and shaped what was perceived to be legitimate behaviour in moral and legal terms. Pluralist principles of international society were arguably manifested in the objections of Russia and China to the use of unilateral force, while NATO states, at least in part, drew on solidarist interpretations in that they sought to protect the rights of individual Kosovars.

For some, the solidarist approach requires that for good international citizens serious human rights violations should take precedence over state sovereignty, necessitating, under certain conditions, the use of force. This perspective is captured most clearly by Wheeler and Dunne whose interpretation of good international citizenship has focused on specific strands within the original concept, namely, human rights and the consequent 'solidarist' or cosmopolitan shift.[32] Thus, law-abiding 'good international citizens not only have to place order before the pursuit of narrow commercial and political advantage but are also required to forsake these advantages where they conflict with human rights'.[33]

Concerns over this approach emerge when looking at the problems raised when certain major powers believe that a humanitarian crisis requires the use of force, but are unable to secure a consensus for such action. Dunne and Wheeler's response is that 'in exceptional cases good international citizens have a duty to use force even if this weakens the rule of law in the society of states'.[34] By advocating a solidarist interpretation of international society, they establish a perspective that not only no longer precludes, but advocates intervention in the affairs of other states on the grounds of human rights if the relevant criteria have been met and if the intervention has the collective legitimation of international society.

Wheeler has made a compelling case for good international citizens to be able to resort to unilateral force in the case of a 'supreme humanitarian emergency', when collective armed force is being blocked by the 'unreasonable veto' or self-interest of a major power within the Security Council.[35] However, while a solidarist interpretation of good international citizenship which supports an emergent norm of humanitarian intervention offers substantive values for international society, it does not indicate what kind of prior communicative process legitimates the moral or legal values which justify the use of force. It blocks out from the dominant narrative of humanitarian need and justice the recognition of other sets of relations (and prior interventions of a different nature) between those intervening and those suffering, as well as possible contestation of the nature and consequences of particular conceptions of justice. Dunne and Wheeler note the importance of dialogue, assuming that participants are prepared to engage in conversation and thus potentially alter their position, but when dialogue breaks down, they argue that good international citizenship requires alternative approaches, including force, to be considered rather than reflection upon the construction and nature of the process which led to the breakdown of dialogue. Human rights, often at the heart of justifications for intervention, offer a powerful means to enter into dialogue, but the 'how' of such dialogue is important. Supplementing the legal and moral conceptions of legitimacy integral to criteria for intervention with a communicative dimension grounded in communicative ethics provides normative standards with which to engage in and critique the justificatory process.

The overarching critique of good international citizenship is that while it retains a normative approach to international politics – the notion that states both can (a descriptive claim about state practice) and should be moral agents – and operates on constructivist premises concerning the potential for the identities of states to change, most interpretations of the concept lack a capacity for critique beyond their own normative terms. Whilst it works within a constructivist methodology, it comes closer at times to rationalism (e.g. strategic action and bargaining strategies) than to critical theory. This is because both rationalist theorists and good international citizenship theorists can justify the use of force (or not) with the intention of changing the target state's behaviour through coercive methods. The difference lies in the way in which this is legitimated. For English school theorists, action is legitimated with reference to the rules and norms of international society, whereas for rationalists it may be legitimated through conceptions of national interests, self-legitimation through domestic norms, hegemonic stability or unipolar responsibilities.

Linklater has argued that 'Good international citizens must challenge the status quo while avoiding recklessness, arbitrariness, and opportunism, but they must convince others of their case, their competence, and their motives.'[36] It is the latter emphasis – the need to *'convince others of their case, their competence, and their motives'* – that highlights the need to establish an evaluative approach to claims to legitimacy derived from communicative ethics. While a communicative dimension is present in the debates surrounding the legitimate use of force which draw on the just war tradition and international law through a recognition of the need to offer justifications, missing from these accounts is a more fundamental ability to contest the communicative practices through which justifications are voiced and legitimacy granted or withheld. Drawing on an emancipatory critique of power, communicative ethics offers not only a recognition of the strategic dimension of legitimation tactics, but also a communicative alternative.

From the 'responsibility to protect' to a responsibility to discuss

The doctrine of *The Responsibility to Protect* published in 2001 by the International Commission on Intervention and State Sovereignty (ICISS) marked a shift from the language of 'humanitarian intervention' and the 'right to intervene' to that of a 'responsibility to protect'.[37] This doctrine reflected the urge felt among practitioners, politicians and cosmopolitan-inclined theorists to address the ambivalence of competing norms intrinsic to contemporary humanitarian intervention by specifying, in a variety of ways, a set of formal criteria for the justification, authorisation and conduct of military force.[38] The prominence of solidarism and the human rights discourse, coupled with ethnic cleansing during the conflict in Bosnia and the inaction of the international community in the face of genocide in Rwanda, initiated a demand for such mass human rights violations to be prevented in future. The responsibility to protect doctrine is one of several versions of criteria put forward, partly in connection with Kosovo, which would effectively institutionalise humanitarian intervention in one way or another: others include those of the IICK; Nicholas Wheeler; and Neta Crawford.

With the exception of Crawford, these attempts to codify our moral responsibility in the face of mass violations of human rights draw heavily on the tradition of just war. All of these approaches, to varying degrees, also recognise the importance of language and justification. The IICK and the ICISS reports seek to constrain the kinds of justifications for humanitarian intervention which might be legitimised through the establishment of criteria. Recognising the importance of justifications, what characterises Wheeler's approach to communication is an explicitly constructivist understanding of the role of legitimacy in enabling and constraining the reasons offered to justify particular actions. Crawford draws on a discourse ethical approach but this is explored in a limited fashion.

In summary, the IICK's framework of principles consists of two parts. First, those threshold principles which must be satisfied in order for any claim of humanitarian intervention to be legitimate, and second, a series of 'contextual principles' which 'enhance or diminish the *degree* of legitimacy possessed by forceful intervention'.[39] There are three threshold principles indicated by the Commission. The first comprises two valid trigger factors for humanitarian intervention: 'severe violations of international human rights or humanitarian law on a sustained basis' and the 'subjection of a civilian society to great suffering and risk due to the "failure" of their state, which entails the breakdown of governance at the level of the territorial sovereign state'. The second principle is that the 'overriding aim of all phases of the intervention involving the threat and the use of force must be the direct protection of the victimized population', while the third is that the 'method of intervention must be reasonably calculated to end the humanitarian catastrophe as rapidly as possible, and must specifically take measures to protect all civilians, to avoid collateral damage to civilian society, and to preclude any secondary punitive or retaliatory action against the target governments'.[40]

The principles developed for military intervention by the responsibility to protect doctrine reflect certain similarities to the above guidelines and draw heavily on the just war tradition to construct four main principles: 1) the just cause threshold (actual or apprehended large-scale loss of life, or large-scale ethnic cleansing); 2) the precautionary principles (right intention, last resort, proportional means, and reasonable prospects); 3) right authority; and 4) operational principles (clear objectives and mandate, common military approach, appropriate rules of engagement, acceptance of gradualism in the application of force, maximum coordination with humanitarian organisations, and acceptance that force protection cannot become the main objective).[41] The doctrine of the responsibility to protect has worked to place these principles within a more developed conceptual context than that indicated by the IICK.[42] First, the debate concerning the 'right to intervene', which has characterised the humanitarian intervention debate, has undergone a discursive shift to a responsibility to protect those at risk. Ideally, its perspective is not that of the prospective interveners, but rather those on whose behalf we claim to act. Second, it was argued that in the absence of the state's will or ability to protect its citizens, a secondary responsibility to protect falls on the wider international community.[43] Thirdly, it makes clear that the responsibility to protect is about more than military intervention and covers three broad strands of action and obligation: 1) the responsibility to prevent situations arising by addressing the root causes and direct causes of conflict and other man-made crises; 2) the responsibility to react; and 3) the responsibility to rebuild.[44]

Wheeler proposes a slightly different interpretation of the minimum criteria required by interventions in order to qualify as humanitarian. Briefly, he claims that these are: supreme humanitarian emergency; necessity or last resort; proportionality; and a positive humanitarian outcome. Wheeler's solidarist argument indicates that in the instance of a supreme humanitarian emergency, state leaders should accept the risk of casualties in order to end human rights abuses.[45] Noticeable by its absence is the requirement of positive humanitarian motive. Wheeler argues, contrary to conventional wisdom, that the primacy of humanitarian motives is not necessary for an intervention to qualify as humanitarian. It is only when either the motives or the means employed serve to undermine a positive humanitarian outcome that the intervention may no longer be counted as humanitarian.[46]

Crawford's guidelines for humanitarian intervention stress a discourse ethical procedure. She asserts that the 'procedural aim must be to conduct a discourse with all potential actors who will then develop an approach to deciding questions of humanitarian intervention'.[47] This is significant because she highlights the need to develop means of avoiding humanitarian crises as well as for managing them. The convention she has in mind should be sufficiently flexible to meet a variety of cases, but would look at such questions as who can legitimately call for humanitarian intervention; who should be authorised to carry out intervention and what means are acceptable; what constitutes a humanitarian intervention; what the limits of humanitarian intervention are; and what kind of humanitarian crises demand an international response.[48] As Crawford points out, it is precisely because humanitarian intervention violates discourse ethical principles that a discourse ethical practice must be used to decide when force can or must be used. Without such a dialogue, humanitarian interventions may come to resemble colonial practices. By emphasising the need for broad and inclusive participation in any conversation that shapes the guidelines for humanitarian intervention, Crawford demonstrates the relevance of a communicative ethics approach, although this is not fully unpacked and operationalised. Dialogue, she notes:

> could help actors see the consequences of their actions, in the long chain of events, which help create humanitarian crises (such as great powers sending arms to authoritarian regimes to promote the 'interests' of the great power), and help actors avoid, prevent, or halt those actions.[49]

Crawford suggests that interventions might be granted greater legitimacy (and under a Convention, greater legality) if the 'entire international community were part of the discourse that leads to a convention on humanitarian intervention'.[50]

Having summarised these contemporary examples of criteria for humanitarian intervention, it remains to elucidate the central concern with such projects. The limitations of just war-informed criteria are cast into relief by communicative ethics in two ways. First, the notion of sovereignty as responsibility enshrined in *The Responsibility to Protect* articulates standards for intervention, but in an attempt to provide answers it does not sufficiently address the need for the prior legitimacy of the communicative process through which consensus on these substantive principles was reached. The danger here is that legitimacy is conflated with morality and legality. Indeed, Wheeler's solidarism offers a substantive set of moral principles which can be used to judge the legitimacy of individual interventions. Actors may draw on these reasons to justify their claim to legitimacy. But this does not indicate what might constitute a legitimate *communicative process* which is burdened with making these decisions and validating claims to legitimacy. In other words, what kinds of communicative practices characterise the decision-making process which settled on these substantive principles or enabled them to be intersubjectively validated when drawn upon in particular cases?[51] While the just war tradition may remain the most sophisticated framework available for engaging with the moral question of intervention and the use of force, it is missing a communicative dimension grounded in communicative ethics. This is relevant given the acknowledgement that criteria for legitimate humanitarian intervention remain ultimately '*political* – subject to interpretation and manipulation' by all actors involved in fighting or attempting to resolve conflict.[52] Second, whether or not criteria have been met in cases like Kosovo remains a question of justification – reason-giving and argumentation – and political judgement.[53] Missing from the just war-informed approaches to humanitarian intervention is an 'analytical tool for understanding the politics involved in the intersubjective definition and implementation of its criteria'.[54] Existing criteria which rely on the just war tradition do not address such procedural concerns as levels of inclusion, the absence of coercion, and reflexive dialogue. What does communicative 'fairness' look like in such contexts, particularly in the face of opposing interpretations of substantive principles, and how should claims to legitimacy be validated? Criteria for intervention neither look for nor are able to recognise forms of communicative distortion which might invalidate claims to legitimacy. The need to give full recognition to the communicative dimension to legitimacy requires developing a communicative ethics capable of judging the validity of varied communicative practices.

The search for legitimating criteria to institutionalise intervention in international law faces further problems. On the one hand, in line with their arguments regarding the strategic use of language, realists would argue that such criteria may simply provide a basis for reasserting and legitimising the rights of the interveners which are likely to be those of the most powerful states. On the other hand, the argument for non-intervention and sovereignty can also be interpreted as legitimising the interests of the powerful and reaffirming the status quo. A further possibility is that the case for institutionalising intervention, for example through the responsibility to protect doctrine, faces the difficult task of responding to situations in which the discourses of law, intervention and human rights have been co-opted by actors in order to justify *non*-intervention. This can clearly be seen in the conflict in Darfur which was considered to be a test case for the responsibility to protect doctrine.[55]

Despite Colin Powell, then US Secretary of State, declaring in 2004 that genocide was taking place in Darfur, the lack of intervention by the international community paved the way for critics of the doctrine to point to its lack of credibility. In an argument that recognises both the ambivalence within the doctrine over where authority lies to determine the shift of responsibility from the state to the international community, and the power of language, Alex Bellamy has demonstrated the challenge that Darfur has posed for advocates of responsibility to protect. Acknowledging that the debate surrounding Darfur drew heavily on the language of a 'responsibility to protect', he nevertheless identifies how this language has enabled '*anti-interventionists* to legitimize arguments against action by claiming that primary responsibility in certain contested states still lies with the state, and not (yet) with an international body'.[56] In other words, the language of the responsibility to protect serves to constrain as much as to enable intervention. By focusing on the contested and ambiguous issue of who has the primary responsibility to protect (the Sudanese government, the African Union, or the Security Council), opponents of intervention were able to legitimise their actions with reference to the dominant discourse of 'responsibility to protect'. Their argument was that the primary responsibility to protect Darfur's civilians still lay with the Sudanese government, thereby rejecting the possibility of external intervention.[57] Bellamy's argument demonstrates that language and meaning are not incontrovertibly fixed and can be drawn on by different normative constituencies for whom judgements about the protection of civilian life goes to the heart of politics. Thus, criteria for legitimate intervention do not, by themselves, avert the problem of potentially equally valid, yet differing interpretations and justifications. Communicative ethics instead shifts the focus from the substantive claim to the conditions which enable it to be voiced and validated.[58]

Legitimacy in international relations

Legitimacy, it can be argued, is an 'essentially contested concept'.[59] It has also become the focus of increasing scholarly attention in IR.[60] Historically contingent, as Martin Wight asserted, international legitimacy is 'the answer given by each generation to the fundamental, ever-present question, what are the principles (if any) on which international society is founded?'[61] Often considered to reside at the 'frontiers of morality and law',[62] much attention has been paid to the legitimacy of NATO's actions in these terms. Less critical attention has been paid to the relationship between legitimacy and communicative action. The premise of constructivism in IR that the social construction of reality is fundamentally a linguistic phenomenon has drawn attention to the notion of legitimacy as a language game and to the need to study its communicative dimension.[63] International legitimacy is conceived of by some as a practice which, while not identical to any one norm, draws on a multiplicity of norms, such as legality, morality and constitutionality, to make its claim.[64] Both a normative and sociological concept, legitimacy is not simply the *acceptance* of governance, which can be derived from coercion or self-interest, but rather the understanding and acceptance that the norm in question is binding within a social order.[65] Legitimacy is a social concept which relies upon 'social perception and recognition'.[66] It is often acknowledged that reason-giving, justification and persuasion lie at the heart of legitimating processes, yet there has been insufficient attention paid to what these processes might look like and how they might be both analytically and normatively understood in IR.

Recognising that argumentation, communication and persuasion are key to legitimacy, the central role that Jürgen Habermas's discourse ethics and theory of communicative action might play in shaping a communicative ethics becomes clearer. While Habermas's discourse ethics is a procedural model of communication, his roots in critical theory ensure that emancipatory intentions remain at the heart of his theory of communicative action. In other words, communicative ethics should not only be able to evaluate the process by which decisions are made, but imbue the notion of 'illegitimacy' with normative and substantive values and indicate that communication, if it wishes to be perceived as legitimate, *should* be conducted in certain ways. Andrew Hurrell recognises that 'political, legal and moral debate necessarily involve providing reasons, and criticizing, debating, accepting or discarding them. Legitimacy is about providing persuasive reasons as to why a course of action, a rule, or a political order is right and appropriate.'[67] The central argument of the book, then, is that communicative ethics secures a critical communicative dimension to legitimacy and the decision-making processes whereby these claims are offered by actors to justify the resort to force.

Within the debates over the nature and role of legitimacy in IR, several dominant approaches may be outlined. The international law approach ties together legitimacy, law, and consent (*pacta sunt servanda*).[68] This conception of legitimacy also brings in notions of procedure and right process. The rationalist approach assumes that the violation of legitimate norms (i.e. those that are institutionalised and widely accepted) is potentially costly. Therefore, the perceived legitimacy of norms acts to constrain states from actions which might jeopardise their reputation or motivate resistance to their plans through the imposition of sanctions or other costs. Legitimacy is thus seen as a resource to be drawn on strategically by states.[69] The constructivist approach emphasises the relationship between legitimacy and persuasion and socialisation of states. In other words, states come to accept norms through processes of arguing, reasoning, and persuasion.[70] The rationalist and constructivist approaches are revisited in Chapter 3 whereupon their respective limitations with regard to the communicative dimension of legitimacy are explored.

A number of issues emerge out of the contestation of legitimacy among advocates of these approaches. A common problem posed by legitimacy debates is the aforementioned relationship between legality and legitimacy. The distinction between legality and legitimacy is one which runs throughout much of the debate over Kosovo, and it is closely linked with arguments concerning morality and the need for justice. Much of the positioning of international lawyers, politicians, and academics centred on this distinction and reflected varying stances on the question of the desirability of a legal norm of humanitarian intervention.[71] To some, this distinction is unfortunate and simply reveals deficiencies in the international legal regime, suggesting the need for legal reform to reflect changing international norms. For legal realists, legitimacy is synonymous with law. This reflects the arguments of international lawyers that the obligation of states to comply with international law derives from their explicit consent. While many of the challenges which have emerged in recent security discourses have centred on this distinction, there are as many dangers in separating legitimacy and legality as there are in conflating them. The emergence of 'humanitarian emergencies' and the subsequent use of force, as well as the development of arguments for 'expanding claims of defensive necessity',[72] referring to pre-emptive war and preventive self-defence, have been both defended and criticised by drawing a distinction between legality and legitimacy.

These arguments reflect the normative positions contained within pluralism and solidarism as set out earlier. Those who claim legitimacy, if not legality, for their actions, often draw on arguments of the 'collective good', the triumph of human rights and the need to protect liberal values of democracy and freedom. In the name of morality and justice, certain circumstances call for action outside the law. On the other hand, the arguments of those who seek to confine legitimacy within the law are not so different. They believe values such as democracy, freedom, and the protection of human rights are best protected by rejecting such reinterpretations of international law which they perceive as threatening the stability of international order. Conflating legality and legitimacy runs the grave risk of concealing the unequal power relations which allow some greater ability to determine what is legal, and therefore legitimate, than others.[73] When legality and legitimacy pull apart, however, the question posed by Richard Falk becomes pertinent: 'Is not, in the end, the danger of relying on legitimacy to overcome the inadequacies of legality a means to assert the primacy of politics and the subordination of law?'[74] This is an argument which not only reminds us of the criticisms of realists, but bears parallels with Habermas's concerns over NATO's inter-vention in Kosovo; although he supported the use of force, he argued that it should have been accomplished through authoritative legal channels rather than relying on claims of moral legitimacy and exceptionalism.[75]

The relationship between law and morality lies at the heart of the debates surrounding legitimacy and draws in issues of power relations, procedure, different social actors, and questions of order and justice. As Ian Clark asks, 'where does legitimacy stand if legality and morality pull apart?'[76] Indeed, this was the question central to the debates on the use of force which surrounded Kosovo and was the sentiment captured by the IICK's verdict. What 'illegal but legitimate' meant in this context was the need for morality, not just international law, to shape the response of the international community. As we will see, in the case of Kosovo this resulted in a debate between two opposing interpretations of the norms of international society.

There are strong moral and legal arguments for favouring either a procedural or substantive understanding of legitimacy. On the one hand, the core intuition of pluralists – who have traditionally favoured a proceduralist legitimacy – that in an international society consistently characterised by deep divisions, conflict and unequal power relations, the focus should be on building acceptance of shared processes, legal sources and a commitment to diplomatic engagement, is a powerful one. On the other hand, the argument favoured by solidarists of different shades and stripes is equally powerful: that shared substantive moral values should underpin the conceptions of justice and legitimacy which enable and constrain actions by international actors. Substantive notions of legitimacy built on concepts of shared values and moral standards face, however, charges of imperialism, of being liberal and Western-centric and therefore inappropriate to or ill-received in other cultures. Substantive legitimacy cannot escape the charge of being determined by unequal power relations within international society and therefore able to make and break the law when it meets with the interests of powerful states. It also cannot escape the problem that it opens the door to moral justification and therefore, in the context of the use of force, moves us to the contested sphere of just war debates and the related critiques of Schmittian exceptionalism, among others.[77]

Reading Kosovo: legitimacy and justification

A methodological sphere of contestation also arises between those who engage in empirical or descriptive analyses of legitimacy and those who adopt a normative, evaluative approach to the concept. The focus of the former tends towards the social functions of legitimacy, whereas the latter is concerned with normative justifications of governance. This methodological divide also emerges in the work of those who explore the communicative dimension of IR. By contrast, communicative ethics brings together the empirical and normative facets of legitimacy theorising. Such an analysis will focus on the manner in which the decision to use force against the Federal Republic of Yugoslavia (FRY) was taken and, contesting the IICK's 'illegal but legitimate' verdict, will offer an account of illegitimacy which is tied to neither morality nor legality.

Conclusion

All schools of thought in IR implicitly or explicitly address the notion of boundaries.[78] While some have argued that it is not possible to reconcile citizenship and humanity,[79] others have argued that the state does not constitute the outer boundary of our moral and political obligations.[80] Good international citizenship and the responsibility to protect doctrine both articulate differing interpretations of the way in which these responsibilities should be constructed and implemented. Both tend to conflate legitimacy, however, with moral and legal criteria. Whilst good international citizenship and the responsibility to protect doctrine recognise the importance of justifications and, therefore, the role of language, they do not have a capacity to critically interrogate the communicative practices which constitute the claims to legitimate political action and are thus unable to recognise the influence of exclusion or coercion on evaluations of legitimacy. It is only by looking to communicative ethics that we secure the interpretive power necessary to identify and evaluate the underpinning linguistic and material conditions which shape communicative practices. The 'politics of legitimacy is ... about asking difficult questions about who is included or excluded from these allegedly shared languages and where the gaps and breakdowns occur'.[81] Communicative ethics offers a critical means with which to ask and answer these difficult questions, thereby holding those involved to account through a critical and normative conception of reason-giving, justification and communication.

Communicative ethics contributes an additional theoretical and empirical element to the concept of legitimacy. It is in a sense *prior* to the competing interpretations of morality, legality and constitutionality and must accompany their political reconciliation. Recognising that legitimacy encompasses and requires a balance between substantive justificatory discourses and a communicative dimension, neither consensus on shared values, nor consensus on right process can ignore the political nature of the questions at stake and the need to address the moments of (frequently contested) interpretation and application to a particular situation. Communicative ethics, understood as a critical theoretically informed framework with which to interrogate empirical communicative practices, is an appropriate framework with which to investigate the justifications that actors give when they claim legitimacy for the use of force in international politics. It offers both a tool for reflection and critique and articulates the procedures and conditions under which agents can address the key question in international politics: how should we legitimately respond to a variety of intersocietal, interethnic or interstate conflicts?

NOTES

1 Independent International Commission on Kosovo, *The Kosovo Report* (Oxford: Oxford University Press, 2000), 186.
2 M. Wight, 'International Legitimacy', *International Relations*, 4:1 (1972), 1.
3 Inis Claude drew attention to the limitations of conceiving legitimacy along the lines of morality or legality, arguing that ultimately both law and morality required their own legitimisation and that the relations between these two concepts varied over time, at times reinforcing each other and at others, in conflict. Claude, 'Collective Legitimation', 368–9. Bjola's study, *Legitimsing the Use of Force in International Politics*, also acknowledges the inadequacy of moral and legal conceptions of legitimacy in determining under what conditions the use of force can be understood as legitimate.
4 Reus-Smit argues that: 'Because of its inherently social nature, legitimacy should not be conflated with other social values. Politicians, journalists, and scholars frequently use the language of legitimacy interchangeably with the language of rationality, justice, legality, and morality. But while legitimacy claims may draw on such values in the politics of legitimation, legitimacy is not their synonym.' Reus-Smit, 'International Crises of Legitimacy', 160.
5 The application of the 'communicative imperatives' to Kosovo in Chapter 6 offers arguably plausible counterfactuals and demonstrates the importance of contingency in the decision-making process. However, given that the aim of the book is not to deliberately construct counterfactuals, the methodology used is not a counterfactual one. It would be a different project to examine the plausibility of the counterfactuals which might be identified (through the lens of communicative ethics) in the context of NATO's intervention in Kosovo. These would have to be examined in terms of their temporal, cultural, technological/military, diplomatic, and political plausibility. See R. N. Lebow, *Forbidden Fruit: Counterfactuals and International Relations* (Princeton: Princeton University Press, 2010); R. N. Lebow, 'What's So Different about a Counterfactual?', *World Politics*, 52:4 (2000), 550–85; P. E. Tetlock and A. Belkin (eds), *Counterfactual Thought Experiments in World Politics: Logical, Methodological and Psychological Perspectives* (Princeton: Princeton University Press, 1996).
6 N. Crawford, *Argument and Change in World Politics: Ethics, Decolonization, and Humanitarian Intervention* (Cambridge: Cambridge University Press, 2002), 402.
7 Resolution 1160, 31 March 1998, 14–0 (China abstained).
8 The broadening interpretation of 'threats to peace and security' includes: migration

and refugee flows, climate change, human rights violations, human security, terrorism and nuclear security. Article 39 of the UN Charter indicates that where the Security Council determines there is a threat to the peace, a breach of the peace, or an act of aggression, it may decide what measures shall be taken to maintain or restore international peace and security, including the use of force or of economic sanctions.

9 Collective security refers to the institutionalised balance of power which requires states to behave in accordance with certain norms and rules to maintain stability and if necessary to act collectively to stop the aggression of individual states or groups of states. See C. A. Kupchan and C. A. Kupchan, 'The Promise of Collective Security', *International Security*, 20:1 (1995), 52–61.

10 B. Simma, 'NATO, the UN and the Use of Force: Legal Aspects', *European Journal of International Law*, 10:1 (1999), 1–22; T. Farer, 'Humanitarian Intervention Before and After 9/11: Legality and Legitimacy', in Holzgrefe and Keohane (eds), *Humanitarian Intervention*.

11 For a variety of arguments see F. R. Tesón, 'Collective Humanitarian Intervention', *Michigan Journal of International Law*, 17:2 (1996), 323–72; Holzgrefe and Keohane (eds), *Humanitarian Intervention*; Simma, 'NATO, the UN and the Use of Force'; A. Cassese, 'A Follow-Up: Forcible Humanitarian Countermeasures and *Opinio Necessitatis*', *European Journal of International Law*, 10:4 (1999), 791–9; N. J. Wheeler, 'Humanitarian Intervention After Kosovo: Emergent Norm, Moral Duty or the Coming Anarchy', *International Affairs*, 77:1 (2001), 113–28.

12 IICK, *The Kosovo Report*, 186. For a different perspective see G Robertson, 'JISB Interview: Intervention, Statebuilding and Security', *Journal of Intervention and Statebuilding*, 3:2 (2009), 259–75.

13 Linklater and Suganami, *The English School*; E. H. Carr, *The Twenty Years' Crisis 1919–1939* (London: Macmillan and Co. Ltd, 1939).

14 G. Evans, *Making Australian Foreign Policy* (Melbourne: Australian Fabian Society, 1989).

15 A. Linklater, 'What is a Good International Citizen?', in P. Keal (ed.), *Ethics and Foreign Policy* (Sydney: Allen and Unwin, 1992), 21.

16 Linklater, 'What is a Good International Citizen?', 28.

17 Evans, *Making Australian Foreign Policy*, 42.

18 See H. Bull, 'The Grotian Conception of International Society', in Herbert Butterfield and Martin Wight, *Diplomatic Investigations: Essays in the Theory of International Politics* (London: Allen & Unwin, 1966); Wheeler, 'Pluralist or Solidarist Conceptions of International Society'; T. Dunne, *Inventing International Society: A History of the English School* (London: Macmillan, 1998); Linklater and Suganami, *The English School*; W. Bain, 'The Pluralist-Solidarist Debate', in R. Denemark (ed.), *International Studies Compendium Project*, vol. IX (Oxford: Blackwell Publishing, 2009).

19 Linklater, 'The Good International Citizen and the Crisis in Kosovo'.

20 N. J. Wheeler and T. Dunne, 'Hedley Bull's Pluralism of the Intellect and Solidarism of the Will', *International Affairs*, 72:1 (1996), 95.

21 Linklater, 'The Good International Citizen and the Crisis in Kosovo', 485.

22 Wheeler, *Saving Strangers*, 29. The main distinction between English School pluralism and realism is that 'even if a state decides to break the rules, it recognises "that it owes other states an explanation of its conduct, in terms of rules that they accept"'. Ibid. 24, citing Bull.

23 R. Jackson, *The Global Covenant: Human Conduct in a World of States* (Oxford: Oxford University Press, 2000), 169–78.

24 Bull, 'The Grotian Conception of International Society', 63. Bull concluded, however,

that based on then current practice, this view of international society was premature. See also N. J. Wheeler and T. Dunne, 'Good International Citizenship: A Third Way for British Foreign Policy', *International Affairs*, 74:4 (1998), 856.
25 P. Lawler, 'The Good State: In Praise of 'Classical' Internationalism', *Review of International Studies*, 31:3 (2005), 427–49; Keal (ed.), *Ethics and Foreign Policy*.
26 Wheeler and Dunne, 'Good International Citizenship', 854.
27 Linklater and Suganami, *The English School*, 170–1; A. Linklater, *Critical Theory and World Politics* (Abingdon: Routledge, 2007); A. Linklater, *The Problem of Harm in World Politics: Theoretical Investigations* (Cambridge: Cambridge University Press, 2011).
28 A comprehensive list of these principles includes, although is not limited to: '(1) states are the basic members of international society; (2) all societies have a right to a separate existence subject to the need to maintain the balance of power; (3) intervention in the internal affairs of member states to promote some vision of human decency or human justice is prohibited; (4) states should relinquish the goal of acquiring preponderant power in the international system; (5) the duty to cooperate to maintain an equilibrium of power is incumbent on all states; (6) diplomatic efforts to reconcile competing interests should proceed from the assumption that each state is the best judge of its own interests; (7) an "inclusive" as opposed to "exclusive" conception of the national interest should be pursued so that other states, and the society to which they belong, are not harmed for the sake of trivial national advantages; (8) because of their unique military capabilities the great powers should assume special responsibilities which are determined by mutual consent for preserving international order; (9) an essential purpose of an "inclusive" foreign policy is to make changes to international society which will satisfy the legitimate interests of rising powers and new member states; (10) force is justified in self-defence and in response to states that seek preponderant power; and (11) proportionality in war should be respected along with the principle that defeated powers should be readmitted as equals into international society.' Linklater and Suganami, *The English School*, 237–40.
29 Ibid., 240.
30 Cox, 'Social Forces, States and World Orders'; Linklater and Suganami, *The English School*, 168.
31 A list of principles for a solidarist understanding of good international citizenship includes: '(1) individuals and the various communities and associations to which they belong are the fundamental members of international society; (2) unnecessary suffering and cruelty to individuals and their immediate associations should be avoided in the conduct of war; (3) pluralist commitments to sovereignty and sovereign immunity should be replaced by the notion of personal responsibility for infringements of the laws of war; (4) superior orders do not justify violations of humanitarian international law; (5) breaches of the laws of war should be punishable in domestic and international courts; (6) the sovereignty of the state is conditional on compliance with the international law of human rights; (7) sovereignty does not entitle states to be free from "the legitimate appraisal of their peers" with respect to human rights; (8) states have responsibilities as custodians of human rights everywhere; (9) individuals have the legal right of appeal to international courts of law when violations of human rights occur; and (10) regard for human rights requires respect for non-sovereign communities and requires the society of states to protect minority nations and indigenous peoples from unnecessary suffering.' Linklater and Suganami, *The English School*, 243–4.
32 Wheeler and Dunne, 'Good International Citizenship'.
33 Ibid., 855. Wheeler and Dunne develop the definition originally offered by Linklater in

34 'What is a good international citizen?'.
34 Ibid., 869.
35 Wheeler, *Saving Strangers*.
36 Linklater, 'The Good International Citizen and the Crisis in Kosovo', 493.
37 ICISS, *The Responsibility to Protect*; G. Evans, *The Responsibility to Protect: Ending Mass Atrocity Crimes Once and For All* (Washington, D C: Brookings Institution Press, 2008); A. J. Bellamy, *Responsibility to Protect* (Cambridge: Polity Press, 2009); D. Bulley, *Ethics as Foreign Policy: Britain, the EU and the Other* (Abingdon: Routledge, 2009); A. J. Bellamy, 'Kosovo and the Advent of Sovereignty as Responsibility', *Journal of Intervention and Statebuilding*, 3:2 (2009), 163–84; J. Pattison, *Humanitarian Intervention and the Responsibility to Protect* (Oxford: Oxford University Press, 2010).
38 R. Fine, 'Cosmopolitanism and Violence', *British Journal of Sociology*, 57:1 (2006), 49–67.
39 IICK, *The Kosovo Report*, 193. Original emphasis.
40 Ibid., 193–4.
41 ICISS, *The Responsibility to Protect*, xii–xiii.
42 R. Thakur, 'Intervention, Sovereignty and the Responsibility to Protect: Experiences from ICISS', *Security Dialogue*, 33:3 (2002), 323–40. On responsibility to protect see E. C. Luck, 'Sovereignty, Choice, and the Responsibility to Protect', *Global Responsibility to Protect*, 1 (2009); Bellamy, *Responsibility to Protect*; Evans, *The Responsibility to Protect*; A. J. Bellamy, 'The Responsibility to Protect – Five Years On', *Ethics and International Affairs*, 24:2 (2010), 143–69. For a critical perspective on responsibility to protect in relation to the role of the international community, see for example M. Mamdani, 'Responsibility to Protect or Right to Punish?', *Journal of Intervention and Statebuilding*, 4:1 (2010), 53–67; D. Chandler, 'The Paradox of the "Responsibility to Protect"', *Cooperation and Conflict*, 45:1 (2010), 128–34; A. Orford, *International Authority and the Responsibility to Protect* (Cambridge: Cambridge University Press, 2011).
43 G. Evans, 'Crimes Against Humanity: Overcoming Indifference', *Journal of Genocide Research*, 8:3 (2006), 333.
44 Evans, *The Responsibility to Protect*, xi. Significantly, it is the theme of prevention (and not military intervention for protection purposes) which dominated the discourse preceding and subsequent to the World Summit Outcome Document of 2005, where one version of the doctrine of the responsibility to protect is officially endorsed (see UN Doc A/RES/60/1, 24 October 2005).
45 Wheeler, *Saving Strangers*, 50.
46 Ibid., 38.
47 Crawford, *Argument and Change in World Politics*, 431.
48 Ibid., 431–2.
49 Ibid. 433.
50 Ibid.
51 One way of interpreting the need for a greater communicative dimension is to consider the question of 'who decides' and the concomitant issue of 'right authority' in the context of criteria for intervention – see N. J. Wheeler, 'Operationalising the Responsibility to Protect: The Continuing Debate over Where Authority Should be Located for the Use of Force', NUPI Report, No. 3 (2008). However, I argue that the concept of right authority does not recognise the need to make evaluations based on the quality of the communicative practices concerning the legitimacy of the process through which claims are validated intersubjectively. Thanks to Nick Wheeler for his help clarifying the distinction between 'legitimacy claims which are raised by actors through justification and public reasoning processes and legitimacy or legitimation

which only comes about if these claims are validated'. See N. J. Wheeler, 'Saving Strangers: A Personal Reflection', Lecture delivered in Rio de Janeiro, 10 December 2010.

52 J. M. Welsh, 'From Right to Responsibility: Humanitarian Intervention and International Society', *Global Governance*, 8:4 (2002), 514. Original emphasis. Bjola makes a similar point in his argument for the need for a deliberative dimension to the legitimate use of force (*Legitimising the Use of Force in International Politics*, 35). Orford also acknowledges that 'how to deal with a situation involving competing loyalties or the clash of rationalities [e.g. statecraft, human rights, international criminal law and so on] is in the end a fundamentally political question. It is a question that has not been resolved by the responsibility to protect concept' (*International Authority and the Responsibility to Protect*, 187).

53 Alex Bellamy acknowledges this in relation to the issue of last resort. He recognises that in relation to the use of force, we have 'no way of judging when "last resort" is reached'. Bellamy, *Responsibility to Protect*, 166. See N. J. Rengger, 'The Judgement of War: On the Idea of Legitimate Force in World Politics', *Review of International Studies*, 31, Special Issue (2005), 143–61; C. Reus-Smit, 'The Liberal Licence to Use Force', *Review of International Studies*, 31, Special Issue (2005), 71–92.

54 Bjola, *Legitimising the Use of Force in International Politics*, 35.

55 A second example of the way in which manipulation of particular discourses can serve to bolster oppositional positions is articulated in Ian Hurd's work on the case of UN sanctions against Libya. Hurd argues: 'Libya's strategy against the sanctions relied on recycling, in opposition, the very claims to legitimation made by the strong states on behalf of the Security Council and the sanctions regime.' I. Hurd, *After Anarchy: Legitimacy and Power in the United Nations Security Council* (Princeton: Princeton University Press, 2007), 140, 149–70.

56 A. Bellamy, 'Responsibility to Protect or Trojan Horse? The Crisis in Darfur and Humanitarian Intervention after Iraq', *Ethics and International Affairs*, 19:2 (2005), 33. Original emphasis.

57 Ibid., 52. The problem of locating jurisdiction and the absence of procedures according to which movement between the jurisdiction of the state and that of the international community is to be negotiated or by whom it should be decided is recognised by Orford in terms of the World Summit Outcome Document on Responsibility to Protect. See Orford, *International Authority and the Responsibility to Protect*, 182.

58 Rightly raising the issue that those actors involved in the dialogues that do take place and are envisaged by the frameworks discussed above are primarily the interveners, Bellamy argues that there appears to be: 'little basis in pragmatic epistemology for claims that link the legitimacy of force to a set of criteria that are removed from lived experiences about the efficacy of armed intervention. Moreover, it is important to bear in mind that the Socratic demand that we collect as many experiences as possible when constructing "good" knowledge means that the experiences of the interveners should not be prioritised, as they appear to be in the move to establish legitimising criteria.' A. J. Bellamy, 'Pragmatic Solidarism and the Dilemmas of Humanitarian Intervention', *Millennium: Journal of International Studies*, 31:3 (2002), 484.

59 A. Hurrelmann, S. Schneider and J. Steffek, 'Conclusion: Legitimacy – Making Sense of an Essentially Contested Concept', in A. Hurrelmann, S. Schneider and J. Steffek (eds), *Legitimacy in an Age of Global Politics* (Basingstoke: Palgrave Macmillan, 2007).

60 See Wight, 'International Legitimacy'; T. Franck, *The Power of Legitimacy Among Nations* (Oxford: Oxford University Press, 1990); A. Linklater, *The Transformation of Political Community: Ethical Foundations of the Post-Westphalian Era* (Cambridge: Polity

Press, 1998); I. Hurd, 'Legitimacy and Authority in International Politics', *International Organization*, 53:2 (1999), 379–408; Shapcott, *Justice, Community and Dialogue*; M. Bukanovsky, *Legitimacy and Power Politics* (New Jersey: Princeton University Press, 2002); I. Johnstone, 'Security Council Deliberations: The Power of the Better Argument', *European Journal of International Law*, 14:3 (2003), 437–80; J. Steffek, 'The Legitimation of International Governance: A Discourse Approach', *European Journal of International Relations*, 9:2 (2003), 249–75; A. Hurrell, 'Legitimacy and the Use of Force: Can the Circle be Squared?', *Review of International Studies*, 31, Special Issue (2005), 15–32; R. Falk, 'Legality and Legitimacy: The Quest for Principled Flexibility and Restraint', *Review of International Studies*, 31, Special Issue (2005), 33–50; Rengger, 'The Judgement of War'; Bjola, *Legitimising the Use of Force in International Politics*; I. Clark, *Legitimacy in International Society* (Oxford: Oxford University Press, 2005); I. Clark, *International Legitimacy and World Society* (Oxford: Oxford University Press, 2007); Hurd, *After Anarchy*; Hurrelmann et al. (eds), *Legitimacy in an Age of Global Politics*; I. Clark and C. Reus-Smit (eds), Special Issue: 'Resolving International Crises of Legitimacy', *International Politics*, 44:2–3 (2007); I. Johnstone, 'The Security Council as Legislature', in B. Cronin and I. Hurd (eds), *The UN Security Council and the Politics of International Authority* (Abingdon: Routledge, 2008); C. Bjola, 'Legitimacy and the Use of Force: Bridging the Analytical-Normative Divide', *Review of International Studies*, 34:4 (2008), 627–44; H. Charlesworth and J.-M. Coicaud (eds), *The Faultlines of International Legitimacy* (Cambridge: Cambridge University Press, 2010).
61 Wight, 'International Legitimacy', 1.
62 Ibid.
63 S. Schneider, F. Nullmeier and A. Hurrelmann, 'Exploring the Communicative Dimension of Legitimacy: Text Analytical Approaches', in A. Hurrelmann et al. (eds), *Legitimacy in an Age of Global Politics*, 131.
64 Clark, *International Legitimacy and World Society*.
65 Steffek, 'The Legitimation of International Governance', 254.
66 Reus-Smit, 'International Crises of Legitimacy', 159.
67 Hurrell, 'Legitimacy and the Use of Force', 24.
68 These three approaches are drawn from J. Steffek, 'Legitimacy in International Relations: From State Compliance to Citizen Consensus' in Hurrellman et al. (eds), *Legitimacy in an Age of Global Politics*, 182–5.
69 Ibid.
70 Ibid.
71 For a range of arguments see: Simma, 'NATO, the UN and the Use of Force'; L. Henkin, 'Kosovo and the Law of Humanitarian Intervention', *American Journal of International Law*, 93:4 (1999), 824–8; C. Chinkin, 'Kosovo: A "Good" or "Bad" War?', *American Journal of International Law*, 93:4 (1999) 841–7; J. Charney, 'Anticipatory Humanitarian Intervention in Kosovo', *American Journal of International Law*, 93:4 (1999), 834–41; S. Chesterman, *Just War or Just Peace? Humanitarian Intervention and International Law* (Oxford: Oxford University Press, 2001); T. Franck, *Recourse to Force: State Action Against Threats and Armed Attacks* (Cambridge: Cambridge University Press, 2002), 177–91; Orford, *Reading Humanitarian Intervention*; N. Blokker and N. Schrijver (eds), *The Security Council and the Use of Force* (Leiden: Martinus Nijhoff Publishers, 2005); E. A. Heinze, *Waging Humanitarian War* (Albany: SUNY, 2009); A. Hehir, *Humanitarian Intervention: An Introduction* (London, Palgrave Macmillan, 2010).
72 Falk, 'Legality and Legitimacy', 33; Reus-Smit, 'The Liberal Licence to Use Force'.
73 Bjola, 'Legitimating the Use of Force'.

74 Ibid., 34.
75 Habermas, 'Bestiality and Humanity'.
76 Clark, *Legitimacy in International Society*, 19. Franck's response to this question is one of mitigation: 'The essence of mitigation is that the law recognizes the continuing force of the rule in general, while also accepting that, in extraordinary circumstances, condoning a carefully calibrated and justifiable violation may do more to rescue the law's legitimacy that would its rigorous implementation.' This argument is rejected by those who perceive mitigation to be the beginnings of a 'slippery slope'. Franck, *Recourse to Force*, 185.
77 C. Brown, 'From Humanized War to Humanitarian Intervention: Carl Schmitt's Critique of the Just War Tradition', in L. Odysseos and F. Petito (eds), *The International Political Thought of Carl Schmitt* (Abingdon: Routledge, 2007), 56–69.
78 See R. B. J. Walker, *Inside/Outside: International Relations as Political Theory* (Cambridge: Cambridge University Press, 1993); Linklater, *The Problem of Harm in World Politics*.
79 M. Walzer, 'Spheres of Affection', in M. Nussbaum, *For Love of Country?* (Boston, MA: Beacon Press, 2002).
80 Linklater, 'What is a Good International Citizen?', 25; Linklater, *The Transformation of Political Community*
81 Hurrell, 'Legitimacy and the Use of Force', 25. Other ways of exploring legitimacy include symbolic power (I. Hurd, 'Legitimacy, Power, and the Symbolic Life of the Security Council', *Global Governance*, 8:1 (2002), 35–51), legitimacy as authority (the normative belief held by an actor that a rule or institution ought to be obeyed, see Hurd, 'Legitimacy and Authority in International Politics') and 'political legitimacy as conceptualized and contested through the medium of political culture' (Bukanovsky, *Legitimacy and Power Politics*). Clark argues that 'legitimacy refers to international society as the subject: it denotes the condition of international society, not the condition of its individual actors and actions'. In doing so, he argues that legitimacy is a first-order, constitutive, principle of international society. Clark's focus is analytic rather than normative: it does not attempt 'to probe from the outside, the justice of the international order, or of any actions to which it gives rise'. Clark, *Legitimacy in International Society*, Chapter 1.

2

Putting out the fire while the coals still burn: Kosovo prior to 1999[1]

> We are instant witnesses in our sitting rooms through the medium of television to human tragedy in distant lands, and are therefore obliged to accept moral responsibility for our response.
>
> Robin Cook[2]

Introduction

THE STORY OF Kosovo has been iterated through a variety of lenses since 1999.[3] In this instance, the story will be told in two parts in order to bring attention to the hitherto neglected question of communicative ethics. The purpose of this chapter is not to reiterate the existing literature but to narrate particular elements of it in order to identify the problem posed by Kosovo and addressed theoretically and empirically in Part II of the book. Whilst most analyses of the intervention focus on the period 1998–99, there is little doubt that an understanding of the process which led to NATO's use of force in March 1999 requires that the story be traced back earlier than to the immediate factors leading to the intervention. By so doing, it is possible to take into account a number of factors which are often overlooked in assessments of the legitimacy of intervention perceived in moral and/or legal terms. Such an alternative account ascribes to legitimacy a communicative dimension grounded in communicative ethics and, consequently, widens the temporal focus beyond 1998–99 and points, crucially, to a number of missed opportunities for dialogue during the 1990s in Kosovo. The second half of the story is told in Chapter 6 where a theoretical account of communicative ethics is applied to the empirical communicative practices through which the justifications for the use of force were offered.

The first section challenges the essentialist ethnic assumption which underpins some interpretations of the conflict and instead focuses on the political and social construction of ethnic tension. The second section identifies a number of key processes and actors which contributed to the marginalisation of Kosovo between 1989–98 and thus to the development of violent conflict.[4] These processes include: the European Community

Conference on Yugoslavia in 1991; the Badinter Arbitration Commission set up in 1991; the London Conference in 1992 and the International Conference on Former Yugoslavia; the development and side-lining of the non-violent resistance movement in Kosovo led by the Democratic League of Kosovo (LDK); the Dayton Accords in 1995; and the Holbrooke Agreement in October 1998. This contextual account highlights missed opportunities for dialogue or non-violent engagement, thereby proposing moments prior to 1998 in which opportunities for dialogue were foreclosed. The actions of the international community raise two key issues relating to communicative ethics: the exclusionary practices which frequently characterised the decision-making processes used to determine Kosovo's status during the 1990s and the construction of the legitimacy of the use of force in 1999 in moral and legal terms.

The third section sets out the conventional narrative concerning events in the UN Security Council and the run-up to the intervention between 1998 and 1999, together with some of the main lines of argument which structured the debates within the Council. These arguments reflected the normative positions concerning law, order and justice contained within the debate between pluralist and solidarist approaches to international society. The focus on the Security Council enables a recognition of the extent to which the justification of last resort underpinned the shift to the use of force and problematises this emphasis in the light of the discussion of missed opportunities for non-violent engagement.

The political and social construction of ethnic tension

A central premise of the book is that in order to understand what happened to precipitate military intervention in 1999, it is necessary to understand earlier events in Kosovo. This section addresses some of the issues which are integral to a nuanced understanding of the conflict and argues that the wars in the former Yugoslavia in general, and the conflict in Kosovo in particular, were due less to the eruption of ancient ethnic hatred and enmity, as has often been suggested, than to the consequence of specific policies and conscious agency.[5] In order to understand the construction of ethnic tension which led to the crisis in 1998–99, it is necessary to explore some of Kosovo's political and social history.

Both Serbian and Kosovar Albanian identities have been constructed in part through perceived ties to Kosovo and influential historical myths.[6] Central to the political importance of Kosovo and the perpetuation of myths are Kosovo's demographics and their historically contested roots. The 1981 Yugoslav census indicates that of Kosovo's total population of 1,585,000, 77.5% were Albanian and 13.3% were Serb. By 1991, despite active policies by Belgrade to increase Kosovo's Serbian population, Albanians constituted 90% of the population and Serbs only 10%. Historical and demographic narratives, therefore, are commonly used to represent difference in Kosovo.[7] Kosovo holds a special place in the history of both Serbians and Albanians; it is not what is true that matters, but rather what people believe to be so, and this approach pervades any interpretation of Kosovo.[8]

Although myths and legends surrounding Kosovo have been passed down through the centuries, 'it was only in the late nineteenth century that they were resurrected as part of the narratives of rival Serb and Albanian national movements'.[9] Despite being populated largely by Albanians, there is little agreement as to 'first possession' of the land. The Serbs viewed Kosovo as the holy place of the Serb nation, where the Serbian Army, under Lazar, was defeated by the Turks at the Battle of Kosovo Polje in June 1389. Kosovo is also home to the Serbian Orthodox Church. The early twentieth century saw continuing conflict in the Balkans and between the Serbs and Albanians over Kosovo. Albanians resisted both Serb and Yugoslav rule not only because it prevented any union with the newly created Albanian state (1912), but also because, in an attempt to address the ethnic balance, the Serbian-dominated authorities encouraged Serbs and Montenegrins to settle in Kosovo.[10] In addition, all key positions were in the hands of a 'largely imported Serbian elite. Every effort was made to obstruct the development of Albanian national consciousness.'[11] In 1937, Vaso Čubrilović drafted a plan calling for the expulsion of Albanians. Čubrilović's suggestions as to how to 'persuade' Albanians to leave are instructive, as they were to be revived later under Milošević:

> The law must be enforced to the letter so as to make staying intolerable for Albanians: fines, and imprisonments, the ruthless application of all police dispositions such as on the prohibition of smuggling, cutting forests, damaging agriculture, leaving dogs unchained, compulsory labor and any other measure that an experienced police force can contrive.[12]

If this failed to work, then there always remained the practice of 'burning down Albanian villages and city quarters'.[13] Such statements may be seen not as evidence of a pre-given identity prioritising ethnic hatred, but as political and discursive interventions in social relations in Kosovo which served to create antagonism and conflict.

In July 1945, Kosovo became an autonomous province within a federal Serbia (which was a constituent part of the new Federal People's Republic of Yugoslavia) and Serbs retained their dominant position in Kosovo. Although demonstrations in 1968 by Albanian students called for the province to be upgraded to a republic and to be given its own Albanian-language university, the demand for republic status was rejected.[14] However, the 1974 Yugoslav

Constitution gave Kosovo republic status in all but name, granting it economic and political autonomy virtually identical to that of the republics. It was represented on the federal presidency, along with Vojvodina (an autonomous Serbian province) and the six republics, which granted it an equal vote in all decisions. Serbs saw the autonomy granted to Kosovo by the 1974 Constitution as the first step towards secession and unification with Albania. While Tito had maintained a balance over the simmering discontent in Yugoslavia, the system began to unravel following his death in 1980, and in 1981 demonstrations and rioting spread across the province which were suppressed harshly by the Yugoslav authorities. The exact number of dead is unknown, but thousands of Albanians were arrested, tried and imprisoned.[15] Many of the protesters who were jailed were later instrumental in founding the Kosovo Liberation Army (KLA). Tim Judah argues that it is crucially important to remember that until 1989 it was Albanian Communists who were ruling Kosovo, not Serbs. Who did what, in and after 1981, contributed to explaining why it was difficult to bring together a representative Kosovo Albanian negotiating team later on.[16]

The events of 1981 were a turning point. Propaganda on both sides played an important role in the construction of hostilities and the degeneration of inter-communal relations. During the 1970s and 1980s, Kosovo was increasingly Albanianised and the case of the Kosovo Serb farmer, Djordje Martinović, became symbolic of the sentiment being nurtured by Serbs concerning their treatment at the hands of Albanians. In May 1985, he was rushed to hospital to have a broken bottle removed from his anus. He claimed to have been attacked by two Albanians, a claim seized upon by the Belgrade media, although some doctors believed the injury to be self-inflicted, which Martinović himself later admitted was the case before subsequently retracting this confession.[17] This incident was an example of the way perceptions of social relations in Kosovo were shaped, fuelling feelings of Serbian victimisation and being portrayed by the Serbian press as an attack by Albanian nationalist separatists on Serbs.

Another important moment in the reproduction of hostile ethnic identities occurred in January 1986, when 216 Serbian intellectuals presented a petition to the Serb and Yugoslav Assemblies declaring that: 'The case of Djordje Martinović has come to symbolize the predicament of all Serbs in Kosovo.' Later that year, the Serbian Academy of Arts and Sciences published a document which became known as the *Memorandum*, the language of which is seen as an important step on the road to war, particularly in its discussion of the position of the Serbs in Croatia and Kosovo. The document spoke of the 'physical, political, legal and cultural genocide' of Serbs in Kosovo and argued that the 'remnants of the Serb nation [...] faced with a physical, moral and psychological reign of terror [...] seem to be preparing for their final exodus'.[18] The use of historic symbols and events by political elites functioned to mobilise and politicise ethnic identity, thereby enabling the construction of the Serbs as victims and underpinning the call to war.[19]

Milošević visited Kosovo on 24 April 1987 at the request of Ivan Stambolić, the Serbian President, to listen to the grievances of the Kosovo Serbs. He arrived in Kosovo Polje – a site of historical and symbolic significance to both Serbs and Kosovars – while thousands of Serbs were clashing with the Albanian police. Drawing on powerful symbolism, Milošević told Serbs, 'Yugoslavia does not exist without Kosovo! Yugoslavia would disintegrate without Kosovo! Yugoslavia and Serbia are not going to give up Kosovo.'[20] Serb and Albanian claims to Kosovo were greatly informed by the view that 'Nationalism holds that they [nations and states] were destined for each other; that either without the other is incomplete, and constitutes a tragedy.'[21]

Between 1987 and 1989, when he assumed the Serbian Presidency, Milošević consolidated and increased his support, primarily through hundreds of rallies held across the country and known as 'Meetings of Truth'. These populist gatherings served the purposes of politicians, nationalist or communist, like Milošević, who manipulated the myth of Kosovo to create nationalist ideology, rhetoric and propaganda.[22] On 17 November 1988, Milošević achieved the removal of Kosovo's Albanian communist leaders. Preparations began to alter the constitutional status of Kosovo, in order to 'reunite' it with Serbia. To legalise this step, Kosovo's own assembly had to vote to approve it and, on 23 March 1989, surrounded by tanks and police and with Serbian officials monitoring the votes of Albanian delegates, the Kosovo assembly voted for the relevant constitutional amendments which were ratified in the Serbian parliament five days later.[23] Those Albanian delegates who stood up to Serbian pressure were expelled from the Assembly, dismissed from their jobs, and threatened with criminal prosecution.[24] The province reverted to its Serbian name of 'Kosovo and Metohija' and Serbia gained control over Kosovo's security, judiciary, finances, and social planning. In this regard, it is important to understand why the provinces still existed even though they had lost their autonomy: Milošević now controlled Montenegro as well as Kosovo and Vojvodina and therefore held four out of the eight votes on the federal presidency.

When the Serbian Assembly adopted the amendments on 28 March 1989, the Assembly President, Borisav Jovic, warned that the Constitution would be 'used without remission' against anyone who dared attack the integrity of Serbia.[25] On 28 June 1989, the six hundredth anniversary of the Turkish victory at Kosovo Polje, Milošević celebrated his triumph over Kosovo in front of a crowd of approximately one million, actively drawing on the history and legends surrounding Lazar's defeat. This erosion of Kosovo's status was compounded by further deliberate actions by both Albanians and Serbs to institute ethnic polarisation and segregation such as the mass sacking of Albanian staff throughout all employment sectors from 1990 onwards, police and paramilitary presence and intimidation, media control, and the Albanian boycott of the December 1990 Serbian elections.[26]

It is conventional when narrating the events leading up to the conflict in 1999 to differentiate between ethnic identities. Although an analysis of the different interpretations of what happened in Kosovo and of the region's history is not the current focus, fundamental to our core concerns is the recognition that representations of identity and of 'ethnic conflict' are contested.[27] There are two common strands to representations of Kosovo: the 'liberal focus on Milosevic and elite manipulation of popular sentiment' and 'the realist characterisation of the outbreak of suppressed hatreds at the end of the Cold War'.[28] As Anna Stavrianakis notes, both accounts construct Kosovo and 'the Balkans' as the 'backward or uncivilized Other of "Europe"; a discursive construction pivotal to policies taken in relation to the region'.[29] Accounts which favour the portrayal of the Balkans as a 'confused, often violent ethnic cauldron' waiting to explode with the revival of 'ancient ethnic hatreds'[30] following the end of the Cold War do not explain, for example, the non-violent resistance of the Kosovo Albanians during the 1990s which had a deep impact on Kosovar politics and identity. This is worth noting because Western accounts of the violence in Kosovo would inform the consequent and, many argue, inadequate response to it.[31]

David Campbell suggests that conflict on the basis of ethnicity is a consequence of the dominance and exclusivity of one identity, rather than the inherently violent nature of ethnic identities themselves.[32] It is, then, the process of 'degrading' othering which may take place through language, religion, race and other social factors, which leads to violence.[33] When the Other is seen as a threat to one's own national identity and feelings of victimhood are created and manipulated, then conflict can emerge. Campbell refuses to accept that ethnicity is a stable or static factor in the explanation of ethnic conflict, arguing that identity can only be perceived in relation to difference and that ethnicity is a term which 'signifies relationships of power in the problematic of identity/difference rather than being a signifier for which there is a stable referent'.[34] Difference, then, can be translated into otherness through policies oriented towards an exclusivist politics. There is no *a priori* subject with fixed characteristics, be it Serb or Kosovar Albanian, which necessitates violent relationships. This approach suggests that history, myth, experience and tradition are central to the ongoing process of identity creation.

The notion that ethnic identities on which claims are based are not in any sense innate, but rather a discursive practice, can be seen in key moments of the run-up to conflict in Kosovo as they involve actors 'reproducing and rearticulating a historical representation and violently deploying it in the present to constitute ... (individual and/or collective) subjectivity'.[35] It is not, taking this to Campbell's logical conclusion, that any identity may be adopted, as 'the pool of resources from which identities can be materialized is never infinite, and in Kosovo it became an ethnicized pool', but rather it is a matter of recognising discursive practices and the use of dialogue to recreate identities for political ends.[36] Identity, then, is not static, but is reflected in its 'dynamics with the Other, which has a constitutive role in the articulation of identity'.[37] This is particularly apt in regard to the constitutive role of education policy in forming a wider political identity. The increasing segregation of both political and social space in Kosovo, particularly after the construction of the Albanian parallel systems in 1992 – in which education was at the core – reflects these dynamics. The appeal to non-violence by the Albanians was both a necessity for survival in the face of superior Serb military strength and a deliberate choice (a chance to reject the negative Serbian portrayal of Albanian identity and to identify themselves with contemporary Europe).[38]

The role of identity and its construction goes some way to understanding how the situation in Kosovo evolved as deliberate policy. This challenges the interpretation of many within the international community who have represented the conflict as tribal, ancient ethnic hatreds. This, in turn, served to shape the way in which they attempted to determine Kosovo's status. Contextualising the emergence and progression of conflict is important because it opens up the possibility of alternative paths of political engagement with its constituent actors. Indicating, moreover, the constitutive relationship between discursive interventions and conflict attunes our awareness to the significance of communication and the concerns central to communicative ethics.

Missing dialogues and non-violent resistance

Focusing on the non-violent resistance movement in Kosovo contributes to the central argument that the call for military intervention in 1999, raised by those who argued that there was no alternative, paid insufficient attention to the myriad of opportunities to influence events in Kosovo over the previous decade. It seeks, to borrow the words of Howard Clark, to 'counter the tendency to write non-violence out of history'.[39] The importance of the extended period of civil resistance, or non-violence, in Kosovo is that it 'demonstrated alternative possibilities to the calamity in Bosnia, averting war for eight years and giving those intergovernmental bodies that claim responsibility for European security time to develop a preventive peace policy'.[40] It is this 'time', this 'space created' by the non-violence movement which will be considered, alongside the way in which it was responded to by the international community. It reveals 'missing dialogues'; opportunities for non-violent engagement which were not taken by the international community and which therefore at the very least question the justification of last resort for the use of force in March 1999. Communicative ethics helps us to 'see' such missing dialogues because it attunes us to the relevance of practices of inclusion and exclusion which shape decision-making processes and thus opens up the potential for alternative patterns of communication which facilitate the transformation of conflict through non-violent means. It also heightens our awareness of the wider, often strategic, dynamics of encounters which enabled Kosovo to be repeatedly excluded from the agenda of the international community.

The focus on missing dialogues and non-violence counters at least two common interpretations. It challenges those who asserted the inevitability of conflict in the Balkans and it counters the interpretation of those whose perspective located responsibility for the conflict solely with Milošević and the KLA without considering the impact of the (in)action of the international community. Robert Jackson suggests that the 'Kosovo disaster was thus created by President Milosevic with the popular support of the Serbs; it was enlarged by certain Kosovar Albanian warlords who enjoyed substantial popular support from among the Kosovo Albanian people'.[41] While this approach rightly attributes responsibility to Milošević and the KLA, it fails to critically evaluate the impact that the international community *did* have on the conflict, whether by virtue of particular actions or a refusal to act.

Following Serbia's unconstitutional assumption of control over Kosovo in 1991, the province lost its status as a legal entity with rights. The Serb authorities passed a series of laws, the effect of which was to erode Albanian rights. They passed laws which prevented Albanians buying land or houses from Serbs, while other measures included incentives to encourage the return of Serbs who had left Kosovo. Public companies such as the electricity organisation were taken over by their Serb counterparts. Workers who were not sacked were forced to resign if they refused to sign loyalty oaths. Many doctors and medical staff were sacked, leading to the closing down of many, particularly rural, medical facilities. The police force was purged, making it in essence an all-Serb force. The police then took over television and radio buildings and large numbers of Albanian journalists lost their jobs. All cultural and other institutions were closed down or merged with their Serbian counterparts.[42] Education became highly contentious as the Serbian curriculum and language was imposed on Albanian students. The financing of Albanian schools and educational materials ceased from March 1991 and the University became a Serb-only institution. From 1991 onwards, the Serbian regime sought to Serbianise all public discourse in Kosovo.⁴³ For many Kosovars who only spoke Albanian, the public sphere became alien and inaccessible. Acts of violence against Kosovars, carried out by Serbian police with impunity, were systemic. A report by Amnesty International indicates the documentation of a 'systematic pattern of human rights violations in Kosovo province, including torture and ill-treatment by police, deaths in police custody, and unfair trials of political prisoners'.⁴⁴

It was from these social and political conditions that the non-violent resistance emerged. Following Milošević's destruction of the Communists in Kosovo, new Albanian political groups began to appear, often growing out of existing groups of intellectuals. Ibrahim Rugova, head of the Kosovo Association of Writers, rapidly rose to prominence, as did Veton Surroi, a journalist and head of the Kosovo branch of the Association for a Yugoslav Democratic Initiative. The Association circulated a petition entitled 'For Democracy, against Violence'. Clark argues that this petition, signed by over 400,000 Kosovo Albanians, played an important role in shaping the strategy of non-violent resistance against increasing Serb repression and was representative of an increasing number of symbolic moments of unity and resistance which became part of everyday life for Kosovo Albanians.⁴⁵ It has been noted that this strategy of non-violence ran counter to Kosovar Albanian tradition (for example, the kaçak tradition), thus demonstrating the construction of political and cultural identity to be an ongoing process and not merely a retreat to innate ethnic characteristics. The LDK, led by Rugova, was founded in December 1989 and rapidly became the focal point of Kosovar politics; it would remain dominant until 1998. Rugova insisted that Kosovo's status should be equal to that of the other Yugoslav republics. Once Yugoslavia had disintegrated, Rugova insisted that Kosovo must become independent.

Clark argues that non-violence is often over-simplified in the case of Kosovo and is usually identified with Rugova's position within Kosovar politics. However, the civil resistance movement went much further than the stance taken by the LDK, who, certainly at first, were the supporters rather than the initiators of such a position. The initiatives which made non-violence a viable strategy in this context came from a number of other sources. Clark identifies the roots of contemporary civil resistance as being in the dignified and non-violent protests of the Trepça miners in November 1988. Out of this grew a movement initiated both by local communities and workers and the *Kosova Alternative*, a group of political and intellectual organisations intent on ending the cycle of domination in Kosovo. This included the Writers Association, the Social Democratic Party, the Youth Parliament, the Parliamentary Party of Kosovo, a Green Party and a feminist group. From 1990, following the establishment of the Council for the Defence of Human

Rights and Freedoms (CDHRF) in November 1989, it became the pattern for activists from the CDHRF or the new parties to go to the scene of any violent incident. This was partly to document what had happened and partly to urge restraint among local populations and to explain the idea behind non-violence.[46]

On 2 July 1990, 114 out of 123 Albanian members of the provincial government voted to declare Kosovo a republic, independent of Serbia, but remaining part of Yugoslavia. Three days later, the Serbian parliament voted to dissolve the Kosovar parliament and the Serb Assembly took over all legislative functions. On 7 September, a secret meeting of Kosovar deputies voted for a constitution for their own Republic of Kosovo, although it was not until fighting was taking place in Croatia that the deputies voted for the Resolution on Independence of Kosovo, on 22 September 1991. On 19 October 1991, the Kosovar 'parliament' voted to confirm the results of a referendum and declared Kosovo to be the independent 'Republic of Kosova'.[47] The Republic of Kosova existed only virtually at this point, as Serbian and Yugoslav institutions remained in control. This is where the non-violent strategy began to develop, leading to the creation of Kosovo's parallel state. According to Judah,

> Instead of trying to mount a violent insurrection to realise this independence, the party began to simulate it in the hope that, by force of demographic and other pressures, Kosovo would, one day, simply drop into Albanian hands like ripe fruit.[48]

The parallel state was created on two levels. New political bodies were created, and practical measures were put into place in order to replace the loss of healthcare and educational provision.[49] On a political level, the LDK created a new government structure and, on 24 May 1992, elections were held for a new Kosovar parliament and to elect a president. The LDK won the election with 76.44% of the votes and Rugova was elected by 99.5% of those who voted, granting Rugova and the LDK a significant measure of legitimacy and authority. Although more than eighteen parties contested the election, none disagreed over the issue of independence. Fourteen seats were left empty for the Serbs and Montenegrins.[50] Despite ignoring the election, the Serb authorities would not allow parliament to convene. Consequently, although parliament never met, thirteen commissions were set up in order to provide policy guidance. Technically, a government comprising six ministers under Prime Minister Bujar Bukoshi and based in Slovenia until May 1992, when it moved to Bonn, had already been set up on 19 October 1991. Despite its exile, this government was more than an exercise in institution building or 'gesture politics', its most important role having been to collect taxes from the large Kosovar diaspora.[51] 90% of these taxes were spent on supporting the parallel education system while the remainder funded the LDK administration, cultural activities, sports and some health care.[52]

The parallel education system became an essential part of Kosovar society, making a significant difference in the teaching of history, geography, music and language and further aiding the construction of incompatible notions of identity.[53] Other organisations were set up which also supported the parallel system. These included, but were not limited to: the Mother Teresa Society, which was established in 1990 and provided aid and health care to Kosovars who were afraid to use the Serb-dominated facilities; the Councils for Reconciliation, which provided a kind of parallel justice system; media outlets; and a number of other NGOs which were concerned with culture and sport, as well as organisations for young people and women, such as the Kosovo Karate Association.[54] The presence of these various attempts to develop an alternative Kosovar political society which rejected the tools of violence serve to cast doubt on the essentialised identities drawn on to support particular justifications for the use of force in 1998–99. Peaceful attempts by Kosovars to transform their situation suggest the potential for alternative political strategies that could have been adopted by the international community. At the very least, they indicate the existence of avenues for dialogue which were not sufficiently acknowledged or responded to by the international community. As Fierke notes, the non-violent resistance movement raises the interesting counterfactual question about the failure to support the campaign and whether a different, more peaceful outcome to the conflict might have been achieved by acting earlier with other forms of intervention.[55] Although it is not possible to prove that non-violent forms of engagement would have prevented conflict, it is highly plausible to argue that the conflict was exacerbated as a result of the failure by the international community to actively support non-violent alternatives.

The argument that these non-violent political acts offered the international community opportunities to pursue alternative strategies is not intended to remove all responsibility or agency from the Kosovo Albanians. Clark offers a detailed analysis of ways in which the civil resistance movement could have developed in a more profitable and fulfilling way, in terms of being more open to the needs and interests of minorities, and encouraging active social, political and economic transformation. Instead, there was a tendency for the movement to stagnate, given Rugova's and the LDK's assurance to the population that help would come from outside.[56] Rugova argued that the politics of non-violence would result in positive treatment by the international community although, in reality, Rugova's strategy to internationalise the conflict met consistently with failure and exclusion from decision-making processes. Thus, the critical view of external action is not intended to depoliticise the Kosovo Albanians, but rather to demonstrate the presence of non-violent resistance and dialogue-based activities which were ongoing in Kosovo and the extent to which these offered the international community (in the form of both states and non-state/civil society actors) possible ways in which to support or influence politics in Serbia and Kosovo prior to the escalation of conflict and the moral dilemma subsequently faced by the international community.[57] Drawing on the example of the successful polio immunisation campaigns in 1996 and 1997, Clark supports this position when he argues that 'internationals wishing to support social development in Kosovo were in a strong position to negotiate inter-ethnic cooperation'.[58] This campaign brought together international agencies (WHO, UNICEF), state (Serbian) and parallel health structures (Mother Teresa Society) which, in their turn, brought in mosques, churches and the media to aid in the mobilisation phase, as well as commitment from the Serbian police not to intervene.

The parallel state system allowed the LDK to deny the legitimacy of Belgrade institutions and to call for support from the international community, which brings us to the issue of the engagement of the international community prior to 1998, or as Louis Sell remarks, the 'pattern of Western neglect that prevailed for most of the decade'.[59] This was a pattern of neglect expressed, in part, through a series of exclusionary and coercive communicative practices.

Having declared independence, Kosovo struggled for recognition by the international community. Rugova was not invited to the July 1991 European Community Conference on Yugoslavia (ECCY) which ended the fighting in Slovenia and marked the beginning of Europe's efforts to broaden the search for a Yugoslav settlement. A request for recognition by the ECCY in 1991 was refused, as were requests to the Organization for Security and Cooperation in Europe (OSCE) to be allowed to express their views.[60] At the same conference, the EC chief negotiator excluded the issue of Kosovo altogether in his attempt to keep Milošević on board. Despite Kosovo's status as a constitutional entity under the 1974 Constitution of the Socialist Federal Republic of Yugoslavia (SFRY), it was not invited to participate in the peace process.[61] In a move which firmly established the exclusion of Kosovo from the international agenda the conference defined Kosovo as an 'internal' problem for Yugoslavia, thus preventing it from facing further international scrutiny and involvement.[62]

The establishment of the ECCY led to the Badinter Commission, created in 1991 to consider the legal elements of constitutional reform as a result of the ongoing dissolution of Yugoslavia. In applying the principle of *uti possidetis*,[63] Robert Badinter limited the right of self-determination to the six Yugoslav republics on the grounds that they were sovereign, founding members of the federation. Eager to avoid setting a precedent for further ethnic unrest in the USSR or in other European states, Badinter rejected

> pleas by Albanians that Kosovo's position as one of the eight federal units in Yugoslavia, as demonstrated by Kosovo's separate membership on the collective

presidency and other Yugoslav institutions, entitled it to be considered for independence on the same basis as the six republics.[64]

The exclusion of Kosovo from participation in the peace talks has met with some controversy. Alex Bellamy argues, also on the grounds of *uti possidetis*, that the Kosovars in fact had a convincing legal case both for independence and for inclusion in the peace process.[65] Kosovo had been a federal entity under the 1974 constitution and had been directly represented in the federal institutions. Consequently, given the dissolution of the Federation, it should also emerge as an entity entitled to constitute itself as a state. The International Crisis Group's report on the issue lists six reasons why Kosovo should be considered for 'intermediate sovereignty':

> 1) the legal and factual similarity between Kosovo and the other Republics of the former Yugoslavia which were deemed by the international community to be entitled to international recognition; 2) the legal precedent of earned recognition established by the international community in recognizing Slovenia, Croatia, Bosnia-Herzegovina and Macedonia; 3) the fact that Yugoslavia has dissolved, and the international community has rejected Serbia/Montenegro's claim to continue its international legal personality; 4) the historical fact that Kosovo, while legitimately part of Yugoslavia, has never been legitimately incorporated into Serbia [referring to the unconstitutional revocation of Kosovo's autonomous status in 1989]; 5) the fact that the people of Kosovo have been subjected to ethnic aggression [to violations of their basic human rights, and denied the right to collectively determine their political fate]; and 6) recent precedent set by the Russian/Chechen Accords and the Northern Ireland Peace Agreement.[66]

The main reason for Kosovo's lack of republic status appeared to be the Yugoslav constitutional distinction which determined that nations, not nationalities, should have republic status. 'Nationalities' such as Albanians were deemed not to be constituent because they had 'home' states outside the borders of Yugoslavia and therefore did not have the right of self-determination. This was a distinction which the commission used to enable it to draw the line between legitimate statehood and secession. Although there was in fact no legal ruling by the commission in response to Kosovo's claim to independence, the international community were clearly opposed to any such outcome. They worried that the FRY's break-up would have disastrous consequences for the former USSR and implications for the Bosnian and Croatian Serbs. This concern reflects key pluralist preoccupations with the maintenance of order.[67] The legal debate over the exclusion of Kosovo from consideration by the ECCY or the Badinter Commission illustrated the problem of legal indeterminacy. Persuasive arguments could be made by both sides. However, when considered both in the wider political context and from the perspective of communicative ethics, the denial of representation for Kosovo, or consideration of its claims in these fora, had significant implications.

Kosovo prior to 1999

The subsequent stage of the process, the London Conference of August 1992, has also been described as representing a '"grotesque" expression of the international sidelining of Kosovo'.[68] Despite presenting their case for inclusion as equals in the talks, the Kosovar delegation was not permitted to enter the chamber or to represent themselves. Rugova was invited to attend, but was not allowed to speak or participate in the proceedings, having to watch the conference on closed-circuit television from an adjoining room.[69] Ironically, in the letter of invitation, Lord Carrington remarked that 'We are thus making *strenuous* efforts to ensure that the views of the Kosovo Albanians are heard.'[70]

At the conference a working group on Kosovo was established, but, at Milošević's insistence, it would only deal with issues on minority rights. The group produced a 'joint Serb-Albanian statement aimed at normalising the divided Kosovo educational system, but the agreement collapsed after the Serbs arrested the rector of the Albanian underground university'.[71] According to Marc Weller, 'Worse than the lack of progress on the education issue may have been that the mere existence of the Special Group gave the impression that the Kosovo problem was now being addressed in some way by an international forum.' No agreement was actually reached until 1996 and nothing concrete ever emerged afterwards.[72] The price of the working group on minority rights (and the desire to keep Milošević engaged in peace talks on Bosnia) was the dismissal of the issue of Kosovo's legal status and any hope of inclusion for the Kosovo Albanians in the peace process.[73]

The Albanian conviction that eventually the justice of their cause as a result of their non-violent resistance would be recognised was aided by the inconsistency and incoherence of signals from the international community. The US Secretary of State, James Baker, came to Belgrade on 21 June 1991 to tell the leaders of the six republics, particularly Slovenia and Croatia, that the US would not recognise them if they tried to secede from Yugoslavia. He also told them, specifically Serbia, that the US would oppose any attempt to prevent secession by force. The EC concurred; seven months later, however, this policy had proved itself worthless and the EC/EU led the world in recognising Croatia and Slovenia. Judah emphasises the importance of this radical policy reversal. From then on, Kosovars never believed that US or European policy was unchangeable when it declared that Kosovo did not have the right to independence because of its provincial status.[74]

A key development in the 1990s which had a significant impact on Kosovar politics was the Dayton Accord, signed in 1995 to bring to an end the conflict in Bosnia.[75] Negotiated by Richard Holbrooke, US special envoy, who was to play a pivotal role in the later conflict in Kosovo, the Dayton peace agreement had been preceded by NATO bombing of Bosnian Serb positions in Operation Deliberate Force. The agreement entailed a formal recognition of two constituent parts to the Republic of Bosnia-Herzegovina – a Muslim-Croat federation and the Serbian Republika Srpska – backed by the presence of a large number of NATO troops. It is undeniable that the agreement signed at Dayton had a crucial impact on the Kosovar Albanians, largely due to the exclusion of the issue of Kosovo at the negotiating table and the subsequent recognition by the EU of the Federal Republic of Yugoslavia which included Kosovo.[76] As Peter Russell argues, the strategic exclusion of Kosovo did not result from lack of knowledge about the conditions in the province, but was the result of a 'deliberate decision on the part of Richard Holbrooke and his team that the severity of the Bosnian war justified focusing on it to the point, if necessary, of excluding any other issue'.[77] This highlights the conflict between order and justice in international society; Holbrooke and the other negotiators decided to prioritise ending the war in Bosnia (the most that it was believed could be achieved with Milošević), despite the potential costs that this implied for the Kosovar struggle for self-determination.

Dayton shocked the Kosovar Albanians largely because they had been led by Rugova to believe that the strategy of internationalisation would bear the fruit of resolution for the Kosovo issue. The failure to internationalise the conflict speaks to failure on the part of the international community as much it does on Rugova's.[78] Holbrooke was defensive about the failure to discuss it at Dayton, asserting that 'Kosovo would have happened anyway, and it is part of the mythology that Dayton was responsible and I don't believe it. What really drove this thing was Rugova's failure to produce results and the Serb crackdown.'[79] Whether or not the international community could or should have done more to address the simmering conflict in Kosovo after Dayton does not change the fact, as Judah argues, that,

> unrecognised in the West at the time, Dayton was an extraordinary trauma for the Kosovo Albanians ... it confirmed to them in the most dramatic and humiliating way that Rugova's policy of passive resistance had failed. And not only that, but that his idea that they would be rewarded for their 'good behaviour' by Western countries had been just plain wrong. While they had had an entity, which had played its part as a federal unity in the old Yugoslavia, they were now without rights while, in their view, the campaign of genocide led by Bosnian Serb leaders was being rewarded.[80]

Among those who consider the exclusion of Kosovo from Dayton in more depth, there is some agreement that Dayton represented more than simply a missed opportunity to address the ongoing conflict in Kosovo. Rather, Dayton 'directly contributed to the course of events which ultimately culminated in NATO's military campaign four years later'.[81] Violence did not break out immediately, nor was Rugova undermined straight away. This was in part because the LDK controlled, either directly or indirectly, most of the Albanian-language media. However, the strategic decisions taken at Dayton led to the rapid emergence of the Kosovo Liberation Army who sought to change the terms of the game from one of non-violence to violent resistance. Founded in 1993, the KLA was the armed wing of the LPK – a small political party called the People's Movement of Kosovo. Support for the KLA came from several sources, including those who were jailed after the 1981 demonstrations; members of the Kosovar diaspora; former Albanian police officers who had been fired or arrested as the Serbs took over Kosovo; and local elders and clan leaders, who, although initially firm supporters of the LDK, became more sympathetic to armed resistance as discontent grew and enabled a massive increase in the grassroots support necessary for the KLA to become a major player in Kosovar politics.[82] Following Dayton, those who had been sceptical of Rugova's non-violent approach felt that it was time to change tactics; the lesson learnt from Dayton was that violence pays.

According to *The Kosovo Report*, it was unlikely that the Dayton process would have arrived at a solution for Kosovo, although either 'the earlier "hands off Kosovo" message of President Bush could have been reiterated; or Dayton could have been used as a forum to encourage FRY acceptance of an NGO presence in Kosovo'.[83] An additional problem unrecognised by the international community while it continued to encourage the non-violent resistance movement were the ongoing strains and difficulties of sustaining the parallel system in the long term. At the same time, in November 1997, a State Department official told NGOs lobbying for support and aid that the US government 'cannot support civil society because it would lead to secession'.[84] This reveals the paradox at the heart of the international community's approach to Kosovo.

The international community continued to give out mixed signals. While Milošević had been warned to stay away from Kosovo, he received repeated assurances that the integrity of Yugoslavia was paramount and that the status of Kosovo within the FRY was an internal matter. In December 1995, after Dayton, Rugova was told by the US administration that the US would insist Milošević begin a dialogue with the Albanians after the deployment of NATO troops to Bosnia. Furthermore, they would maintain sanctions until Kosovo's autonomy was restored.[85] Once again, however, nothing happened. In early 1997, the EU lifted sanctions and resumed political and economic relations with the FRY, which meant that it acknowledged Kosovo as part of Serbia. Those few voices calling for further international engagement in Kosovo were essentially ignored.[86] Although the leaders remained firmly attached to their demands, there were enough 'signs of moderation on both sides of the ethnic divide to suggest that if Dayton had been promptly followed by a major, US-led diplomatic offensive, it might not have been too late to broker a compromise settlement in Kosovo'.[87] None of the available alternative ideas were taken up. One option being considered by some Serb intellectuals, for example, suggested the partition of Kosovo with the predominantly Serb-populated northern part, together with areas around Serb monasteries and other historical sites, remaining part of Serbia, and the rest of Kosovo being allowed to go its own way.[88] Other alternatives included Adem Demaçi's Balkania (a confederation of sovereign states consisting of Kosovo, Serbia, and Montenegro), and Fehmi Agani's plan for a negotiated transition under a UN Protectorate.[89] The Transnational Foundation for Peace and Future Research proposed the United Nations Temporary Authority for a Negotiated Settlement (UNTANS) in 1996,[90] which listed a number of imaginative procedural and dialogic suggestions, as did the European Action Council for Peace in the Balkans.[91] The International Helsinki Federation for Human Rights also called for a Dayton-like conference in January 1998 to resolve the conflict.[92]

The Kosovo Report highlights the failure to respond adequately at each stage of the developing conflict and discusses a number of moves that the international community might have made in order to try and prevent conflict. In an acknowledgement that at 'each stage in the conflict, the diplomatic options narrowed', the report comes to the conclusion that:

> The decision not to deal seriously with the Kosovo issue in 1991 created obstacles to action in 1992–3. The decision not to confront the intransigence of Milosevic in 1993, and above all the neglect of Kosovo during the Dayton negotiations, contributed to the developments that were to escalate the conflict in 1996–7. The inadequacy of diplomatic efforts in the period 1997–8 was to culminate eventually with Rambouillet where the space for maneuver was extremely limited.[93]

It is precisely for this reason that communicative ethics must apply to a more comprehensive timeframe. *The Kosovo Report* suggests that conflict prevention should have focused on establishing an armed presence on the ground to provide protection against human rights abuses, to support and facilitate parallel institutions and to encourage dialogue. More effort should have been aimed at ensuring a strong international presence in Kosovo, improving conditions of everyday life and 'fostering communication among Serbs and Albanians inside Kosovo' and elsewhere. More could also have been done to support the initiatives of the parallel society. Universities, for example, in other nations did little to support the alternative educational system developed in the early 1990s.[94] The LDK was a willing diplomatic partner and open to forms of non-forceful pressure that might have been applied. Their commitment to non-violence provided 'potential avenues of civilian international involvement that were less intrusive, and not as threatening to the sovereignty and security concerns of the FRY as an armed presence'.[95] While this does not deny that the LDK became increasingly inflexible and uncompromising in their demands for independence, by failing to take the demands of the non-violent movement seriously at an early stage, the international community sent out the signal that 'violence produces results and is a more effective political strategy'.[96]

The establishment of the parallel state in Kosovo and its effective functioning at the political and societal level provides a classic example of the transformative strategy of acting 'as if' the situation were already different; as if Kosovo was already recognised as an independent state.[97] Yet the assertion of realist power dominance signalled by the lessons drawn from Dayton foiled the attempt by the non-violent movement to establish a different set of rules in conjunction with the failure of the international community to engage with the conflict in ways which might have prioritised dialogue and alternative forms of political engagement.

The political and social collapse of Albania in 1997 helped to move the Kosovo Albanians closer to an armed resistance, leaving many arsenals unprotected and so providing a supply of weapons to the KLA. The first significant armed actions in Kosovo by the KLA took place in early 1996.[98] On 14 February 1996, the KLA, still only consisting of approximately 150 men, issued communiqué 18 which stated that

> Dialogue about withdrawing the military and police from the Republic of Kosova should start immediately. We call on powerful international centres such as the USA to recognise the independence of Kosova for which the Albanians have declared themselves in a referendum otherwise war in Kosova is inevitable.[99]

In August 1997, events indicated a further shift away from non-violent resistance. Students in Priština began protesting at the failure of the authorities to implement the 1996 Rome agreement on education. In December 1998, the KLA issued their first public statement, which warned that the 'Serb "occupiers" would face increasing resistance and – warning against continued Western reluctance to deal with the KLA – said the movement would accept no agreement on Kosovo's status that it had not been a party to'.[100]

By 1998, a series of offensives by KLA and Serbian security forces were ratcheting up the levels of violence. Serbian forces concentrated their attacks on the strongholds of the KLA in the Drenica Valley using heavy weapons and air power to drive the KLA out of urban areas in central and western Kosovo.[101] This triggered a wave of internal displacement in a preview of what was to come as some 200,000 Kosovars were driven from their homes. This escalation of the conflict quickly attracted the closer attention of the Security Council.

The Security Council and the road to war

As a result of the increasing levels of violence now developing in Kosovo and the acknowledgement that Serbian forces were targeting civilians, the matter became subject to scrutiny by the Security Council. I turn now to a narrative of events which took place in the Council between 1998 and 1999, because the justifications and arguments presented there paved the way for the unprecedented use of force by a regional organisation – NATO – without a Council mandate. During this period a number of resolutions were passed by the Security Council which were intended to halt the violence.

The first of a series of resolutions (UNSCR 1160) was adopted by the Security Council on 31 March 1998 under Chapter VII of the UN Charter, by a vote of 14 in favour to none against, with 1 abstention (China). By adopting the resolution under Chapter VII, the Council determined that the situation represented a 'threat to international peace and security'. The resolution established an arms embargo on the FRY, including Kosovo, and banned the sale or supply of arms and all related material. In addition, a Sanctions Committee was established with responsibility for monitoring the ban, examining information concerning violations and recommending appropriate measures in response. The Council urged all parties to enter 'without preconditions into a meaningful dialogue on political status issues' and requested the Office of the Prosecutor of the International Criminal Tribunal for the Former Yugoslavia to begin gathering information relating to the violence in Kosovo which might fall within its jurisdiction. The resolution called for an end to the violence by both the Serbs and the KLA, whilst at the same time supporting the non-violent approach of Rugova and the LDK. Although no member state voted against the resolution, Russia and China expressed serious reservations concerning the intervention of the Security Council in matters which they considered to be the preserve of national sovereignty and therefore subject to the domestic jurisdiction of the FRY. Russia and China acknowledged that there was cause for concern over the situation in Kosovo, but remained adamant that it did not constitute a threat to international peace and security and had not reached the threshold of last resort. The situation did not, therefore, either permit Article 2(4) to be overridden or justify the application of enforcement measures under Article 2(7).[102] It is important to remember, however, that no member state in the Council supported the secessionist aims of the Kosovar Albanians, and this resolution, as did all those that followed, emphasised the territorial integrity of the FRY.

On 10 June 1998, the then British Prime Minister Tony Blair called for military action if diplomacy was unable to end the crisis quickly. The scale of Serbian counter-attacks against Albanian villages led to increased pressure to take action and on 11–12 June 1998, NATO defence ministers ordered the organisation's military chiefs to prepare a range of options, should the use of force become necessary. This call for action was complicated by two key issues. First, NATO was determined not to become the KLA's air force or support their aim of secession and second, the issue of whether the Alliance could or should act without explicit authorisation from the Security Council was highly controversial.[103] Both factors would complicate the wider public reception and interpretation of NATO's actions when it later moved to intervene militarily.

On 12 June, the Contact Group, the main informal body undertaking negotiations with Milošević, which comprised France, the Russian Federation, the United Kingdom, the United States, Germany and Italy, called for an immediate ceasefire and the 'withdrawal of security units used for civilian repression' from the province, and demanded that the Kosovo Albanian leadership 'make clear its rejection of violence and acts of terrorism'.[104] On 15 June 1998, NATO began an aerial exercise, Operation Determined Falcon, which involved military flights over Albania and Macedonia in a show of force. According to Sell, 'General Naumann [Chair of NATO's Military Committee] later assessed that Milošević "rightly concluded that the NATO threat was a bluff... and finished his summer offensive."'[105]

In the face of escalating tensions in Kosovo, Resolution 1199 was adopted on 23 September 1998 under Chapter VII, again with fourteen members in favour and one abstention (China). Although key member states such as Britain, under Prime Minister Tony Blair and Secretary of State for Foreign Affairs Robin Cook, had been looking for a UN resolution to back the use of force, it became evident by September that this was not going to happen. Once again, Russia and China made it clear that they would veto any suggestion of the use of force against Milošević.[106] The resolution reaffirmed the sovereignty and territorial integrity of the FRY, called for the cessation of all action by the security forces affecting the civilian population and ordered the withdrawal of security units used for civilian repression. It required the FRY to facilitate the safe return of refugees and internally displaced persons, to allow unimpeded access for humanitarian organisations and aid, to enable effective international monitoring in Kosovo and to make rapid progress towards a clear timetable for dialogue. It insisted that the Kosovo Albanian leadership condemn all terrorist action, reminded states of their obligations concerning the prohibitions imposed by Resolution 1160 and decided, 'should the concrete measures demanded in this resolution and resolution 1160 (1998) not be taken, to consider further action and additional measures to maintain or restore peace and stability in the region'.[107] The demands were not, however, backed up by the threat of military actions, due in part to the constraints imposed by Russia, China and the other non-permanent Council members.

In addition, the resolution requested that the Secretary-General, Kofi Annan, conduct an assessment of the levels of compliance by both parties, a report which, when presented on 3 October, concluded that he was 'outraged by reports of mass killings in Kosovo'.[108] Britain, holding the Presidency of the Council at that time, proposed a draft resolution specifying the use of 'all necessary means' – the terminology understood to permit the use of force – to end the atrocities in Kosovo. Russia and China indicated that any such resolution would be vetoed. Shortly afterwards, US Special Envoy Richard Holbrooke was sent to Belgrade by the Contact Group to try to reach a settlement with Milošević.

Holbrooke returned to Belgrade in October 1998 with two aims: to put in place a verification system on the ground in Kosovo to monitor Serb behaviour, and to draw up an interim agreement between Serbs and Kosovo Albanians based on an existing draft drawn up by Christopher Hill, US special envoy for Kosovo, in September. The first draft had been presented to Serbs and Albanians on 1 October and attempted to avoid the issue of the status of Kosovo and focus on the assignment of powers to different levels of administration. Both sides reacted uneasily but did not reject it outright. The draft allowed for power to be located not in Kosovan public institutions but in the individual communes or local districts. Consequently, Kosovo 'as an entity would not enjoy any significant element of legal personality . . . In deference to Serbia, the draft also contained very detailed provisions which, it was feared, would subject Kosovo to devisive [sic] ethnic politics'.[109] The communes would retain significant powers of self-administration and could unite to form 'self-administering regions comprising multiple communes' which, technically, enabled those few Serb majority communes to form an ethnic Serb entity within Kosovo.[110] Furthermore, another layer of authority was added in the form of 'national communities', in other words all ethnic groups would enjoy additional rights regardless of whether or not they constituted an ethnic majority in a particular commune, and would be granted additional institutions for self-administration, and even courts. Kosovo was opposed to this concept, which was based on ethnic division rather than a multicultural society with equal rights for all. Serbs, however, saw it as a means to secure a separate status for themselves, since, although the Assembly in Kosovo would enjoy fairly wide legislative competence, voting could be blocked by any national community and the FRY would retain power in relation to territorial integrity, a common market, monetary policy, defence and foreign policy and a federal police presence.[111]

While Kosovar political representatives formulated their response to the first draft, however, the Holbrooke agreements were concluded without consultation with the Kosovars. In order to encourage Milošević to take seriously these negotiations, NATO approved a plan for air strikes against

Serbian targets if no agreement was reached within 96 hours. Despite the concerns some NATO members had over the legality of relying on Resolutions 1160 and 1199, the Activation Order was justified in terms of existing Security Council resolutions.[112] An agreement was reached on 12–13 October which stated that Serbian military and police would withdraw to their pre-war levels, serious negotiations would begin with the Kosovars, and two thousand 'verifiers' would be dispatched to Kosovo under the auspices of the OSCE (the Kosovo Verification Mission). NATO would have the right to make aerial surveillance flights to ensure that Serbia was in full compliance.

Resolution 1203, which was adopted on 24 October 1998 under Chapter VII with thirteen votes in favour (Russia and China abstained) repeated the terms of 1160 and 1199, endorsed the Holbrooke agreement signed in October between Holbrooke and Milošević and noted the commitment of the FRY to complete negotiations on a full settlement by 2 November. The unilateral eleven-point, strategically formulated, statement issued by Serbia claiming to present the basis for a political settlement to be completed by 2 November, unlike the Hill draft, strengthened the element of territorial integrity and sovereignty of the FRY, thus continuing the subordination of Kosovo within the FRY.[113] Serbia reneged on its agreement to commit to the Hill plan on 2 November, thus throwing away an opportunity to achieve a settlement that might have been accepted by all parties.[114]

During this time, NATO maintained its Activation Order, ensuring that a credible threat of force was in place against Milošević. This met with growing dissatisfaction on the part of Russia and China, both of whom emphasised their concern over the bypassing of the Security Council and the unilateral threat of force used by NATO to coerce an agreement.[115] They were not the only states uncomfortable with NATO's assumption of the authority to use force. Council members such as Brazil and Costa Rica articulated the same concern over the decision to use force being removed from the purview of the Security Council. Costa Rica argued that 'any action which implies the use of force – with the very limited exception of the right of legitimate defence – thus requires clear authorisation by the Security Council for each specific case'.[116] Mirrored in the Rio Group's March 1999 statement expressing disquiet over the intervention, Brazil declared its concern over the question of regional organisations acting without express Council authority. As the Brazilian representative stated,

> According to the Charter, non-universal organisms may resort to force only on the basis either of the right to legitimate self-defence, as stipulated in Article 51, or through the procedures of Chapter VIII, in particular Article 53, which imposes on them the obligation of seeking Security Council authorization beforehand and abiding by the Council's decision ... There is no third way.[117]

Despite the operative threat of force by NATO, the ceasefire established by the Holbrooke agreement did not hold and the KLA continued to attack Serb forces which retaliated against Kosovar civilians. In January 1999, it was clear that the Holbrooke Agreement was disintegrating. On 15 January, fighting broke out around the village of Račak and Serbian police entered the village. The final death toll was forty-five. Nine KLA soldiers were also found dead. The next day, William Walker, head of the Kosovo Verification Mission, immediately accused the Yugoslav authorities of being responsibile.[118] Many argue that Račak was the trigger factor for the use of force, since, although not the only atrocity, it was picked up by the international media. After Račak, Madeleine Albright put together a new strategy 'under which both sides would be presented with an ultimatum to accept by a certain date an interim deal that would establish Kosovo as an international protectorate with a NATO force on the ground to implement it'.[119] Albright felt that the situation was 'emerging as a key test of American leadership and of the relevance and effectiveness of NATO',[120] a later point of contention when critics argued that concern for a future role for NATO dictated the pace and direction of the talks rather than a desire to come to terms through dialogue.[121] Albright went on to say that alongside the celebrations for NATO's fiftieth birthday, the Alliance would 'look like fools proclaiming the Alliance's readiness for the twenty-first century when we were unable to cope with a conflict that began in the fourteenth',[122] an unhelpful view in terms of a full understanding of the dynamics of the conflict, given its willingness to subscribe to certain, essentialised, representations of identity.

Consequently, Serbs and Albanians were summoned to talk peace at a château in Rambouillet, south-east of Paris on 6 February 1999.[123] The diplomatic half of Albright's strategy required them to negotiate Kosovo's future on the basis of draft proposals already worked out which raises questions over how far the negotiations were influenced by considerations of coercion. The other half of the strategy, supplied by the credible use of force, was supported by the threats announced by the North Atlantic Council (NAC) on 30 January 1999. The agreement, on the basis of which the Albanians agreed to come to Rambouillet, stipulated that there would be a transitional period of three years for Kosovo, after which the future of the province would be decided. Although the Serbs would retain a limited security presence, the Kosovar Albanians would have a significant degree of autonomy in the areas of policing and the judiciary and they would have a democratically elected Assembly. The Serbs were told to conform to the commitments agreed with Holbrooke in October and to end their 'excessive and disproportionate use of force'. In the absence of these steps being taken, 'NATO is ready to take whatever measures are necessary ... The [North Atlantic] Council has therefore agreed today that the NATO Secretary General may authorise air strikes against targets on FRY territory'.[124] Keen to prevent what they perceived to be an impending humanitarian catastrophe, Western leaders had decided that a peace deal without a NATO-led force would never be implemented. Russia did not object to a peacekeeping force, in which it was certain to participate, as long as it was invited into Kosovo by the Yugoslav authorities.[125] This was to become a matter of contention during the negotiations when the scope of the military annex was revealed, and was to impede agreement once more. With the talks breaking down on 15 March, Serbian forces recommenced their ethnic cleansing of the province and Milošević refused to sign the agreement, despite being fully aware of the consequences.[126]

On the night of 24 March 1999, NATO governments took the decision to carry out airstrikes against the FRY. There were four key justifications offered by the Alliance to support their intervention in Kosovo. First, that their action was aimed at avoiding an imminent humanitarian disaster; secondly, that NATO's credibility was at stake, as indicated by Madeleine Albright's statements; thirdly, that ethnic cleansing could not be allowed to happen once more in Europe and it posed a serious threat to regional peace and security; and lastly, that NATO's use of force was in conformity with existing Security Council resolutions given the failure of the FRY to comply with Security Council demands under Chapter VII.[127] What was *not* included in the rationales offered for justification was an explicit doctrine of humanitarian intervention. Underpinning these justifications was the motivating belief that this was indeed a 'just war' on the part of US President Bill Clinton and Prime Minister Blair. This was reflected in Blair's speech to the Economic Club of Chicago on 22 April 1999, when he argued that this was a war 'based not on any territorial ambitions but on values'.[128]

NATO's rationales were rejected by Russia who viewed them as violations of the principles of the UN Charter. Russia, supported by Namibia, China, Belarus, and India (who spoke in favour of the draft resolution despite not being a member of the Council at the time), tabled a draft resolution on 26 March 1999 which called for an immediate cessation of NATO's illegal military action and the resumption of diplomatic efforts. The draft was defeated by twelve votes to three (Russia, China and Namibia). On 24 March, the Russian Federation had made clear its principled outrage at the 'unilateral' use of force in 'violation of the Charter of the United Nations and without the authorization of the Security Council'. NATO countries must, Russia argued, 'realize the heavy responsibility they bear for subverting the Charter and other norms of international law and for attempting to establish in the world, de facto, the primacy of force and unilateral diktat'.[129]

Whilst the positions articulated by the Russians and the Chinese tended to be perceived as deliberately obstructive by other members of the Security

Council and the Contact Group states in particular, this neglects the possible interpretation of their position as a principled one.[130] Russia's central critique was the threat NATO's actions posed to international stability and international law. They were concerned that a precedent for intervention was being set which would fundamentally de-stabilise states with national minorities by effectively sanctioning ethnic secessionism in multi-ethnic states.[131] The prudential and pluralist concerns articulated by Russia and China highlight the difficulties of establishing the motives behind the resort to particular justifications and thus raise the question of whether Russia and China were using language strategically. The problem is that while they may have been disguising their self-interests under the cloak of principled reasoning, these arguments might also have reflected a genuine belief that last resort had not been reached in March 1999 and that as a result the crisis did not warrant the use of force. Similar views were voiced by some Western critics of intervention who perceived the military intervention to be highly damaging to US–Russian and US–Chinese relations and thus divisive of the unity of the great powers.[132] This concern resonated with Robert Jackson's pluralism:

> The states who are in a position to pursue and preserve international justice have a responsibility to do that whenever and wherever possible. But they have a fundamental responsibility not to sacrifice or even jeopardize other fundamental values in the attempt. International order and stability, international peace and security, are such values. In my view, the stability of international society, especially the unity of the great powers, is more important, indeed far more important, than minority rights and humanitarian protections in Yugoslavia or an other country – if we have to choose between these two sets of values.[133]

The use of force by NATO brought into stark relief the political divisions between members of the Security Council which echoed the disagreements between pluralism and solidarism. Russia rejected outright NATO's actions in line with pluralist principles of territorial integrity and non-intervention, concern over setting precedents, and legal objections. Although not adopting a solidarist position, other non-aligned states such as Malaysia and Gabon did not accept the pluralist position offered by Russia and China. Instead, they offered principled regrets for the military action taken outside the sphere of the Security Council which potentially curtailed the possibility of a diplomatic resolution to the conflict.[134] Despite their more nuanced reactions, these non-Western states voted against the Russian draft resolution tabled on 26 March condemning NATO's bombing. Contrary to the arguments of some, the failure of the Russian draft resolution does not equate to a positive endorsement of NATO's arguably solidarist actions as would have been the case had a resolution in support of the intervention been adopted through the normal procedures of the Security Council. This is reflected in the consensus among the members of the Council who voted against the resolution that this was an exceptional action which should not set a precedent for a doctrine of unilateral humanitarian intervention.

Conclusion

Whilst many of the issues surrounding the intervention are frequently covered in broad brushstrokes, by painting an oversimplified picture a number of important nuances connected with the potential for dialogue are lost in the entrenchment of international norms, be it territorial integrity, sovereignty and non-intervention, or human rights, the victimisation of the Kosovars, and emerging arguments for military intervention. A lack of contextual sensitivity to the position of Kosovo within the dissolution of Yugoslavia, a preference for ethnic animosity as the root cause of conflict thus minimising the agency of the Kosovars, and the absence of in-depth knowledge of domestic politics, render these accounts bereft of the subtleties of the negotiations, interests and positions held by all actors involved in the crisis.

Underpinning the justifications offered by NATO for the use of force was the notion that Kosovo satisfied the criterion of 'last resort', namely a situation where all credible diplomatic alternatives had been exhausted. However, as Richard Falk suggested, this ignores the alternative paths which might have been taken. He argued that:

> [Critics] point to the exclusion of Russian diplomatic participation prior to NATO's recourse to war, the rigidity of the Holbrooke/Rambouillet formula, the absence of any evident diplomatic effort to induce China and Russia to accommodate the Security Council majority by shifting their veto to an abstention. Critics of the NATO intervention compare this pattern of prewar negotiation with the success of the war-ending diplomacy, which was based on a major Russian role and face-saving gestures toward Belgrade that included willingness to 'conceal' the NATO-led peacekeeping force beneath a UN cover story.[135]

By establishing the political construction of the conflict by agents both internal and external to the FRY and exploring the non-violent resistance in some detail, the dissonance between the missed opportunities identified for non-violent engagement and the (contested) justification of last resort becomes clearer.

Practices of inclusion, exclusion and coercion, *inter alia*, as demonstrated by a number of decisions concerning the structure of dialogue and negotiation over Kosovo, all served to shape the decisions that were taken by the parties. The narrative unfolded thus far has revealed a series of communicative practices on the part of the international community throughout the 1990s which include the foreclosure of dialogic opportunities, the exclusion of actors, state-dominated interactions and questions concerning the strategic or communicative use of language. Consequently, there is a need to subject to close scrutiny the justifications offered in the Security Council regarding the claim that there was no alternative but to use force to end the humanitarian crisis in Kosovo. This critical interrogation will be undertaken in depth in Chapter 6. The next step in the argument is to develop the critical tools with which to apply the lens of communicative ethics to Kosovo, and the following chapter begins this endeavour by examining the insights opened up by the communicative turn in IR.

NOTES

1 The chapter title draws on a phrase by Julie Mertus in relation to the Dayton Accord: 'To be sure, giving the Albanians of Kosovo a place at the table might infuriate Mr. Milosevic. But to try to reach peace in the Balkans without addressing the Kosovo issue is to try putting out a fire while leaving the coals burning.' *International Herald Tribune*, 23 October 1995.

2 R. Cook, 'Mission Statement', 12 May 1997. Available online: www.guardian.co.uk /indonesia/Story/0,2763,190889,00.html (accessed 24 November 2010).

3 For a variety of perspectives on the intervention, see R. Falk, 'Kosovo, World Order, and the Future of International Law', *American Journal of International Law*, 93:4 (1999), 847–57; M. Ignatieff, *Virtual War* (London: Vintage, 2000); Wheeler, *Saving Strangers*; N. J. Wheeler, 'Legitimating Humanitarian Intervention: Principles and Procedures', *Melbourne Journal of International Law*, 2:2 (2001), 550–67; ICISS, *The Responsibility to Protect*; K. Booth (ed.), *The Kosovo Tragedy: The Human Rights Dimension* (London: Frank Cass Publishers, 2001); K. E. Smith and M. Light (eds), *Ethics and Foreign Policy* (Cambridge: Cambridge University Press, 2001); M. Kaldor, *New and Old Wars* (Cambridge: Polity Press, 2001); D. Chandler, *From Kosovo to Kabul: Human Rights and International Intervention* (London: Pluto Press, 2002); A. J. Bellamy, *Kosovo and International Society* (Basingstoke: Palgrave Macmillan, 2002); Holzgrefe and Keohane (eds), *Humanitarian Intervention*; D. K. Chatterjee and D. E. Scheid (eds), *Ethics and Foreign Intervention* (Cambridge: Cambridge University Press, 2003); Hehir, *Humanitarian Intervention*; S. Chesterman, 'Legality Versus Legitimacy: Humanitarian Intervention, the Security Council, and the Rule of Law', *Security Dialogue*, 33:3 (2002), 293–307.

4 This builds on Bellamy's claim that there was 'an interdependent relationship between international responses to the conflict and events in Kosovo themselves'. Bellamy, *Kosovo and International Society*, 12. He describes seven periods of engagement: 1) Non-engagement (January 1991–August 1992); 2) Limited engagement (August 1992–June 1993); Malign non-engagement (June 1993–March 1998); 4) Debating Intervention (March 1998–October 1998); 5) Unarmed intervention (October 1998–January 1999); 6) Coercive diplomacy (January 1999–March 1999); 7) Limited war (March 1999–June 1999).

5 H. Clark, *Civil Resistance in Kosovo* (London: Pluto Press, 2000), 7; Amnesty International, *Kosovo: The Evidence* (London: Amnesty International, 1999); F. Bieber and Ž. Daskalovski (eds), *Understanding the War in Kosovo* (London: Frank Cass, 2003). See also K. M. Fierke, *Diplomatic Interventions: Conflict and Change in a Globalizing World* (Hampshire: Palgrave, 2005), 15. In line with Fierke's argument, these policies can be seen as forms of 'intervention' which shaped and constituted the lines of conflict.

6 A. Pavković, 'Kosovo/Kosova: A Land of Conflicting Myths', in M. Waller, K. Drezov and B. Gőkay, *Kosovo: The Politics of Delusion* (London: Frank Cass, 2001).
7 For example, C. Layne, 'Blunder in the Balkans: The Clinton Administration's Bungled War against Serbia', *Policy Analysis*, 345, 20 May (1999), 4.
8 Mertus, *How Myths and Truths Started a War*, 2–10.
9 IICK, *The Kosovo Report*, 33.
10 Malcolm, *Kosovo: A Short History*, 278–86.
11 L. Sell, *Slobodan Milosevic and the Destruction of Yugoslavia* (Durham, NC: Duke University Press, 2002), 74.
12 Cited by Malcolm, *Kosovo: A Short History*, 284.
13 Ibid.
14 Pristina University opened in 1970, strengthening ties with Albania.
15 T. Judah, *Kosovo: War and Revenge* (New Haven: Yale University Press, 2002), 40.
16 Ibid., 41.
17 Mertus, *How Myths and Truths Started a War*, 100–14.
18 IICK, *The Kosovo Report*, 40
19 See Fierke, *Diplomatic Interventions*, 126.
20 Judah, *Kosovo*, 52–3; IICK, *The Kosovo Report*, 40–1.
21 D. Kostovicova, *Kosovo: The Politics of Identity and Space* (London: Routledge, 2005), 10, citing Ernst Gellner. A look at Albanian literature and poetry indicates that the 'natural features of the terrain became "poetic spaces" when imbued with historical memories, myths and legends, as well as with the heroic deeds of brave ancestors, all of which were told and retold in the nationalist language' (Kostovicova, *Kosovo*, 14–15). For example, see A. Podrimja, *A Split Stone: An Anthology of Albanian Poets for Kosova* (Prishtina: DÇJ Rozafa, 2006).
22 Mertus, *How Myths and Truths Started a War*, 7.
23 Judah, *Kosovo*, 56.
24 Sell, *Slobodan Milosevic and the Destruction of Yugoslavia*, 87; A. J. Bellamy, 'Human Wrongs in Kosovo 1974–99', *International Journal of Human Rights*, 4:3 (2000), 105 26.
25 Sell, *Slobodan Milosevic and the Destruction of Yugoslavia*, 87.
26 Clark, *Civil Resistance in Kosovo*, 71–85.
27 It is worth noting that fairly static ethnic identities are also at times portrayed by Serbian and Albanian writers which aided the entrenchment of particular 'truths': 'The Serb campaign of terror did not begin on March 24, 1999, the day NATO began bombing Serbia, nor in March 1998, when the massacres of Drenica happened, nor in 1988 or 1981. Rather, it has been an entire period of hatred and cultivating racism by Serbs pushing the idea that they are superior to the Albanians, a period that has lasted at least from 1912 to the present.' B. Haxhiu: 'Kosova: A Place Where the Dead Speak', in W. Buckley (ed.), *Kosovo: Contending Voices on Balkan Interventions* (Cambridge: Wm. B. Erdmans Publishing Co., 2000), 180.
28 A. Stavrianakis, 'A Tale of Two Ethnicities? An Analysis of Approaches to "Ethnic Conflict": The Case of Kosovo', *Global Politics Network*, Fall (2002), 1.
29 Ibid. See Henry Kissinger, 'Doing Injury to History', *Newsweek Magazine*, 5 April 1999. For a critical perspective of this discursive construction, see E. Dauphinee, 'Rambouillet: A Critical (Re)Assessment', in Bieber and Daskalovski (eds), *Understanding the War in Kosovo*.
30 R. Kaplan, *Balkan Ghosts: A Journey Through History* (New York: Vintage Books, 1993), xi–xii. See discussion in R. Holbrooke, *To End a War* (New York: Random House, 1998), 22–4.

31 J. Husanović, '"Post-Conflict Kosovo": An Anatomy Lesson in the Ethics/Politics of Human Rights', in Booth (ed.), *The Kosovo Tragedy*, 277.
32 D. Campbell, *National Deconstruction: Violence, Identity, and Justice in Bosnia* (Minneapolis: University of Minnesota Press, 1998), 88–93.
33 Mertus, *How Myths and Truths Started a War*, 4.
34 Campbell, *National Deconstruction*, 92.
35 Ibid., 83.
36 Stavrianakis, 'A Tale of Two Ethnicities?', 16.
37 Kostovicova, *Kosovo: The Politics of Identity and Space*, 12.
38 Clark, *Civil Resistance in Kosovo*, 67. The campaign to reconcile blood feuds is an example of communicative attempts to break out of traditional and violent practices and thus a shift in identity (60).
39 Ibid., 5.
40 Ibid. It would be an interesting counterfactual to ask whether a more peaceful outcome to the conflict could have been secured had the international community not failed to support the non-violent resistance movement.
41 Jackson, *The Global Covenant*, 292.
42 Judah, *Kosovo*, 62; Bellamy, *Kosovo and International Society*, Introduction; Sell, *Slobodan Milosevic and the Destruction of Yugoslavia*, 93–4; M. Weller, *The Crisis in Kosovo 1989–1999: From Dissolution of Yugoslavia to Rambouillet and the Outbreak of Hostilities*, vol. 1 (Cambridge: Documents & Analysis Publishing Ltd, 1999), Chapters 6 and 14, 347.
43 Bellamy, *Kosovo and International Society*, 9.
44 Amnesty International, *Kosovo: The Evidence*, 33.
45 Clark, *Civil Resistance in Kosovo*, 57; Sell, *Slobodan Milosevic and the Destruction of Yugoslavia*, 89.
46 Clark, *Civil Resistance in Kosovo*, 59.
47 Judah, *Kosovo*, 61.
48 Ibid., 66.
49 Ibid., 67–8.
50 Ibid.
51 Ibid., 68–9.
52 IICK, *The Kosovo Report*, 46.
53 Kostovicova, *Kosovo: The Politics of Identity and Space*, 22–7. See D. Kostovicova, 'Albanian Schooling in Kosovo 1992–1998: "Liberty Imprisoned"', in Waller *et al.* (eds), *Kosovo: The Politics of Delusion*.
54 IICK, *The Kosovo Report*, 47; Clark, *Civil Resistance in Kosovo*, 95–121.
55 Fierke, *Diplomatic Interventions*, 94. Intervention might be considered to take legal, economic, cultural, therapeutic, diplomatic, military, or moral forms.
56 Clark, *Civil Resistance in Kosovo*, 128–41. See H. H. Perritt Jr, *Kosovo Liberation Army: The Inside Story of an Insurgency* (Chicago: University of Illinois Press, 2008), 143. Perritt illustrates the tensions within the Kosovar political sphere, citing Bujar Bukoshi, PM in exile, who indicated that 'Failing to recognize that diplomacy requires pressure, Rugova was passive in the execution of his strategy.' He sought to represent himself as being in control over the situation, thereby offering the international community an easy reason for inaction.
57 Dialogue activities for 'dialogue's sake' were attempted in a number of ways both by local individuals and groups, such as the Belgrade-based Women in Black, some Kosovo and FRY political parties, between the Belgrade and Prishtina Helsinki Committees, by LDK Youth, and by external organisations such as the Norwegian Nansen Peace Academy,

Mens Sana, and the Open Society Fund/Soros. Clark, *Civil Resistance in Kosovo*, 142–3.
58 Ibid., 170–1.
59 Sell, *Slobodan Milosevic and the Destruction of Yugoslavia*, 108.
60 Letter from Dr Rugova to Lord Carrington, Peace Conference on Yugoslavia, 22 December 1991 where he requests that 'the Republic of Kosova be recognised as a sovereign and independent state'. Weller, *The Crisis in Kosovo*, 347. Bellamy notes that Carrington never responded to the letter and never took the issue seriously. Bellamy, *Kosovo and International Society*, 26.
61 Bellamy, *Kosovo and International Society*, 22–4. He points to the general consensus that Milošević's decision to revoke Kosovo's autonomy in 1989 was unconstitutional, and the European Parliament's call to include Kosovo and Vojvodina in the ECCY.
62 IICK, *The Kosovo Report*, 57.
63 The International Crisis Group's report, *Intermediate Sovereignty as a Basis for Resolving the Kosovo Crisis*, no. 46, 9 November 1998, states that *uti possidetis* 'generally provides that an entity in legitimate possession of territory at the time of a dispute over ownership or at the time of the decolonization or dissolution of a state be entitled to retain and be granted permanent legal right to such territory and that in such circumstances the borders of the territory as they exist at such time should not be modified. In particular, the doctrine provides a valid basis for declaring that the borders of a Kosovo holding international status would be exactly the same as the internal borders established by the 1946 and 1974 constitutions' (25).
64 Sell, *Slobodan Milosevic and the Destruction of Yugoslavia*, 109. Weller writes of the Commission that: 'Self-determination was not deemed applicable to territorially defined enclaves within former federal entities where a minority formed a local majority. The most striking examples are Kosovo and Krajina, which were granted the right to self-determination only in the sense of minority and human rights, notwithstanding, at least in the former case, that preexisting structures of autonomous government were in place.' M. Weller, 'The International Response to the Dissolution of the Socialist Federal Republic of Yugoslavia', *American Journal of International Law*, 86:3 (1992), 606.
65 See Bellamy, *Kosovo and International Society*, 28; Clark, *Civil Resistance in Kosovo*, 26–8; A. Bellamy, 'Lessons Unlearned: Why Coercive Diplomacy Failed at Rambouillet', *International Peacekeeping*, 7:2 (2000), 104. See also R. Caplan, 'International Diplomacy and the Crisis in Kosovo', *International Affairs*, 74:4 (1998), 748; M. Weller, 'The Rambouillet Conference on Kosovo', *International Affairs*, 75:2 (1999), 211–51; Weller, *The Crisis in Kosovo*, 76; see Opinion No. 1 of the Arbitration Commission on the former Yugoslavia, 11 January 1992 and Kosovo Memorandum to the International Conference on the Former Yugoslavia, 26 August 1992, Weller, *The Crisis in Kosovo*, 81, 86–8; S. Terrett, *The Dissolution of Yugoslavia and the Badinter Arbitration Commission* (Aldershot: Ashgate, 2000), 125. Terrett also notes that the Kosovars enjoyed less access to the Commission than the Republika Srpska which had no formal status under Yugoslavia's constitution and had been created through conflict (154).
66 ICG, *Intermediate Sovereignty as a Basis for Resolving the Kosovo Crisis*, ii.
67 Jackson, *The Global Covenant*, 325–35.
68 Judah cited in Bellamy, *Kosovo and International Society*, 29.
69 Letter from Lord Carrington, Chairman, Conference on Yugoslavia to Dr I. Rugova, 17 August 1992: 'As it will not, for practical and other reasons, be possible to grant your delegation access to the Conference chamber itself, the organisers will set up a "Salle d'ecoute" to which the formal Conference proceedings will be relayed live.' Weller, *The Crisis in Kosovo*, 86; Interview with Rugova, in *La Question du Kosovo, Entretiens realisés*

par Marie-Françoise Allain et Xavier Galmiche (Paris: Fayard, 1994), 170–1. Interestingly, in the context of this interview, Rugova uses this example to indicate that diplomatic progress was being made and that the Kosovars were better represented at international summits than previously.
70 Letter from Lord Carrington to Rugova, emphasis added. Weller, *The Crisis in Kosovo*, 86.
71 Sell, *Slobodan Milosevic and the Destruction of Yugoslavia*, 109.
72 St Egidio Education Agreement, 1 September 1996, Weller, *The Crisis in Kosovo*, 93.
73 Bellamy, *Kosovo and International Society*, 31. The focus on minority rights also tied Kosovo's position to that of minorities such as the Krajina Serbs. This ignored the constitutional position Kosovo had had under the 1974 constitution.
74 Judah, *Kosovo*, 76.
75 C. Rogel, 'Kosovo: Where It All Began', *International Journal of Politics, Culture and Society*, 17:1 (2003), 167–82; C. Chinkin, 'The State That Acts Alone: Bully, Good Samaritan or Iconoclast?', *European Journal of International Law*, 11:1 (2000), 34; IICK, *The Kosovo Report*, 59.
76 For discussion on the exclusion of Kosovo see P. Russell, 'The Exclusion of Kosovo from the Dayton Negotiations', *Journal of Genocide Research*, 11:4 (2009), 487–511; Bellamy, *Kosovo and International Society*.
77 Russell, 'The Exclusion of Kosovo', 504.
78 Bellamy, *Kosovo and International Society*, 54.
79 Judah, *Kosovo*, 124, citing Holbrooke.
80 Judah, *Kosovo*, 124–5. Kosovar Prime Minister Bukoshi declared that '"our greatest concern is that Kosovo could be forgotten or marginalized in" Dayton, and that if it was, the resistance to Serbia would not remain peaceful. "You can create moderates or you can create radicals, and this is a situation that can create radicals."' Cited in Russell, 'The exclusion of Kosovo', 500. See also See H. Thaqi: 'Kosova', in W. Buckley (ed.), *Kosovo: Contending Voices on Balkan Interventions* (Cambridge: Wm. B. Erdmans Publishing Co., 2000), 190; Caplan, 'International Diplomacy', 750; J. Pettifer, 'The Kosovo Liberation Army: The Myth of Origin', in Waller *et al.* (eds), *Kosovo: The Politics of Delusion*, 26.
81 Russell, 'The Exclusion of Kosovo', 499. Judah and Bellamy make similar arguments.
82 Sell, *Slobodan Milosevic and the Destruction of Yugoslavia*, 278; J. Pettifer and M. Vickers, *The Albanian Question: Reshaping the Balkans* (London: I. B. Tauris, 2007), Chapters 7 and 8; Perritt Jr, *Kosovo Liberation Army*.
83 IICK, *The Kosovo Report*, 60.
84 Ibid., 61.
85 Sell, *Slobodan Milosevic and the Destruction of Yugoslavia*, 274.
86 Ibid., 275. There were a number of local initiatives which called for non-violent engagement prior to 1999, such as: the Humanitarian Law Foundation, the Soros Foundation, the Belgrade Circle, and the Helsinki Committee for Human Rights in Kosovo. See International Crisis Group, 'Kosovo Spring', Report 32 (March 1998), 34–5; S. Troebst, *Conflict in Kosovo: Failure of Prevention? An Analytical Documentation 1992–1998* (Flensburg: European Centre for Minority Issues, Working Paper No. 1, 1998).
87 Troebst, *Conflict in Kosovo*, 23–5.
88 Sell, *Slobodan Milosevic and the Destruction of Yugoslavia*, 276.
89 Clark, *Civil Resistance in Kosovo*, 162; Judah, *Kosovo*, 95; Caplan, 'International Diplomacy', 757; Troebst, *Conflict in Kosovo*, 24; *The Economist*, 'Welcome to Balkania: Kosovo' (7 September 1996).

90 Transnational Foundation for Peace and Future Research, *UNTANS – Conflict Mitigation for Kosovo. A UN Temporary Authority for a Negotiated Settlement* (1996).
91 Troebst, *Conflict in Kosovo*, 87–9.
92 International Helsinki Foundation for Human Rights, *From Autonomy to Colonization: Human Rights in Kosovo 1989–1993* (Vienna: IHF, November 1993).
93 IICK, *The Kosovo Report*, 62–3.
94 Ibid.
95 Ibid., 64
96 Ibid.
97 See Fierke, *Changing Games*, Chapter 8.
98 Ibid., 279.
99 Judah, *Kosovo*, 131.
100 Sell, *Slobodan Milosevic and the Destruction of Yugoslavia*, 279.
101 Wheeler, *Saving Strangers*, 258; IICK, *The Kosovo Report*, 67–70. Perritt attributes to the KLA a keen understanding of the necessary strategy to pursue their aims: they opposed any terrorist attacks on civilian targets; they sought to internationalise the conflict where Rugova had failed to do so; they maintained a viable military force against Milošević's forces, thus playing on the fears of the international community concerning the conflict spreading; they avoided any links with militant Islam; they publicised the repression by the Serbian authorities and worked with local and Western media to do so; they lobbied foreign governments through influential members of the diaspora (*Kosovo Liberation Army*, 130–51).
102 UN Security Council Document (hereafter referenced by number) S/PV.3868, 31 March 1998.
103 Wheeler, *Saving Strangers*, 260.
104 Judah, *Kosovo*, 165.
105 Sell, *Slobodan Milosevic and the Destruction of Yugoslavia*, 287.
106 S/PV.3930, 23 September 1998, 3.
107 S/RES/1199 (1998), 5.
108 S/1998/912, 3 October 1998.
109 Weller, *The Crisis in Kosovo*, 349.
110 Ibid.
111 Ibid.
112 Wheeler, *Saving Strangers*, 262.
113 For the eleven-point statement detailing the Yugoslav government's interpretation of the Holbrooke agreement see S/1998/953, 14 October 1998.
114 See Bellamy, *Kosovo and International Society*, 109–10.
115 S/PV.3937, 24 October 1998. China stated: 'However, very regrettably, almost at the same time as [the Holbrooke] agreements were being concluded, a regional organization concerned made the decision to take military actions against the Federal Republic of Yugoslavia and interfere in its internal affairs. More disturbingly, that decision was made unilaterally, without consulting the Security Council or seeking its authorization' (14).
116 Ibid., 6. Costa Rica went on to declare in clear opposition to the exercise of unilateral (unauthorised) force that 'The Security Council alone can determine whether there has been a violation of its resolutions, adopted in the exercise of its mandated powers. Only the Security Council can authorize the use of force to ensure compliance with its resolutions, in exercise of its primary responsibility for the maintenance of international peace and security' (7). See D. Sarooshi, 'The Security Council's Authorization of Regional Arrangements to use Force: The Case of NATO', in V. Lowe, A. Roberts,

J. Welsh and D. Zaum (eds), *The United Nations Security Council and War: The Evolution of Thought and Practice since 1945* (Oxford: Oxford University Press, 2008).
117 S/PV.3937, 24 October 1998, 10–11. See also the communiqué issued by the Rio Group, A/53/884–S/1999/347, 25 March 1999.
118 Judah, *Kosovo*, 193.
119 Sell, *Slobodan Milosevic and the Destruction of Yugoslavia*, 295.
120 M. Albright and B. Woodward, *Madam Secretary – A Memoir* (London: Macmillan, 2003), 391.
121 P. Robinson, 'Ready to Kill But Not to Die', *International Journal*, 54:4 (1999), 671–82.
122 Albright, *Madam Secretary*, 391.
123 S/1999/96, 29 January 1999.
124 Judah, *Kosovo*, 195.
125 Ibid., 196.
126 See Holbrooke's record of his last meeting with Milošević prior to the commencement of the bombing. Judah, *Kosovo*, 227.
127 Wheeler, *Saving Strangers*, 265; M. J. Matheson, 'Justification for the NATO Air Campaign in Kosovo', *American Society of International Law Proceedings*, 94 (2000), 301; S/PV.3989, 26 March 1999.
128 Speech by British Prime Minister Tony Blair to the Economic Club of Chicago, 22 April 1999: www.pbs.org/newshour/bb/international/jan-june99/blair_doctrine4-23.html (accessed 8 December 2011). It is worth noting that, unlike the US, the UK developed a legal justification for intervention.
129 S/PV.3988, 24 March 1999, 1.
130 Chesterman, *Just War or Just Peace?*, 221; S/PV.3989, 26 March 1999.
131 Jackson, *The Global Covenant*, 283.
132 Ibid.
133 Jackson, *The Global Covenant*, 291.
134 S/PV.3988, 24 March 1999.
135 Falk, 'Kosovo, World Order', 851.

3

Communicative action in International Relations

Introduction

The growing significance which has been attributed to language and communication in IR responded to the critical turn in social and political theory. Its impact on IR manifested itself variously in the insights of social constructivism, the application to the world stage of the critical theory of the Frankfurt School, the philosophy of language, feminism, and the continental philosophy of those such as Foucault and Derrida, among many others.[1] As a leading proponent of the linguistic turn whose work has been substantially appropriated by IR scholars, the significance Habermas accords to communicative action in the public sphere makes this an appropriate place from which to further develop the analytic and normative potential of the nexus between legitimacy and communicative ethics.[2]

Broadly speaking, Habermasian influences can be detected in two branches of IR theory. First, in the work of critical theorists who have sought to appropriate Habermasian concepts to establish a critical theory of IR, and second, in the work of social constructivists who, in seeking to construct a social theory of international politics, have paid considerable attention to the influential role of argumentative processes in international politics. The purposes underlying these theoretical approaches remain somewhat different and neither, as they have been articulated to date, fully captures the potential offered by a Habermasian-informed analysis of the role of justifications for the use of force. By engaging in a close analysis of the work of two scholars who draw respectively on the constructivist and critical theoretical approaches, it is possible to explore limitations relating both to the broad theoretical aims and their particular empirical analyses. The contributions of Ian Johnstone and Corneliu Bjola in particular are assessed because they tie together the tripartite themes central to this book, namely, a communicative-theoretic approach, a concern with justifications for the legitimate use of force, and the intervention in Kosovo.

Habermas's work was initially drawn on by some scholars of IR as a critical tool to challenge the dominance of positivist approaches in the discipline, notably the theorising that underpinned neorealism and neo-liberalism.[3] The end of the Cold War, which no theoretical approach in IR had predicted, dealt a powerful blow to neorealism given the latter's understanding of the limits of change in an anarchic system.[4] Neorealism became the target of criticism that it reified a particular international order which privileged the interests of certain dominant states and therefore served particular political ends. As such, the epistemological, ontological and methodological premises of neorealism were called into question by those who recognised the need to challenge neorealism's claim that the structure of international politics is immutable.[5]

Habermas's writings contributed to the critique of positivism and the shift towards a focus on communication and language in IR in two crucial ways. Firstly, he argued that positivism's tendency to view all human problems as technical problems which could be addressed with technical solutions failed to understand that the aim of knowledge about the human world should be to foster greater freedom and autonomy, not greater control.[6] Critical theorists were asking questions about the nature of knowledge claims and the historical contingency of knowledge, the constitution of meaning and truth, and the division adhered to by neorealists between 'facts' and 'values'. Habermas demonstrated that it was not necessary to resort to either essentialism about human nature or metaphysical assumptions about reason, instead grounding his critique on the reconstruction of the assumptions which underpin our everyday language use. Secondly, his theory of communicative action revealed fundamental concerns with the relationship between power and discourse.[7] At its heart is the notion of mutual agreement through the exchange of arguments. He set out the key distinction previously noted between communicative and strategic rationalities and explored ways in which instrumental and strategic processes within society lead to increasing distortion of communication.

Given the critical theoretical concern with autonomy and emancipation, the analytical distinction between strategic and communicative rationalities lends itself to analysing how communicative practices contribute to enabling, perpetuating or transforming conflict and inequality in the international sphere. Habermas's writings offer a clear counterpoint to those who wish to challenge the emphasis on instrumental rationality and strategic action which permeate many conventional paradigms in IR. Recognising the importance of communication, the broad church of constructivism and critical theory has countered the dominant position of strategic action in international politics as conceived by neorealism and rationalism.

A brief aside is necessary here to indicate that although conscious of the fact that both realism and rationalism belong to complex and rich political and theoretical traditions, justice cannot be done to them within the scope of this book. In the context of strategic language use in IR, reference is made both to rationalism as a methodology (which informs and shapes the idea that politics amounts to utility-maximising strategic action and subordinates the role and significance of language) and to those realist writers who fall into two camps: a) those who accept rationalist tenets and come under the umbrella of neorealism, and b) those who do not draw on rationalism as a methodology, but who nonetheless recognise ways in which language can be used strategically. As such, there are elements within these bodies of thought which overlap with the concept of strategic action found in Habermas's work. Similarly, there are overlaps between constructivists in IR who are concerned with the constitutive power of language, the strategic use of language, and Habermas's concepts of strategic and communicative action. While these concepts may be used interchangeably in practice, Habermas's terms should not be conceptually conflated with their related positions in IR as this would be to oversimplify both theoretical traditions.

The dichotomy between strategic and communicative action as represented by this broad set of theoretical positions opens up the question of the merits of communicative ethics. A central criticism of neorealism and rationalism is that the focus on strategic action, bargaining and rhetoric fundamental to their interpretation of behaviour in international politics enables practices which enact a politics of exclusion or enable particular discourses to remain dominant. The conceptual focus on communicative action adopted by both social constructivism and Habermasian critical theory challenges these assumptions and offers alternative methods of interpretation and political action. In addition, the communicative ethics approach highlights the need for those persuaded by the 'communicative turn' to take into their theoretical considerations the appropriate relationship *between* these rationalities. As already noted, Habermas has been criticised for setting up this dichotomy, not least because it is considered untenable in the real world where both rationalities intermingle in complex environments.[8] Despite the difficulties entailed, it will be argued that retaining an imperfect sense of the distinction is necessary in order to hold on to the critical leverage which communicative ethics promises.

The 'communicative turn' in international relations

The influence of critical theory in IR emerged in the early 1980s, notably with the work of Robert Cox, Richard Ashley and Andrew Linklater.[9] Broadly speaking, critical theory can be split into four main strands: Frankfurt School critical theory, neo-Gramscian theory, feminism and post-structuralism.

These are not the only variants of critical influence, but they remain significant ones. They are also, in and of themselves, heterogeneously composed. Given that the theoretical framework in this book derives its influence predominantly, although not solely, from the Frankfurt School, it is this strand which will be focused on. Those who work in this tradition tend to focus on emancipation conceived in dialogical terms: the removal or correction of communication distorted by power and interests.[10]

Cox's well-known distinction between 'problem-solving' theory and 'critical theory' in IR drew on Max Horkheimer's 1937 classic essay 'On Traditional and Critical Theory' which has become one of the founding essays of the Frankfurt School. One of the central challenges which critical theory presented to the dominant, positivist trend in IR was that it recognised the theorist as situated within their historical and political context – not as a neutral outside observer of social phenomena – leading to Cox's seminal observation that 'Theory is always *for* someone and *for* some purpose.'[11] A key contribution of critical theory to IR therefore has been the idea of 'immanent critique': that is, in understanding the particular historical context, theorists seek to understand how and why it came to be as it is and what possibilities for change there might be implicit within it.[12] This is echoed in Linklater's claim that central to critical theory is a capacity to reflect upon the 'social construction and effects of knowledge and to consider how claims about neutrality can conceal the role knowledge plays in reproducing unsatisfactory social arrangements'.[13] The dominant strand of Frankfurt critical theory in IR has undoubtedly emerged in Linklater's work and it is in his writing that we can also see the centrality of Habermas's thought for theoretical debates in IR. He argues that:

> critical theory judges social arrangements by their capacity to embrace open dialogue with all others and envisages new forms of political community which break with unjustified exclusion. Realist and neo-realist arguments that communities must deal with one another in the currency of military power is rejected by critical theory which envisages the use of unconstrained discourse to determine the moral significance of boundaries and to examine the possibility of post-sovereign forms of political life.[14]

Encompassed within this claim for critical theory are four key elements: first, an account of transformation and social learning through unconstrained dialogue; second, a normative, emancipatory intent; third, a recognition that change must come from immanent possibilities within society; and fourth, a perspective that reaches beyond the Marxist focus on class as the fundamental form of social exclusion.[15]

Constructivism shares with critical theory a concern to challenge the view of the world of positivist IR. Constructivists have developed a sociological explanation of world politics which focuses on the importance of 'normative as well as material structures, the role of identity in the constitution of interests and action, and the mutual constitution of agents and structures'.[16] It is worth noting that the emancipatory element of critical theory emerges to a greater or lesser degree in constructivist theorising.[17] Like other theoretical perspectives in IR, constructivism is a heterogeneous and contested church; only that branch of it, therefore, which adopts a focus on the theory and practice of communicative action will be considered here.[18] Central to both the Habermasian-inspired communicative ethics of critical theory and constructivism is a shared concern with the intersubjectivity and dynamics of communication. For constructivists, Christian Reus-Smit argues that the insight offered by communicative action enables the 'development of an *empirical* theory of norm formation, one that emphasises the way in which actors negotiate new norms by "grafting" them discursively to established intersubjective meanings'. Communicative ethicists, by contrast, are concerned with an *ethical* theory of norm formation.[19]

Richard Price and Reus-Smit have argued that much of the early work on critical theory focused on the metatheoretical project, making little effort to 'apply the conceptual and methodological apparatus of either modern or post-modern critical theory to the sustained empirical analysis of issues in world politics'.[20] In contrast, the task of developing a social theory of international politics has been central to the efforts of constructivists who have undertaken considerable theoretical and empirical work looking at the role of communication in international politics. The central claim shared by constructivists and critical theorists is that argument and justifications matter in international politics.

Indeed, argument, reasoning and justification together constitute a crucial pillar in the construction of our understanding of the functioning of international institutions, state actions and the constitution of norms and values. As demonstrated by the debates over Kosovo, international legal norms provide one of the most common sources of reason and justification. The role of the Security Council as the executive body responsible for the maintenance of international peace and security locates it as a critical focus for much of the empirical work which has been carried out into communication and its effects. Ian Johnstone contends that legal arguments as justificatory discourse have a demonstrable influence on decision-making processes within the Security Council. He argues that 'voting arrangements are not the only gauge of legitimacy in international organizations; one must also look at the quality of deliberations that precede and follow decisions taken'.[21] Not only do institutions serve as information-rich environments, but they also provide a framework which structures interactions.[22]

This attention to communication and its effects challenges the theoretical premises of other traditional paradigms in IR. Inclined to be suspicious of the value of justifications, those of both realist and rationalist persuasions dismiss them as strategic or manipulative instruments, as 'cheap talk' intended to mask the reality of power politics. Instead of recognising how processes of language shape actions, realists suggest that language, like international law, reflects the prevailing power of material capabilities and interests.[23] Realists argue that justifications can always be found to justify action; they are adopted instrumentally when needed and international law is subordinate to politics.[24] Claims to incorporate communication through a variety of strategies, such as signalling games or cheap talk, which could loosely be termed 'rhetorical action', are, in many cases, flawed because these types of communication strategies often retain an instrumental orientation to communication which assumes the operation of underlying rationalist tenets and reflects the tension between strategic and communicative rationalities.[25] Not only does strategic action of this kind make little allowance for the communicative orientation to language which is so important for Habermas, but also missing is theoretical recognition of the need to explore the relationship between these rationalities.

The crux of the debate is that whereas rationalists think norms are exogenous to state behaviour which is premised on the utilitarian calculations of interests, they are constitutive of state action for constructivists.[26] Constructivists, and critical theorists, influenced by the linguistic turn in social and political theory, argue that perspectives which focus on the strategic use of language are unable to sufficiently explain the constitutive formation of identity and interests of states which takes place through deliberation, justification, and socialisation. The need to account for communicative action is demonstrated in the very existence of pre-negotiations. On the rationalist/utilitarian reading, there would be no need for such exchanges, as the interests of the parties and the structure of the situation are clear.[27] Contrary to this perspective, however, actors may engage in dialogue with the aim of reaching a mutual understanding based on a reasoned consensus, thus suggesting a fundamentally different orientation to language than that subscribed to by realists or rationalists.

The advantages of the constructivist recognition of the importance of communication to understanding the appeal to norms in the Security Council concerning the use of force include an explicit recognition of the intersubjectivity of language and the construction of norms. In order to understand an action in the constitutive terms of constructivism, we not only need to understand the actor's perspective, but crucially be familiar with the intersubjective understandings that tell us about the meaning of the act.[28] Along these lines Friedrich Kratochwil argues that 'we have to understand how the social world is intrinsically linked to language and how language, because it is a rule-governed activity, can provide us with a point of departure for our inquiry into the function of norms in social life'.[29]

Those constructivists most influenced by the linguistic turn claim that language cannot be manipulated infinitely and have demonstrated that there are limits to the manner of justifications which can be offered in international society. There is, Fierke argues, a relationship between the '*language of manoeuvre* by states, that is, the strategic use of language, and the *entanglement* of states in their own public justifications'.[30] In other words, (continually evolving and historically contingent) parameters on what are considered to be acceptable reasons or justifications are drawn from international norms and law. The constraining effect of norms on justifications can be explained in terms of reciprocity. Even though states may benefit in the short term from violating international law, they almost always refrain from doing so because they do not want to jeopardise the structure of international legal obligations more fundamentally.[31] Similarly, Risse argues that argumentative 'self-entrapment' has an analogous effect. The force of 'argumentative self-entrapment' is that it works to induce states to match words with deeds, assuming that they take seriously the 'need to legitimate'. Once states have accepted a legal norm 'they begin to argue over its interpretation and its application to the particular case at hand, rather than the validity of the law itself'.[32] The constraining power of norms, even on actors who act strategically, has been set out by Quentin Skinner in an argument which is worth quoting at length. Skinner argued that it does not follow

> from the fact that someone's professed principles may be *ex post facto* rationalisations that those principles play no role in explaining their behaviour. As I have argued, this is to ignore the implications of the fact that people generally possess strong motives for seeking to legitimise any conduct liable to appear questionable. One implication is that they will generally find it necessary to claim that their actions were in fact motivated by some accepted principle. A further implication is that, even if they were not motivated by any such principle, they will find themselves committed to behaving in such a way that their actions *remain compatible* with the claim that their professed principles genuinely motivated them. To recognise these implications is to accept that the courses of action open to such agents will in part be determined by the range of existing principles they can hope to profess with some degree of plausibility.[33]

For Skinner, two conclusions emerge from this argument which are relevant for advocates of the significance of language in international politics. First, he argues that 'any course of action will be inhibited to the degree that it cannot be legitimised'. Second, he indicates that 'the range of terms that innovating ideologists can hope to apply to legitimise their behaviour can never be set by themselves'.[34] While argumentation may begin as rhetorical and reflect strategic adaptation to external pressures, it may also end, as Risse suggests, with a shift towards real argumentative rationality as the actors gradually accept each other as valid interlocutors, try to establish some common definition of the situation and agree on the norms guiding it.[35] In this sense, argumentative self-entrapment offers a bridge between strategic language use and communicative action and a counter to the position that states only engage in strategic bargaining. The bridge offered by Risse's argumentative self-entrapment does not, however, extend to encompass the critical and reflexive orientation of communicative ethics as regards the nature of communicative practices and their legitimacy.

Communicative ethics encourages individuals/groups as members of societies to negotiate their needs and interests without harming each other by granting everyone equal access to and equal voice in decision-making procedures that may affect them. Both critics of Habermas and his advocates have noted that there is a disjuncture between the ideal, utopian nature of the demands placed upon participants in discourse and political reality. This misses the purpose of ideal theory in this context, however, for while acknowledging that communication is always imperfect and not a goal to be realised concretely, as John Forester has insisted, 'deviations from the formal idealization might still be usefully identified and assessed'.[36] In other words, as will be unpacked further in the following chapter, Habermas offers a powerful critical and evaluative tool in the shape of discourse ethics and the ideal speech situation. Such an ideal of complete participation coupled with immanent claims to legitimacy voiced by real political actors enables the generation of a theoretical framework intended to examine the legitimacy of real moments of participation in international politics and it is this premise that underpins the theoretical formulation of communicative ethics and the empirical analysis of Kosovo.

Communicative action, Kosovo, and the use of force

Having identified the merits, broadly speaking, of the 'communicative turn', it is to analyses of Kosovo which we now turn in order to examine the empirical strength of existing approaches and to draw attention to their conceptual limitations. An illustration of the limits of applying sociological approaches to the legitimacy of the use of force can be seen in Ian Johnstone's analysis of the debates in the Security Council over Kosovo. Johnstone's constructivism recognises the constraining power of norms, especially legal ones, and sheds important light on the character of the Security Council's deliberations in relation to NATO's intervention. The other analyst whose assessment of the legitimacy of the intervention in Kosovo is examined is Corneliu Bjola. The latter adopts a critical orientation through his conceptual framework of deliberative legitimacy but, despite employing Habermasian insights, it will be shown that his approach, like Johnstone's, does not fully embrace the theoretical and empirical potential offered by a Habermasian-inspired critical theory of IR.

Johnstone's argument is an exemplary illustration of the influence of the communicative approach in shaping decision-making processes. Contrary to those accounts which emphasise the strategic use of language in international politics, Johnstone charts how legal arguments were invoked to justify the different positions taken by states in the Security Council debates over Kosovo.[37] He argues that language is not simply epiphenomenal (the strategic language use argument) because 'norms are invoked to explain, defend, justify and persuade'.[38] Johnstone brackets his reading of the justifications offered in the Council with the periods immediately prior to and after NATO's airstrikes which began on 24 March 1999. He identifies a number of key features within the Security Council debates which all point to the relevance and active presence of what he calls an interpretive legal community.

Of the main features of the Kosovo debates identified by Johnstone, two will be highlighted here in order to illustrate the influential presence of legal argumentation. First, there was a significant range of legal arguments drawn upon by states who presented cases both supporting and attacking the intervention's legality. On the one hand, on 26 March 1999, Russia argued that,

> The aggressive military action unleashed by NATO against a sovereign state without the authorization and in circumvention of the Security Council is a real threat to international peace and security and a gross violation of the UN Charter and other basic norms of international law. Key provisions of the Charter are being violated. In particular Article 2, paragraph 4, which requires all Members of the United Nations to refrain from the threat or use of force in their international relations, including against the territorial integrity or political independence of any State; Article 24, which entrusts the Security Council with the primary responsibility for the maintenance of international peace and security; Article 53, on the inadmissibility of any enforcement action under regional arrangements or by regional agencies without the authorization of the Security Council as well as others.[39]

Contrary to Russia's legal argument, the UK was among those who made the most emphatic legal defence of the intervention. The UK representative, Sir Jeremy Greenstock, argued that,

> The action being taken is legal. It is justified as an exceptional measure to prevent an overwhelming humanitarian catastrophe ... Every means short of force has been tried to avert this situation. In these circumstances, and as an exceptional measure on the grounds of overwhelming humanitarian necessity, military intervention is legally justifiable.[40]

These contrary legal positions identified the key norms and law which were then drawn on in order to justify the two opposing positions adopted concerning the legality and morality of intervention. Russia drew on pluralist notions of sovereignty, non-intervention and the primary responsibility of the Security Council to maintain international peace and security, whereas the UK and states including the Netherlands, the United States, Canada, France and Slovenia, drew on solidarist norms of human rights protection and (questionable emerging norms of) humanitarian necessity.[41]

The second key feature Johnstone identifies is that the difficulty of justifying the intervention on legal grounds caused NATO governments (with the singular exception of the UK) to refrain from insisting upon its legality, choosing instead to rely on more general claims to legitimacy derived from the exceptional and moral nature of the intervention. The US, for example, relied on a general claim of legitimacy, substantiated by a variety of factors rather than a single specified legal justification.[42] This shows how language can be constraining on state actions because if law were simply the servant of power, then the United States would surely have been able to defend its use of force by appealing to legal arguments relating to self-defence and even humanitarian intervention. Instead, recognising that a justification of self-defence would lack credibility in the eyes of the international community, the Clinton Administration had to then decide whether to invoke a justification of unilateral humanitarian intervention. It decided against this for two reasons which emphasise how actors worry about becoming entangled in their own justifications: on the one hand, the United States wished to avoid setting a legal precedent which might be drawn on by other states to justify interventions which might affect international order or harm US interests, and, on the other, to avoid establishing expectations that it would act similarly again in comparative circumstances in the future.[43] This reasoning only makes sense if the United States understood that they might be bound to act in certain ways if they lent their actions particular public justifications.

In order to make these claims about the constraining power of legal norms, Johnstone employs the idea of 'interpretive communities'. This concept has been previously employed in literary interpretation by Stanley Fish, and Johnstone sought to adapt it to show how the Security Council was such an interpretive community. An 'interpretive community' is best understood in terms of its function in any type of interpretive practice. It reflects the 'power of institutional settings or disciplines, within which assumptions and modes of arguments are deeply entrenched'.[44] Thus, interpretive communities offer meaning, constrain interpretation, and pass judgement on particular discursive practices within the legal community. In so doing, they avoid the dangers of either pure objectivity or subjectivity. In an intersubjective process, the parameters of meaning are determined by those engaged in a field of practice; as such, they deny the radical indeterminacy of meaning.[45] Interpretive authority 'resides in neither the text nor the reader individually, but with the community of professionals engaged in the enterprise of treaty interpretation and implementation'.[46] Interpretive communities draw on accepted conventions, traditions and practices within a known social horizon, albeit through the lens of a particular issue. They are produced by repeated and frequent communicative interactions which produce the kind of 'common lifeworld' that Johnstone perceives the Security Council to be.

Johnstone establishes two important elements which draw on a sociological interpretation of Habermas's theory of communicative action. First, he places interpretive communities at the centre of his analysis, thus embracing an intersubjective approach with which to understand communicative practice. Crucially, interpretive communities cannot operate as a monological interpretation of international law, but refer to processes which take place intersubjectively, dialogically, and are subject to the force of the better argument.[47]

Second, in order to utilise the notion of an interpretive community, he makes the case for the existence of a common lifeworld in the Security Council. In doing so, he draws on the key Habermasian concept of the 'lifeworld' which Thomas Risse has defined as 'a supply of collective interpretations [actors have] of the world and of themselves, as provided by language, a common history, or culture'.[48] The common world, or 'overlapping lifeworlds' which Johnstone refers to 'does not simply come out of the shared beliefs and attitudes of its inhabitants but in fact generates those beliefs and attitudes through common participation'.[49] In reality, the UN operates according to a set of regimes, conventions, practices, enduring relationships and, to a greater or lesser degree, shared understandings, particularly on issues such as human rights and trade.[50] In a similar fashion, the Security Council operates according to both a set of common procedures and a set of (evolving) norms concerning the maintenance of 'international peace and security'.

This leads to the proposition that the presuppositions for argumentative rationality, including a common lifeworld and 'the mutual recognition of speakers in a non-hierarchical relationship', are more common in international interactions than might be thought.[51] Johnstone has argued that we can identify 'overlapping lifeworlds' in international society through practice within the Council;[52] that 'language is the glue that holds the "overlapping lifeworlds" together' and 'whether driven by the "civilizing" force of strategic argumentation or the logic of true reasoning and mutual persuasion, arguments based on norms can have an independent impact on behaviour';[53] and lastly that, despite the evident asymmetry of power in the Council, 'there are features of deliberations which suggest that raw material power is not the only thing that matters'.[54] Johnstone argued that whilst the normative framework was not sufficiently developed to produce a single 'right' answer in the case of Kosovo – evidenced by competing interpretations of norms – it was enough to distinguish between good arguments and bad arguments and, as indicated above, he maps out the ways in which legal discourse shaped and constrained the justifications put forward by NATO countries to support the intervention.[55]

Interpretive communities are linked to a complex combination of strategic and communicative action which once again highlights the tension between these rationalities in reality. To persuade others that a particular position is justified, actors follow certain norms or language rules, which enable our interaction. Johnstone argues that governments, due to the nature of the legal interpretive communities they find themselves in, are forced to justify their positions in terms other than those of narrow self-interest. Arguably, however, this does not mean that self-interest may not be driving their actions but, returning to the difficulty posed by Habermas's distinction between strategic and communicative rationality, that the interpretive community may have provided a legitimating framework to cloak real strategic interests and motives. Johnstone suggests that we do not in fact need to worry overly about whether arguments are driven by strategic concerns or the logic of arguing in order to ascertain that argumentation matters when it draws on norms. Thus, Johnstone draws on Jon Elster's classic argument referring to the 'civilizing force of hypocrisy': 'even if impartial arguments are used hypocritically, they often lead to concessions to the general interest and more equitable outcomes from the debate'.[56] By utilising the concept of interpretive communities, Johnstone implicitly operationalises Skinner's position at the international level by showing that there is 'a limit to which any legitimating language, including the language of law, plausibly can be stretched'.[57] In support of this position, Johnstone cites Ambassador Danilo Turk, Permanent Representative of Slovenia to the UN during the Kosovo crisis, who acknowledged that 'arguments based on national interest are often couched in quasi-judicial terms because the legitimizing role of the Council is valued'.[58]

Whilst it is clearly the case that the influential presence of legal argumentation in interpretive communities impels states to justify their actions in accordance with accepted norms, once a decision has been taken states may fear to challenge or criticise it as they are unwilling to be seen as failing to comply with international law or the accepted interpretation of the community. Johnstone indicates that interpretive communities are 'composed of the participants in a field of practice who set the parameters of what constitutes reasoned argumentation for that practice'.[59] Thus, challenges to what is, effectively, the status quo remain difficult as 'sustained insistence' on an interpretation considered 'wrong', in that it cannot be reconciled with the conventions and practices of the relevant interpretive communities, is 'symptomatic of a breakdown in the relationship or a dissolution of the community'.⁶⁰ This perpetuates particular kinds of practices, including, potentially, exclusionary practices. Thus, interpretive communities may at times appear closed off from critical reflection or outside influences and rejecting of those interactions or interpretations which do not 'fit' the accepted, dominant, practices of the community.⁶¹

Although Johnstone asserts that the strategic or communicative orientation motivating states does not detract from the impact upon state behaviour once justifications have been articulated which draw on existing norms, he somewhat underplays the tension which permeates the relationship between strategic and communicative rationalities and its impact upon perceptions of legitimacy and the force of argumentation. Certainly, Russia remained convinced that NATO, and the United States in particular, was manipulating Resolutions 1160, 1199 and 1203 to justify the use of force.⁶² Whilst it is true that if language were unimportant then NATO states would not have had to work so hard or rely on such thin legal ice to justify their actions, it also remains the case that the perception by those such as Russia of the tenuous nature of NATO's justifications for the use of force succours the realist belief in the role of power.

Johnstone's argument powerfully demonstrates the importance of justifications – of which legal argumentation is one particular form. He offers empirical evidence that the influence of language in shaping what can and cannot be legitimated in the Council is significant. Moreover, it highlights the degree to which this has been internalised by the actors themselves, since all states drew on norms to legitimate their position within the debates over Kosovo. Johnstone's argument is normative in the sense that it is descriptive of the norms and values of the actors themselves, and hence explains why argumentation matters in terms of enabling and constraining state actions. However, this descriptive or sociological approach to norms does not provide an ethical judgement of the legitimacy of the decisions reached, or the decision-making procedures which led to them.⁶³ Sheldon Wolin argues that 'Democracy was born in transgressive acts, for the demos could not participate in power without shattering the class, status, and value systems by which it was excluded.'⁶⁴ It is by transgressing those obstacles which prevent greater dialogical inclusion and fairness, and generating greater reflexivity concerning the constraints on public discourse, that the development of greater deliberative freedom along critical theoretical lines may emerge. It is in these tasks that the potential offered by a communicative ethics approach becomes evident.

By contrast with Johnstone, Corneliu Bjola has explicitly drawn on the emancipatory focus of Habermas's theory of communicative action to develop his concept of 'deliberative legitimacy' which he argues is analytically and normatively superior to framing legitimacy in legal or moral terms.⁶⁵

Deliberative legitimacy is defined as 'the appropriateness of the manner in which consensus about the decision to use force is attained'.[66] Recognising that language can be used strategically, Bjola establishes three conditions which an action has to meet to satisfy the test of deliberative legitimacy. These are drawn directly from Habermas's communicative-theoretic principles and aim to bring together the analytic and normative facets of Habermas's work:

1. The facts supporting decisions regarding the use of force are truthful and complete, as informed by the best evidence available.
2. All interested parties must be allowed to participate in the argumentative discourse, and all participants should have equal rights to present an argument or to challenge a validity claim.
3. Participating actors show genuine interest in using argumentative reasoning for reaching an understanding on the use of force.[67]

Like Johnstone, Bjola recognises the common lifeworld within international institutional settings such as the UN, which operate on a basis of a 'dense and tested network of collective understandings, rules and diplomatic norms'.[68] Bjola, however, more explicitly acknowledges the 'various power asymmetries' between actors which *control access* to the deliberative process as well as affecting the 'weight' of the arguments presented.[69] With increasing contestation over the scope of application of existing international law, of which the conflict in Kosovo remains a prime example, there is a greater need for closer scrutiny of the procedures by which decisions are made and the conditions under which argumentation takes place. Clarifying his argument which rests on procedure and emphasises the strong Habermasian influence, Bjola argues that deliberative legitimacy 'represents the platform on the basis of which the points of contention between actors' justifications to use force can be ascertained and validated'.[70]

Bjola's application of a Habermasian approach to deliberations surrounding the use of force adheres more closely to the critical orientation of the Habermasian project. He begins to illustrate the capacity intrinsic to Habermasian critical theory to intervene in the underlying premises of communication and demonstrates how Habermas gives us tools to challenge the validity of justifications offered in the public sphere. This is evident in his recognition of the need for a 'hermeneutics of suspicion' as illustrated by the argument that the

> conflation of the concept of the legitimacy of the use of force with what is lawful, as agreed upon by a small number of major international actors, overlooks those situations in which legal standards are rendered instruments of political deception and manipulation in the hands of the most powerful actors.[71]

Significantly, Bjola ventures further into the realm of ethical judgements of the legitimacy of decisions and concludes that the deliberations over Kosovo in the Council constituted a sufficient legitimacy claim.[72] This claim is based on an application of his three key criteria: 1) accuracy of justifications (truth); 2) deliberative context (inclusiveness); and 3) argumentative reasoning (truthfulness), through which he establishes that the 'accuracy of the justifications and the interest in argumentative reasoning of the supporters of the intervention were both strong, while the formal framework of debate was moderately inclusive and transparent'.[73]

Bjola's claim, however, that the deliberations over Kosovo met his second and third tests of deliberative legitimacy, is vulnerable on empirical grounds. Taking the second criterion first, Bjola argues that the deliberative process preceding the intervention in Kosovo was 'fairly balanced'. In support of this claim, he argues that both supporters and opponents of intervention were able to express their opinions freely and without coercion. The Yugoslav representative to the UN was able not only to present and defend Yugoslavia's position directly to the Security Council on several occasions, but he also benefited from the support of the Russian ambassador to the UN.[74] While Bjola acknowledges that the Kosovar Albanians were never invited to address the Council, they were, he suggests, able to rely on the United States and the United Kingdom to defend their interests.[75]

However, given that one of the key pre-conditions for effective discourse from a Habermasian perspective is the degree to which all parties enjoyed equal opportunities to participate in the argumentative discourses that preceded the adoption of the UN Security Council resolutions, it is hard to see how this exclusion of the Kosovars meets the inclusiveness test of deliberative legitimacy. The claim that the Kosovar Albanians' interests were ably and accurately represented by the United States and the United Kingdom is highly questionable when considering, as shown in Chapter 2, these countries' previous engagement, or lack of it, over the Kosovo issue and the missed opportunities for dialogue, their preference for retaining the territorial integrity of the FRY, and their labelling of the KLA as terrorists. In supporting NATO's position that other options had been exhausted prior to the use of force, Bjola does not acknowledge the earlier repeated exclusions of the Kosovars from dialogue and the consequences of this for his claim that the just war criterion of last resort had been met. Overlooked by Bjola is the fact that control of the decisions lay largely with members of the Contact Group[76] and while this is raised in the discussion of the deliberative context (his second criterion), he does not acknowledge the communicative distortion that this might have imposed on discussions. The question thus remains one which will be returned to in Chapter 6: were the arguments opposing intervention genuinely insufficiently persuasive, or did the power balance within the

Security Council, weighted in favour of the Contact Group/Permanent 5, distort the communicative process?

Bjola also addresses the issue of how far the debates satisfied the criterion of argumentative reasoning – the willingness of actors to change their beliefs in order to reach consensus on the decision to use force. He argues that 'unlike the Russians and the Chinese, the Americans and Europeans made genuine efforts to move beyond an instrumental logic of action and to take into account the interests of the other actors as well'.[77] The evidence for this lies, he suggests, in the reiterated Western affirmation of the territorial integrity of Yugoslavia (and thus the denial of independence for Kosovo) in response to the Russian and Chinese refusal to consider embracing a broader interpretation of the principle of sovereignty in relation to human rights violations. Similarly, he ascribes a willingness to engage in argumentative reasoning as the cause of the restraint by Western leaders from supporting, as policy, a doctrine of humanitarian intervention.[78] The problem with Bjola's interpretation of American and European positions rests with his assumption that their policy was determined by their willingness to engage in argumentative reasoning and to respond to Russian and Chinese concerns. As illustrated in Chapter 6, a contrary reading of the considerable empirical evidence indicates that Western leaders would not at that time – regardless of Russia and China's position on these issues – either have supported the Kosovar political aim of independence, or advocated a more permissive doctrine of humanitarian intervention. So, while Bjola believes that the debates over Kosovo meet his third test of argumentative reasoning, he provides little empirical support for the case that the West was behaving communicatively and Russia and China were behaving strategically. Moreover, this account of argumentative reasoning does not consider the possibility that Russia and China offered genuine and principled pluralist reasons for their opposition to the use of force.[79] What is missing is sufficient recognition of the difficulties of establishing whether actors are behaving with strategic or communicative orientations given the plausible alternative interpretation that Western countries had strategic reasons for avoiding the adoption of a stronger doctrinal approach to humanitarian intervention.

Further evidence for the claim that American and European leaders were open to argumentative reasoning can, Bjola suggests, be found in the key area of dispute within the Council concerning the potential for diplomacy to resolve the conflict, whereby 'the supporters of the intervention made reasonable efforts to find a peaceful resolution to the conflict, but their proposals were not reciprocated by the Serbian side or by their backers in the UN Security Council'.[80] While it is true that the United States, United Kingdom, and France did, initially, push for unconditional dialogue and diplomacy over violence (particularly in 1998), did engage Russia and China in an attempt to forge consensus, did call for an end to violence on both sides and did set up the talks at Rambouillet, their *modus operandi* is not free from criticism. As is shown in Chapter 6, there was little reflexivity over the structure, pre-conditions, or procedures guiding the talks prior to Rambouillet, nor does Bjola engage with the oft-cited argument that Rambouillet was in itself an example of strategic action on the part of the Contact Group.[81] There is little consideration of the coherence (one of Bjola's conditions under the criterion of 'truth') between the actions of states and their calls for dialogue. Furthermore, although Bjola argues that, from the outset, the international community tried to achieve a balance between the competing claims of the belligerent parties, he provides little analysis as to the deliberative legitimacy or implications for each side of the preconditions informing dialogue or the political settlements such as the Holbrooke agreement in October 1998 and the Rambouillet negotiations in 1999. Consequently, Bjola exaggerates how far the decision-making process surrounding the decision to use force in Kosovo can claim to have been a legitimate one in terms of his own criteria of what counts as deliberative legitimacy.

Bjola's contention that NATO's use of force against the FRY met the test of deliberative legitimacy is, like much of the debate over Kosovo, temporally limited to the crisis period in 1998–99. This excludes from the discussion a broader historical context and narrative of international involvement, disengagement and missed opportunities for non-violent action and so has an important bearing on the legitimacy of the claim that Kosovo met the criterion of last resort. Despite strong arguments for the appropriateness of communicative action for analysing the legitimacy of decisions to use force, however, the adoption of such principles into IR is not unproblematic. Bjola rightly argues the need to challenge the dominant legal and moral conceptions of legitimacy and suggests that Habermas's theory of communicative action is able to offer a framework for IR which brings together both the descriptive and emancipatory elements of his work. Far less clearly substantiated are the theoretical and methodological implications of applying such principles to analyses of the legitimacy of the decision to use force.

As will become apparent in Part II, such difficulties include the role of immanent critique for communicative ethics; a consideration of the limits to theory (established both intentionally by Habermas and by theoretical critiques of his approach); the implications of accepting Habermas's principle of universalisation; the difficulties entailed in shifting from the theoretical realm of justification embodied in discourse ethics to the practical realm of the application of moral norms; the reflexive relationship between critical theory and emancipatory practice, and, not least of all, the scope and operationalisation of criteria of truth, inclusion, and truthfulness. The latter issue raises the following kind of questions: How might we theorise coherence in relation to the 'truth' criterion? How can we satisfy (theoretically and in practice) the implications of Habermas's principle of inclusion which concerns 'all affected'? Should the burden of legitimacy lie on the one who seeks to exclude other voices or the one who seeks to be included in debate? What counts as internal or external coercion in communication?[82] These remain important theoretical and empirical issues requiring further consideration in the context of a communicative ethics.

Conclusion

The centrality of Habermas's theory of communicative action to attempts to provide a comprehensive transformation of interpretive analysis in IR opens up questions regarding how the descriptive and the critical/emancipatory elements of his theory might be integrated in order to maximise the import of communicative ethics for international politics. Two central components of such a communicative ethics emerge from the above discussion: first, a strong sense of the evaluative capacity of communicative ethics and its ability to provide critical (re-)readings of the legitimacy of the decision to use force in particular cases; and second, the need for a broader temporal focus embraced by a communicative ethics which enables the adoption of a more historical and contextual approach to evaluations of legitimacy.

As we have seen, there is a tendency among social constructivists to focus on the effects that language may have in international politics rather than drawing on the more critical and emancipatory orientation intrinsic to Frankfurt School critical theory which has appeared in the work of IR theorists such as Andrew Linklater, Mark Hoffman, Kimberley Hutchings, Nancy Fraser, and Jürgen Haacke.[83] This reflects, at least in part, a disjuncture between attempts to use Habermas's work to develop a critical theory of IR and attempts to develop a social theory of international politics. Theorists such as Johnstone, Risse and Müller are primarily concerned with the latter as they establish, through careful empirical work, the case for the relevance of communicative action in international politics.

Such empirical analysis is equally central for a critical theory of IR and indeed was at the heart of the Frankfurt School's research agenda. Understanding whether and when argument impacts upon the identities or preferences of actors is important and there is little doubt that arguing both takes place and shapes debate within fora such as the Security Council. It does not, however, exert critical leverage concerning either the process or substance of deliberation. Crucially, the normative and immanent dimensions of claims to legitimacy contained within justificatory discourse are not subjected to critical or evaluative analysis. Given Price and Reus-Smit's claim that constructivism can contribute to the critical project through an engagement with the parameters and dynamics of moral community – determined in part by practices of inclusion and exclusion – this explicit theoretical claim remains muffled in the work of those constructivists who have engaged with communicative-theoretic approaches.[84]

Part II of the book seeks to rectify the disjuncture between the critical and social aspects of Habermasian IR with regard to justifications for the use of force by developing the concept of communicative ethics. This acknowledges the call to arms issued by Price and Reus-Smit that 'dialogue between those focusing on the normative and sociological aspects of communal inclusion and exclusion is essential before any progress can be made on the praxeological front'.[85] Engaging with both Habermas's rich conceptual oeuvre and a range of critical interventions around his work will enable the generation of a new theoretical framework with critical empirical intent. It will be shown that communicative ethics is not synonymous with Habermasian discourse ethics, but rather emerges out of a conversation among critical theorists, whilst retaining key Habermasian insights at its core. The following chapter sets out the relevant Habermasian theoretical concepts and debates which provide the foundations for articulating in Chapter 5 a framework of communicative ethics. The latter is operationalised in terms of a series of 'communicative imperatives' which are intended to help us recognise the crucial link between communicative practices and legitimacy. Chapter 6 then moves the spotlight back to the empirical terrain of Kosovo by applying the communicative imperatives to the communicative practices which shaped the decision to intervene in Kosovo. So doing challenges those accounts which have applied the label 'legitimate' to the decision-making process that led to NATO's decision to use force in March 1999.

NOTES

1 This is a vast and growing literature and so, for reasons of scope and clarity, the literature addressed in this chapter will predominantly focus on the merits of the arguments of those who have primarily relied on Habermas's work to locate their own analyses of international politics.

2 For example, see: Linklater, *The Transformation of Political Community*; M. Lynch, 'The Dialogue of Civilisations and International Public Spheres', *Millennium*, 29:2 (2000), 307–30; T. Risse, 'Let's Argue!: Communicative Action in World Politics', *International Organization*, 54:1 (2000), 1–39; Shapcott, *Justice, Community and Dialogue*; Crawford, *Argument and Change in World Politics*; M. Lynch, 'Why Engage? China and the Logic of Communicative Engagement', *European Journal of International Relations*, 8:2 (2002), 187–230; Steffek, 'The Legitimation of International Governance'; Johnstone, 'Security Council Deliberations'; I. Johnstone, 'Legal Deliberation and Argumentation in International Decision Making', in Charlesworth and Coicaud (eds), *The Faultlines of International Legitimacy*; H. Müller, 'Arguing, Bargaining and All That: Communicative Action, Rationalist Theory and the Logic of Appropriateness in International Relations', *European Journal of International Relations*, 10:3 (2004), 395–435; Bjola, 'Legitimating the Use of Force'; A. Linklater, 'Dialogic Politics and the Civilising

Process', *Review of International Studies*, 31:1 (2005), 141–54; J. Mitzen, 'Reading Habermas in Anarchy: Multilateral Diplomacy and Global Public Spheres', *American Political Science Review*, 99:3 (2005), 401–17; N. Deitelhoff and H. Müller, 'Theoretical Paradise – Empirically Lost? Arguing with Habermas', *Review of International Studies*, 31:1 (2005), 167–79; J. Dryzek, *Deliberative Global Politics: Discourse and Democracy in a Divided World* (Cambridge: Polity Press, 2006); M. Albert, O. Kessler and S. Stetter 'On Order and Conflict: International Relations and the "Communicative Turn"', *Review of International Studies*, 34, Special Issue (2008), 43–67; Bjola, 'Legitimacy and the Use of Force'; E. Jordaan, 'Dialogic Cosmopolitanism and Global Justice', *International Studies Review*, 11:4 (2009), 736–48; J. Brassett and W. Smith, 'Deliberation and Global Civil Society: Agency, Arena, Affect', *Review of International Studies*, 36:2 (2010), 413–30; Bjola, *Legitimising the Use of Force in International Politics*.
3 This debate drew on a particular variant of positivism in IR and the social sciences. See Smith *et al.* (eds), *International Theory*.
4 For example, see R. K. Ashley, 'The Poverty of Neorealism', in R. O. Keohane (ed.), *Neorealism and its Critics* (New York: Columbia University Press, 1986).
5 See A. Linklater, 'The Achievements of Critical Theory', in Smith *et al.* (eds), *International Theory*, 279–98; Linklater, *The Transformation of Political Community*.
6 J. Habermas, *Knowledge and Human Interests* (Boston: Beacon Press, 1972); Diez and Steans, 'A Useful Dialogue?', 129. This was a criticism aimed at neorealists by Ashley who identified a link between 'technical cognitive interests' and 'technical realism' or neorealism. See R. K. Ashley, 'Political Realism and Human Interests', *International Studies Quarterly*, 25:2 (1981), 204–36. Habermas distinguished between three types of knowledge: empirical-analytical (the natural sciences), historical-hermeneutic (concerned with meaning and understanding), and critical sciences (concerned with emancipation). Each type of knowledge has its own set of 'cognitive interests', respectively, those of a technical interest in control and prediction, a practical interest in understanding, and an emancipatory interest in enhancing freedom. See S. Smith, 'Positivism and Beyond', in Smith *et al.* (eds), *International Theory*.
7 J. Habermas, *TCA*, vols 1 and 2.
8 See Müller's discussion in 'Arguing, Bargaining and All That', 414–15. For a distinct but related line of argument, see H. Toros, *Terrorism, Talking and Transformation*, PhD thesis, Aberystwyth University (2009).
9 Cox, 'Social Forces'; Ashley, 'Political Realism and Human Interests'; Linklater, *Men and Citizens*.
10 R. Shapcott, 'Critical Theory', in C. Reus-Smit and D. Snidal (eds), *Oxford Handbook of International Relations* (Oxford: Oxford University Press, 2008), 331.
11 Cox, 'Social Forces', 128. Original emphasis.
12 N. Rengger and B. Thirkell-White (eds), *Critical International Relations Theory after 25 Years* (Cambridge: Cambridge University Press, 2007), 6.
13 Linklater, 'The Achievements of Critical Theory', 279.
14 Ibid., 280.
15 Most relevant for the purposes of this book is Linklater's statement of critical international theory in *The Transformation of Political Community*.
16 R. Price and C. Reus-Smit, 'Dangerous Liaisons? Critical International Theory and Constructivism', *European Journal of International Relations*, 4:3 (1998), 259.
17 N. Onuf, *World of Our Making: Rules and Rule in Social Theory and International Relations* (North Carolina: University of North Carolina Press, 1987); F. Kratochwil, *Rules, Norms, Decisions: On the Conditions of Practical and Legal Reasoning in International Relations and Domestic Affairs* (Cambridge: Cambridge University Press, 1989); A.

Wendt, *Social Theory of International Politics* (Cambridge: Cambridge University Press, 1999); L. G. Lose, 'Communicative Action and the World of Diplomacy', in K. M. Fierke and K. E. Jørgensen (eds), *Constructing International Relations: The Next Generation* (New York: M. E. Sharpe, 2001) 179–200. For more critical discussions of constructivism, see Price and Reus-Smit, 'Dangerous Liaisons?'; Fierke, *Changing Games*; R. Shapcott, 'Solidarism and After: Global Governance, International Society and the Normative "Turn" in International Relations', *Pacifica Review*, 12:2 (2000), 147–65; C. Reus-Smit, 'In Dialogue on the Ethic of Consensus: A Reply to Shapcott', *Pacifica Review*, 12:2 (2000), 305–8; M. Zehfuss, *Constructivism in International Relations: The Politics of Reality* (Cambridge: Cambridge University Press, 2002); Fierke, *Diplomatic Interventions*. The claim that reality is socially constructed was present in sociology, social theory, and philosophy before it emerged in IR. Indeed, the sociological debates strongly influenced Habermas's work. Similarly to constructivism in IR, it is also taken up more or less critically in other disciplines. For example, see P. Berger and T. Luckmann, *The Social Construction of Reality: A Treatise in the Sociology of Knowledge* (New York: Penguin Putnam Inc., 1966); L. Wittgenstein, *Philosophical Investigations* (Oxford: Basil Blackwell, 1958).

18   Although definitions of what constructivism is and who may be counted as a constructivist vary significantly (ranging from the boundaries of rationalism to poststructuralism), this debate goes beyond the scope of this book. For further discussion see: E. Adler, 'Seizing the Middle Ground: Constructivism in World Politics', *European Journal of International Relations*, 3:3 (1997), 319–63; Price and Reus-Smit, 'Dangerous Liaisons?', 259; J. T. Checkel, 'The Constructivist Turn in International Relations Theory', *World Politics*, 50 (1998), 324–48; Wendt, *Social Theory*; Fierke and Jørgensen (eds), *Constructing International Relations*; Zehfuss, *Constructivism in International Relations*; B. Buzan and L. Hansen, *The Evolution of International Security Studies* (Cambridge: Cambridge University Press, 2009), Chapter 7; I. Hurd, 'Constructivism', in Reus-Smit and Snidal (eds), *Oxford Handbook*; R. Price, 'The Ethics of Constructivism', in Reus-Smit and Snidal (eds), *Oxford Handbook*.

19   Reus-Smit, 'Society, Power, and Ethics', 286. By this he is referring to Habermas's 'universalisation principle' whereby a rule or norm can only be considered legitimate if '*all* affected can accept the consequences and the side effects its *general* observance can be anticipated to have for the satisfaction of *everyone's* interests (and those consequences are preferred to those of known alternative possibilities for regulation)'. See J. Habermas, *Moral Consciousness and Communicative Action* (Cambridge: Polity Press, 1990).

20   Price and Reus-Smit, 'Dangerous Liaisons?', 262–3.

21   Johnstone, 'Legal Deliberation', 175.

22   Risse, 'Let's Argue!', 33.

23   See Carr's *The Twenty Years' Crisis*.

24   N. J. Wheeler, 'The Kosovo Bombing Campaign', in Reus-Smit (ed.), *The Politics of International Law*, 193. Wheeler cites Sir Arthur Watts, a former legal adviser to the UK Foreign and Commonwealth Office: 'all governments need to do is "advance a legal justification for their conduct which is not demonstrably rubbish. Thereafter, political factors can take over, and the international acceptability or otherwise of a State's conduct can be determined by considerations of international policy rather than international law."' See Jackson, *The Global Covenant*, 67–71; S. D. Krasner, *Sovereignty: Organized Hypocrisy* (Princeton: Princeton University Press, 1999), 6; T. Dunne, 'New Thinking on International Society', *British Journal of Politics and International Relations*, 3:2 (2001), 223–44.

25 Deitelhoff and Müller, 'Theoretical Paradise – Empirically Lost?', 169. See also Lynch, 'Why Engage?'; Risse, 'Let's Argue!', 11–12; C. Grobe, 'The Power of Words: Argumentative Persuasion in International Negotiations', *European Journal of International Relations*, 16:1 (2010), 16–29'; Müller, 'Arguing, Bargaining and All That'. Müller notes that integrating rationalism and communicative action theory is ontologically incompatible as they favour individualist and holist ontologies respectively. However, he goes on to suggest a hierarchy whereby consequentialism and communicative action are integrated into the logic of appropriateness, thus bridging the rationalist-constructivist divide. To do this, he argues that bargaining, as much as arguing, is embedded in both strategic and communicative rationalities and is norm-regulated behaviour.

26 Dunne, 'New Thinking on International Society', 18.

27 See Müller's argument on international negotiations: 'International Relations as Communicative Action', in K. Fierke and K. E. Jørgensen, *Constructing International Relations: The Next Generation* (New York: M. E. Sharpe, 2001), 166–7. See also empirical cases examined in T. Risse, 'International Norms and Domestic Change: Arguing and Communicative Behavior in the Human Rights Area', *Politics and Society*, 27:4 (1999), 529–59; Risse, 'Let's Argue!'; Lynch, 'Why Engage?'. It should be noted that a distinction has been drawn in the literature between negotiations and dialogue. Fierke notes that they are 'distinct forms of life. Each is constituted by particular language games and rules.' Negotiations are linked to 'the distinct identity and autonomy of the parties', whereas dialogue is seen to relate to 'moral discourse'. See Fierke, *Changing Games*, 135–7; Toros, *Terrorism, Talking and Transformation*, 81–8.

28 Kratochwil uses the example of a game of football: 'Kicking a ball into a goal means something if I consider it in terms of the background conditions of a game of soccer. If I provide only an account in terms of the intentions of the actor, I might miss the mark as much as when I am satisfied with a description of the act in terms of the underlying physical laws. The meaning of "kicking a goal" is antecedent to the actor's intention and understandable only in terms of the "game" that is being played.' F. V. Kratochwil, 'Constructivism as an Approach', in Fierke and Jørgensen (eds), *Constructing International Relations*, 30.

29 Kratochwil, cited in Zehfuss, *Constructivism in International Relations*, 99.

30 Fierke, *Changing Games*, 6–7. See Hollis and Smith, *Explaining and Understanding International Relations*; Wheeler, *Saving Strangers*, 4; T. Dunne, 'Sociological Investigations: Instrumental, Legitimist and Coercive Interpretations of International Society', *Millennium*, 30:1 (2001) 67–91; Johnstone, 'Security Council Deliberations'; J. Elster (ed.), *Deliberative Democracy* (Chicago: University of Chicago Press, 1998); Q. Skinner, *Visions of Politics, Volume 1: Regarding Method* (Cambridge: Cambridge University Press, 2002).

31 Wheeler, 'The Kosovo Bombing Campaign', 195. See Franck, *The Power of Legitimacy Among Nations*, Chapter 4.

32 Johnstone, 'Security Council Deliberations', 454.

33 Skinner, *Visions of Politics*, 155. See also Q. Skinner, 'Language and Political Change', in T. Ball, J. Farr and R. L. Hanson (eds), *Political Innovation and Conceptual Change* (Cambridge: Cambridge University Press, 1989).

34 Ibid., 156. Skinner's figure of the 'innovating ideologist' refers to both the perlocutionary and illocutionary effects of the speaker on the listener or reader. The former includes effects 'such as inciting or persuading or convincing their hearers or readers to adopt some novel point of view'. The latter refers to 'evincing, expressing or soliciting approval or disapproval of the actions they describe' (156).

35 Risse, 'Let's Argue!', 32.
36 Forester (ed.), *Critical Theory and Public Life*, xv.
37 See Chapter 2.
38 Johnstone, 'Security Council Deliberations', 439. This argument is forcefully made in I. Johnstone, 'Discursive Power in the UN Security Council', *Journal of International Law and International Relations*, 2:1 (2005–6), 73–94.
39 Ibid., 467: citing Ambassador Lavrov, Permanent Representative of the Russian Federation to the United Nations, 3989th meeting of the Security Council, 26 March 1999, S/PV.3989.
40 Ibid., 467: citing Sir Jeremy Greenstock, Permanent Representative of the United Kingdom to the United Nations, 3988th meeting of the Security Council, 24 March 1999, S/PV.3988.
41 For discussion see N. J. Wheeler, 'The Humanitarian Responsibilities of Sovereignty: Explaining the Development of a New Norm of Military Intervention for Humanitarian Purposes in International Society', in Jennifer Welsh (ed.), *Humanitarian Intervention and International Relations* (Oxford: Oxford University Press, 2004), 29–51; N. J. Wheeler, 'Humanitarian Intervention After Kosovo: Emergent Norm, Moral Duty or the Coming Anarchy', *International Affairs*, 77:1 (2001), 113–28.
42 Johnstone, 'Security Council Deliberations', 468; see also Wheeler, *Saving Strangers*, 265.
43 Wheeler, 'The Humanitarian Responsibilities of Sovereignty', 42; Johnstone, 'Security Council Deliberations', 476; Johnstone, 'Discursive Power in the UN Security Council'.
44 Johnstone, 'Legal Deliberation', 182.
45 Johnstone, 'Security Council Deliberations', 445.
46 I. Johnstone, 'Treaty Interpretation: The Authority of Interpretive Communities', *Michigan Journal of International Law*, 12:2 (1991), 371–419; Johnstone, 'Security Council Deliberations', 372.
47 Johnstone's language clearly draws on Habermasian-informed approaches to communication: 'decision-makers must make their case for a decision on the basis of reasons that are shared or can be shared by all who are affected, even if they do not agree with the decision itself'. 'Discursive Power in the UN Security Council', 87.
48 Risse, 'Let's Argue!', 10, citing Habermas, *TCA*, vol. 2.
49 Johnstone, 'Security Council Deliberations', 386.
50 Problems concerning the establishment of a shared lifeworld include: cultural differences; a weak sense of community established by international law; different perceptions of justice, and linguistic differences.
51 Risse, 'Let's Argue!', 33; see also Grobe, 'The Power of Words'.
52 Johnstone, 'Security Council Deliberations', 461.
53 Ibid., 455. Here Johnstone combines strategic and communicative rationalities.
54 Ibid., 461.
55 Johnstone, 'Security Council Deliberations', 460. See also Wheeler, 'The Kosovo Bombing Campaign', 195: 'NATO might have failed to win the legal argument over Kosovo, but it certainly recognised the need to justify its conduct in terms of the existing normative framework of international law.'
56 Johnstone, 'Security Council Deliberations', 454. The constructivist-rationalist debate recognises this problem when it identifies the presence of arguing as a means to rationalise positions taken for strategic reasons. This raises the question of whether justification equates to motivation. The constructivist response as illustrated by Risse, Johnstone and Wheeler would be that even if the motivation differs from the public justification, the utterance of reasons in the public sphere then entangles the actor in

ways which mean that he must behave *as if* they were the same. Here the significance of examining the historical context and the relationship between coherence and justification become apparent. If actors are inconsistent in their actions and justifications over a period of time, then there is reason to subject their justifications to closer scrutiny. Crawford also makes this point in *Argument and Change in World Politics*, 126. See also Müller, 'Arguing, Bargaining and All That', 407, 425.
57 Johnstone, 'Legal Deliberation', 181. See Wheeler, *Saving Strangers*, 292.
58 Johnstone, 'Security Council Deliberations', 454, footnote 69, referring to an interview with Ambassador Turk, 21 August 2001.
59 Johnstone, 'Security Council Deliberations', 439. Bjola also accepts and draws on the premises of interpretive communities, thus the same criticisms may be relevant. See Bjola, *Legitimising the Use of Force in International Politics*, Chapter 4.
60 Johnstone, 'Treaty Interpretation', 385.
61 See A. Goldsmith, 'Is There Any Backbone to this Fish? Interpretive Communities, Social Criticism, and Transgressive Legal Practice', *Law and Social Inquiry*, 23:2 (1998).
62 Wheeler, *Saving Strangers*, 263, 276.
63 This is a common position for constructivists within IR whose work tends to focus on the explanatory role of language. For example, see Grobe, 'The Power of Words'; Fierke and Jørgensen (eds), *Constructing International Relations*.
64 S. Wolin, 'Fugitive Democracy', *Constellations*, 1:1 (1994), 17.
65 Bjola, *Legitimising the Use of Force in International Politics*, 11.
66 Bjola, 'Legitimating the Use of Force', 267.
67 Bjola, *Legitimising the Use of Force in International Politics*, 76. Bjola links the degree to which these conditions have been met with the degree of legitimacy pertaining to the process: 'First, if none of the three validity claims is met, then the legitimacy of the intervention is clearly *absent*, regardless of whether the majority of the actors involved eventually agree to authorize the use of force. Second, if participants are primarily oriented toward claims to truth and truthfulness (the first and third conditions), then a *sufficient* claim of legitimacy can be invoked in support of respective intervention. This is so because actors express genuine concerns about the need to use force and they make systematic efforts to listen to the arguments of the others and to engage in argumentative reasoning ... Consequently, a *strong* claim of legitimacy can be invoked only when these two conditions are supplemented by a deliberative framework that is inclusive and allows participants to coordinate their action plans on the basis of the "best argument" available' (ibid., 78).
68 Bjola, 'Legitimating the Use of Force', 279.
69 Ibid., 277–8, emphasis added.
70 Ibid., 279.
71 Bjola, 'Legitimating the Use of Force', 266.
72 Details of Bjola's interpretation of the deliberative basis of NATO's intervention in Kosovo can be found in Bjola, *Legitimsing the Use of Force in International Politics*, 120.
73 Ibid., 90.
74 Ibid., 116–17.
75 Ibid., 117.
76 The Contact Group consisted of France, the Russian Federation, the UK, the USA, Germany and Italy, and was the main actor driving the agenda concerning engagement with and negotiations over Kosovo with Milošević.
77 Bjola, *Legitimising the Use of Force in International Politics*, 118.
78 Ibid., 119.
79 See discussion of these points in Chapters 2 and 6.

80 Ibid., 119.
81 For example, E. Herring, 'From Rambouillet to the Kosovo Accords: NATO's War against Serbia and Its Aftermath', in Booth (ed.), *The Kosovo Tragedy*; R. Falk, '"Humanitarian Wars", Realist Geopolitics and Genocidal Practices: Saving the Kosovars', in Booth (ed.), *The Kosovo Tragedy*; IICK, *The Kosovo Report*, 151–61.
82 Some of these concerns are alluded to in potential criticisms of deliberative legitimacy which Bjola raises briefly and addresses through the concepts of fairness and tractability. However, the scope of inclusion, for example, does not seem to be fully explicated by the principle of pragmatic intersubjectivity which Bjola offers. *Legitimising the Use of Force in International Politics*, 80–8, 156–65.
83 A. Linklater, 'The Question of the Next Stage in International Relations Theory; A Critical-Theoretical Point of View', *Millennium: Journal of International Studies*, 21:1 (1992), 77–98; Linklater, *The Transformation of Political Community*; M. Hoffman, 'Critical Theory and the Inter-Paradigm Debate', *Millennium: Journal of International Studies*, 16:2 (1987), 231–49; M. Hoffman, 'Conversations on Critical International Relations Theory', *Millennium: Journal of International Studies*, 17:1 (1988), 91–5; N. J. Rengger, 1988. 'Going Critical? A Response to Hoffman', *Millennium: Journal of International Studies*, 17:1 (1988), 81–9; N. Fraser, 'What's Critical about Critical Theory? The Case of Habermas and Gender', *New German Critique*, 35, Special Issue 1 (1985), 97–131; K. Hutchings, 'Speaking and Hearing: Habermasian Discourse Ethics, Feminism and IR', *Review of International Studies*, 31:1 (2005), 155–65; K. Hutchings, 'Happy Anniversary! Time and Critique in International Relations theory', in Rengger and Thirkell-White (eds), *Critical International Relations Theory*; J. Haacke, 'The Frankfurt School and International Relations: On the Centrality of Recognition', *Review of International Studies*, 31:1 (2005), 181–94; J. Haacke, 'Theory and Praxis in International Relations: Self-Reflection, Rational Argumentation', *Millennium: Journal of International Studies*, 25:2 (1996) 255–89; C. Brown, 'Turtles All the Way Down: Anti-Foundationalism, Critical Theory and International Relations', *Millennium: Journal of International Studies*, 23:2 (1994), 213–36; M. Neufeld, *The Restructuring of International Relations Theory* (Cambridge: Cambridge University Press, 1995); M. Weber, 'The Critical Social Theory of the Frankfurt School, and the "Social Turn" in IR', *Review of International Relations*, 31:1 (2005), 195–209; J. M. Hobson, 'Is Critical Theory Always for the White West and for Western Imperialism? Beyond Westphilian Towards a Post-racist Critical IR', in Rengger and Thirkell-White (eds), *Critical International Relations Theory*; R. Devetak, 'Between Kant and Pufendorf: Humanitarian Intervention, Statist Anti-cosmopolitanism and Critical International Theory', in Rengger and Thirkell-White (eds), *Critical International Relations Theory*.
84 Price and Reus-Smit, 'Dangerous Liasons?', 264. Indeed, Shapcott argues that constructivism 'suffers because it retains the fact/value distinction of *verstehen* social sciences and so doing separates questions of "is" from "ought"'. In so doing, it therefore provides few criteria with which to evaluate the norms it identifies and explains. See Shapcott, 'Critical Theory', 333.
85 Price and Reus-Smit, 'Dangerous Liaisons?' 288.

II

Communicative ethics and the use of force

4

The Habermasian project: dialogue as normative grounds and object of critique

The concept of reflexivity has been illustrated in the example of a person who at dusk stands before a window and simultaneously sees her reflection in the window and sees herself looking beyond the reflection to the world outside. Reflexivity means being able to stand back from the world and to see how one's actions are shaped and influenced by what is assumed about the world or by past conditioning. This does not necessarily contribute to the elimination of war. It does, however, increase the space within which actors at all levels of international society can make choices rather than acting as if war were the only option.

Karin Fierke[1]

Introduction

THIS CHAPTER begins the task of developing a communicative ethics approach which may be applied to the legitimacy of decisions on the use of force by engaging with both Habermas's rich conceptual oeuvre and a range of critical interventions around his work.[2] The first section lays out the key precepts of the Habermasian project necessary for the development of a communicative ethics operationalisable in IR with its dual understanding of dialogue as both *normative grounds* and *object of critique*. It will address the distinction between the lifeworld, the system and the consequent distinction between communicative and strategic action; the presuppositions of argumentation; the ideal speech situation and discourse ethics, and the distinction between the moral and the ethical (the right and the good). Habermas equips us, therefore, with a set of sophisticated conceptual tools with which to cast a critical and reflexive eye on the procedures, institutions and interactions which sustain, shape and constrain norms concerning the use of force. His concern with emancipation through communicative rationality resonates with the preoccupations of those sensitive to relations of power and domination and the presence of distorted communication within international politics. As we have seen, this work has been embraced by some within IR precisely because it offers a means to challenge and critique these forms of domination, whilst at the same time providing a means to contest and make

Communicative ethics and the use of force

accountable the actions of states and international institutions. Those concerned with the 'democratic deficit' of international institutions have looked to Habermas's theory to identify ways in which institutional arrangements might be improved, thus preventing the resort to force to settle international disputes.[3] Similarly, those interested in questions of legitimacy and decision-making within the international sphere have found resources in Habermas's normative and procedural approach to discourse ethics.[4]

The second part of this chapter looks at a variety of critical interventions which have contributed to reformulations of discourse ethics and how these themes have played out in the application of Habermasian theory to IR. Exploring the conversation between Habermas and those who have adopted and critiqued his theoretical position within IR serves to frame the wider debates concerning Habermas's project and sets out a number of key concerns with his approach. Such concerns elucidate why communicative ethics as it is developed herein cannot simply map onto Habermas's own theoretical position. Thus, an alternative conception of communicative ethics is developed in this and the following chapter which takes its inspiration from but is not synonymous with Habermas's position. It will be argued that this framework allows for a greater sensitivity to both the sociological and critical orientations intrinsic to Habermas's project, and in so doing rectifies the theoretical and empirical lacunae identified earlier in existing approaches to communicative action in IR.

Ideal speech as normative grounds

The theoretical notion of ideal speech offers powerful, if not necessarily straightforward, normative purchase for a communicative ethics relevant to international politics. Having developed strong normative justifications for the primacy of communication, Habermas locates this firmly within the traditions of critical theory which seeks to retain a practical intent; in other words, a recognition of the importance of the relationship between theory and practice. In doing so, he both adheres to and departs from the intellectual positions of his predecessors in the Frankfurt School of critical theory: Theodor Adorno and Max Horkheimer.[5] While he shares their commitment to social justice, emancipation, reflexivity, and a critical orientation as regards positivistic approaches to knowledge and understanding in the social sphere, Habermas refuses to succumb to their eventual view of reason as purely instrumental and bound to technological domination. Instead, retaining some hope in progressive rationality, he re-casts emancipatory reason as latent in linguistic interaction.[6] Speech, for Habermas, 'generates an immanent, nonmetaphysical form of rationality against which individual and social behaviour may be measured'.[7]

The question underlying Habermas's theory of communicative action is 'how is social action possible' and how can we understand the 'social construction and management of political consent'?[8] Habermas perceives this question to be related to two key spheres of action: technical-instrumental (dealing with problems of control and the ordering of the object world) and moral-practical (dealing with problems of legitimacy and the solidarity of social relations).[9] The relationship between the two spheres of action is demarcated by Habermas's concepts of the 'rationalization of the lifeworld' and the 'colonization of the lifeworld'. Habermas argues that the process of rationalization – when done communicatively – minimises the interference between the imperatives of the lifeworld and the system; we should, he indicates, 'view society as an entity that, in the course of social evolution, gets differentiated both as a system and as a lifeworld'.[10] However, the differentiation of system and lifeworld in a capitalist society also leads to their 'uncoupling' and hence to the 'colonization of the lifeworld' as the range of social systems which are coordinated communicatively shrink. A definition of the latter concept signals an ongoing preoccupation with the nature of communication in different spheres of interaction in Habermas's writings. As such, Forester argues that,

> Habermas's notion of colonization is not a matter of voluntaristic action; it reflects the structural effects on people's ordinary lives of systemic developments: the increasing penetration of economic markets into previously nonmarket spheres and increasing concentrations of power in the form of private capital or within the bureaucratic labyrinth of the state. The catch-phrase *systematically distorted communication* has long suggested Habermas's dual concern with social structure and social action.[11]

The lifeworld, then, is concerned with communicative action and is discursively coordinated.[12] The emergence of the system indicates a different kind of rationality operating through instrumental or strategic reason (derived from Enlightenment reason, scientific/logical positivism). The lifeworld is concerned with the symbolic reproduction of cultures, values, social relations, and lived experiences: 'Everyday communicative practice is, as we have seen, embedded in a lifeworld context defined by cultural tradition, legitimate orders, and socialized individuals.'[13] The system encompasses mechanisms such as the economy, the market, and bureaucracy. The distinction between them is clear: the lifeworld is based on action oriented towards understanding, whereas the system is based on action oriented towards success.[14]

The relationship between the system and the lifeworld is developed in Habermas's *Theory of Communicative Action* (vol. 2), where he sets out the vulnerability of the lifeworld to encroachment by the system.[15] He argues that when the system encroaches too far into areas of the lifeworld which are coordinated communicatively, then politics becomes distorted. He identifies the media of money and power and the parallel processes of juridification[16] and commodification as central to colonisation of the lifeworld. Unlike earlier Frankfurt School theorists, he believed that by developing communicative structures, the instrumentalisation of the lifeworld, and in particular the public sphere, could be reversed, and instrumental rationality would be restricted to the domain of the system. For Habermas, communicative action remains the primary means of social integration and strategic action is secondary. Thus, the distinction he draws between communicative action and strategic action is crucial in order to give discourse normative force and to recover an emancipatory understanding of reason.[17]

However, Maeve Cooke has argued that the analytical primacy Habermas affords to communicative action does not necessarily lead to a functional primacy.[18] Consequently, the stark distinction Habermas draws between communicative and strategic action has been criticised for two important reasons which are relevant for its ability to speak successfully to conflict resolution practices in international politics. First, it has been argued that 'all communication, both communicative and strategic, is intersubjective and dependent on shared rules for its meaning'.[19] Certainly this recognition was reflected in Johnstone's argument that it is not necessary to locate arguments in the Security Council over Kosovo within either a purely strategic or communicative rationality in order to determine that arguments matter when they draw on norms. Second, and relatedly, the consequence of privileging communicative rationality (oriented to understanding) risks leaving it unable to contribute to conflict resolution practices when the parties are unwilling to communicate. This is because, according to discourse ethics, parties cannot be convinced to start resolving conflicts through deliberation by means of an appeal to their own strategic self-interests.[20] Discourse ethics relies on the willingness of participants to enter into reflective deliberation, but it cannot create willingness where it is absent.[21] The distinction between strategic and communicative rationalities is relevant to international politics because of the central premise concerning strategic rationality which underpins much of IR theory, notably those parts of it which are rooted in rational choice assumptions.[22] Communicative ethics seeks to acknowledge and provide some redress to this tension by retaining the critical leverage of Habermas's analytical distinction while recognising that actors are unlikely to separate these orientations in their interactions.

Communicative rationality, for Habermas, refers to a post-metaphysical conception of reason which is already operative in the everyday linguistic practices of modern societies. Habermas reconstructs the presuppositions of argumentation which form the universal conditions of possible understanding in order to demonstrate that communicative rationality is already present within our everyday communicative practices.[23] The reformulation of rationality along communicative lines is seen most clearly in the construction of an 'ideal speech situation'.[24] Although it would be a mistake to consider Habermas's notion of an ideal speech situation to be a concrete reality, it is nonetheless intended to serve as a critical tool. Without such a normative ideal, Habermas argues, it is impossible to critique current standards of communicative action or recognise distorted communication. Grounding communicative action on the fundamental notion of language and our intrinsic ability to form consensus through language, the *telos* of communicative rationality, Habermas develops the ideal speech situation in order to be able to distinguish genuine communication from false or pseudo-communication. To do this, he engages in a rational reconstruction of empirical communicative competences[25] which requires consideration of the linguistic competences possessed by ordinary speakers in order to communicate verbally with other participants. Habermas believes that 'communicative competence is not something we possess over and above our ability to speak a language; on the contrary, to understand language as such requires a theoretical comprehension of the kinds of understanding available through language'.[26] Not all forms of language use are aimed towards mutual understanding, and these other, strategic, forms of language use Habermas considers as 'parasitic upon speech oriented toward achieving genuine understanding'.[27]

This leads to the question of what constitutes a 'consensual speech act'? What presuppositions exist which rely upon a background of meaning within the lifeworld? Habermas argues that for moral norms to be universalisable they must express a 'general will'. Those norms which cannot be expressed as universal laws are invalid. There is an important divergence between Kant and Habermas in relation to the manner in which the justification and consequent legitimation of norms is arrived at. Habermas argues that for Kant, the procedural test for universal applicability was decided monologically, through a private reasoning process which the individual engaged in with himself. Whereas Kant's categorical imperative requires that an individual should not act in any way but that he or she could will such a maxim to become a universal law, Habermas's principle of discourse ethics (D) reflects his communicative turn, requiring that the principle of universalization (U) cannot be answered satisfactorily by a single individual, but must take place within an intersubjective dialogue.[28] This shift from a monological to a dialogical exercise is fundamental in order to continue to justify any notion of the normative cosmopolitan project in the face of challenges to it posed by poststructuralists, postmodernists, realists and communitarians (among others). This shift means that universalisability is now defined as an intersubjective procedure of argumentation; the aim is communicative agreement rather than the Kantian version which looked at what each individual rational moral agent could will to be a universal maxim for all without contradiction.[29]

For speech to be considered genuine communication, Habermas stipulates four validity claims linked to understanding and justifying a norm of action. These are: comprehensibility, truth, rightness and sincerity.[30] The background consensus to which Habermas refers implies that the speaker implicitly makes these claims and that they could be justified if this were required. If, therefore, the validity of any of these claims were to be questioned, we could engage in a discourse which would allow us to reach consensus as to their validity. The distinction Habermas draws between action and discourse remains relevant for communicative ethics. As he says: 'In action, the factually raised claims to validity, which form the underlying consensus, are naively assumed. Discourse, on the other hand, serves the justification of problematic claims to validity of opinions and norms.'[31]

Briefly, the validity claim to comprehensibility requires that what is said is actually intelligible and understandable. The claim to sincerity requires that the speaker be honest in what he or she says and that we believe the speaker is being honest with us. Truth – a correct statement about the external or objective world – cannot be discursively redeemed by a direct comparison between statements and reality as advocated by correspondence theories of truth and Enlightenment reason. Rather, truth must be 'defined in terms of a projected consensus': 'The condition for the truth of statements is the potential agreement of everyone else.'[32] In a similar fashion to rightness, truth claims can only be redeemed by means of argumentation and a rational consensus. Rightness requires that what the speaker says and consequently does, is right or appropriate in the light of existing values and norms; that there is a normative basis for the utterance.[33] This is, therefore, like justifications for the use of force, a moral claim and if this validity claim is challenged, agreement can only be achieved through communicative action oriented towards understanding and consensus.

What happens when we cannot reach an agreement? Habermas offers several scenarios relevant to such a predicament in international politics: we can shift towards a strategic approach, we can break off communication altogether and resort to force, or we can enter into a different type of communicative interaction, where contested truth and rightness claims are 'treated as hypotheses in need of thoroughgoing justification and defence'. This opens up a new form of reflective communication called 'discourse': 'As opposed to ordinary communication ('interaction'), the goal of discourse is systematically to examine and test problematic truth and normative claims in their own right.'[34] It is intended to allow participants to reach a 'rationally motivated consensus' concerning controversial claims.[35] Habermas's argument concerning the presuppositions involved in speech acts – that they are truthful, sincere, comprehensible, and right/justified – are compelling when one considers, for example, lying.[36] Lying, as a social concept, would be meaningless if we did not assume that validity claims were unavoidably raised by speech acts.[37]

There are certain pragmatic rules which constitute an ideal speech situation or a discourse free from distorted communication which derive from Habermas's principle of Universalization (U) and his principle of discourse ethics (D). Norms and values which are manifested in particular societies must, for Habermas, conform to (U), which states that:

> Every valid norm has to fulfil the following condition: *All* affected can accept the consequences and the side-effects its *general* observance can be anticipated to have for the satisfaction of *everyone's* interests (and these consequences are preferred to those of known alternative possibilities for regulation).[38]

(U) cannot operate alone however, and requires the location of intersubjectivity in real processes afforded by principle (D) which states that 'only those norms can claim to be valid that meet (or could meet) with the approval of all affected in their capacity *as participants in a practical discourse'*.[39] These principles can be broken down further into procedural elements. There are two conditions of ideal speech which Seyla Benhabib calls the symmetry condition and the reciprocity condition. The symmetry condition concerns speech acts while the reciprocity condition refers to existing action contexts.[40] The symmetry condition refers to two rules for practical discourse: 'first, each participant must have an equal chance to initiate and to continue communication; second, each must have an equal chance to make assertions, recommendations, and explanations, and to challenge justifications'.[41] The reciprocity condition refers to a set of relations that should exist between participants.[42] Such relations require that:

> all must have equal chances as actors to express their wishes, feelings, and intentions; and ... the speakers must act *as if* in contexts of action there is an equal distribution of chances 'to order and resist orders, to promise and to refuse, to be accountable for one's conduct and to demand accountability from others.'[43]

These 'procedural rules express (D) and are those whereby (U) is achieved'.[44] All participants must be motivated by the desire to reach a consensus about the truth of statements and the validity of norms, and discourse should be free from coercion or constraint. The ideal speech situation also requires that the 'force of the better argument prevails'.

Habermas argues that these criteria are anticipated in every act of argumentation. An ideal speech situation effectively forms an ideal of fair communication, offering a position from which to evaluate social practices and, in particular, to assess the legitimacy of norms. While it is clear that Habermas does not suggest that this situation should be realised, it is a 'regulative ideal' as we have to assume its possibility through the very nature of the discursive presuppositions.

Despite discourse ethics being a universalistic moral theory, Habermas accepts the fallibility of discursive practices. In other words, any agreement reached today concerning the validity of a claim does not mean that in the light of further information, reinterpreted needs or changing social conditions, agreement will still hold tomorrow. It may well be necessary to enter into discourse again.[45] In this sense, it is important to highlight once more that what Habermas is offering here is a set of 'universally valid procedural criteria appropriate to judging the justness of proposed norms', not the substantive content of those norms.[46]

The emphasis in discourse ethics, which encapsulates the notion of an ideal speech situation, is on procedure. Habermas claims that the processes that constitute discourse ethics, as identified above, do not determine or ascertain any particular outcome, because this can only be determined by the participants themselves. He argues that discourse ethics is concerned with both needs and wants, and the respective problems of inclusion and exclusion. As the 'revision of values used to interpret needs and wants' draws on intersubjectively shared traditions, this cannot be a decision taken monologically but must take place from within 'real' dialogue between participants.[47] Practical discourse is conceived as:

> the *public* practice of a shared, reciprocal taking over of perspectives: everyone finds him- or herself required to take over the perspective of each other person, in order to test whether a ruling is also acceptable from the perspective of everyone else's understanding of the world and of themselves.[48]

For Habermas, the dialogical engagement is a process of both 'making and finding'.[49] As new forms of suppression are revealed and stripped away, then new understandings can develop, based on the concepts of moral or normative learning and the discourse criterion that although participants enter into discourse from their own particular context, they cannot *a priori* know who may learn from whom.[50]

Interaction and learning are both important parts of Habermas's theory of communicative action. However, the reproduction of certain interactions does not necessarily constitute 'learning'. Forester makes the point that if 'a policy encouraging oil exploration reproduces consumer-monopolist interactions on the market, consumers and suppliers may exchange signals, but little learning will take place'.[51] The information offered by the market is likely to be distorted and misrepresentative of '"true costs of production" – a fact that the consumer will never learn as a participant in a monopoly-dominated interaction'.[52] The kinds of 'imperfect communication' that might be considered as interactions include bargaining, negotiation, and arbitration. Ordinary communicative action concerns the 'recreation in everyday life of particular relations of belief – construction, consent-granting, trust-giving, and attention investment';[53] consequently whilst interactions can reproduce particular patterns of knowledge, awareness, trust, and consent, they do not guarantee learning, nor can they step outside of these interactions in order to challenge them. The issue Forester raises demonstrates the relevance of Habermas's theory of communicative action to everyday practice at all levels of society, including the international: how are we able to distinguish between true social, political and economic learning, and manipulation and deliberate distortion? While ordinary communicative action is also based on the aforementioned validity claims, discourse ethics provides the theoretical tools with which to test these claims without the threat of coercion or constraint. The ability to identify social, political or economic constraints on discourse offers access to a powerful account of political legitimacy particularly relevant for the morally and legally challenging questions surrounding the decision to use force in international politics.

Habermas's distinction between the 'right' and the 'good' is particularly evident in his theory of communicative action. The subject of some controversy, it is necessary to clarify this distinction in order to place the following arguments in context. This clarification is required because discourse ethics – as a deontological ethics – is primarily concerned with justice rather than addressing questions of the good or happiness. Habermas's tripartite model of discourse relates to three different types of world: objective, social, and subjective.[54] Respective types of discourse are pragmatic, moral, ethical and they 'address different understandings of the same paradigmatic practical question: "What should I do?"'[55] Pragmatic discourses approach the question from the perspective of strategic or instrumental action, so seek to find the 'best way of attaining what is *useful*'.[56] Moral discourses are those which take place when the actions of an individual begin to 'violate the interests of others and to lead to conflicts which stand in need of a consensual regulation'.[57] The individual now has to determine whether everyone else would also agree on the choice of a particular course of action. Ethical discourses approach the question from the 'perspective of a life-project oriented to one's own *good*'.[58]

Habermas adhered to this distinction, despite the criticism it has received, because he intended his theory to be limited; he did not wish it to become the means of dictating how people should live their lives in concrete situations.[59] The 'good' refers to subjective and identity-forming issues such as aesthetics, tastes, and preferences. For Habermas, the 'good' lays out a sphere of autonomy where individuals cannot be told how to live or what to believe. The 'moral' however, is based on normative claims of rightness. It deals with '*moral* questions, which can in principle be decided rationally in terms of criteria of *justice* or the universalizability of interests'.[60] Such questions, which include the use of force in international relations, are those which have a greater impact on the social intersubjective world and are those which result in binding decisions. Redeemed in 'discourse' through reasons, such issues are subject to the 'force of the better argument'. In response to critics such as Carol Gilligan[61] who argues that this distinction privileges certain orientations over others (e.g. formalism and justice over the ethics of care and responsibility), Habermas acknowledges that it is problematic. However, he argues that

> [the question of the] context-specific application of universal norms should not be confused with the question of their justification. Since moral norms do not contain their own rules of application, acting on the basis of moral insight requires the additional competence of hermeneutic prudence, or in Kantian terminology, reflective judgement.[62]

The distinction Habermas draws between justification and application, allows, for him at any rate, the satisfaction of both types of demands.[63] Effectively, this distinction states that we cannot apply the same kind of judgement to individual ways of life as we can to a specific norm.[64] We cannot, Habermas argues, expect a generally valid answer when we ask what is good for me, or good for them. Instead, only the question 'what is *equally good for all?*' can be impartially assessed, referring to those 'action-related conflicts which can be resolved with reference to a generalizable interest; those which are questions of justice'.[65] It is not that ethical questions are less important, simply that they can only be judged from the perspective of the particular. However, as Habermas has admitted, 'Moral judgements, decoupled from concrete ethical life (*Sittlichkeit*), no longer immediately carry the motivational power that converts judgements into actions.'[66] Such a distinction erects certain limitations around Habermas's theory, limitations which are both useful, as in the retention of self-determination and autonomy,[67] and problematic, as with Gilligan's argument that it privileges certain ways of thinking/being over others, or the idea that we can ever know what is 'moral' or 'equally good for all'.

The Habermasian project

Critical interventions: adapting discourse ethics

The Habermasian project has been subject to a number of critiques from within critical and social theoretical spheres in ways which suggest that a communicative ethics which desires to maintain both theoretical and empirical purchase on the legitimacy of real communicative practices should not be tied too tightly to Habermas's discourse ethics. Further critiques from within IR direct our awareness to a number of issues which emerge specifically, although not exclusively, within the international sphere. Central to the debates in IR, as demonstrated by pluralist and solidarist theories of international society, is the degree to which the construction of moral and political boundaries shape our perceptions of interests, identities and responsibilities, and guide the foreign policy of states. As such, a communicative ethics which speaks to the relationship between legitimacy and justification in the context of conflict and the use of force requires, at its core, a theoretical defence and empirical awareness of practices of inclusion and exclusion and their consequences. Similarly, the debates encountered over the theoretical and empirical validity of the distinction between strategic and communicative action draws our attention to the respective roles that coercion and reflexivity play in international politics.

The cosmopolitanism of Andrew Linklater develops directly out of an engagement with Habermas's oeuvre and its application to international politics. He calls for a triple transformation of political community, grounded on a dialogic ethics, which is concerned with creating and enhancing social relations which are more 'universalistic, less unequal and more sensitive to cultural difference'.[68] His vision of a cosmopolitan community which is sensitive to the construction of communities and how this may systematise problems of inclusion and exclusion is not blind to the totalising potential of universalism. Rebuilding the critical project in the light of Kant and Marx, recognising and reworking the weaknesses in their respective theories, requires a shift towards more inclusive communication communities which creates space for dialogue between radically different individuals and communities. It challenges the boundaries of traditional concepts of political community, expands the spheres of social interaction that are governed by dialogue, and calls for the creation of socio-economic preconditions for effective dialogic participation for all members of a universal communication community. He attempts to expand the values of the *polis* into the international sphere, whilst simultaneously striking a balance between universalism and particularism principally through the discursive dimension drawn from Habermas.

Linklater identifies three dimensions central to a critical theory of IR which he develops through a Habermasian-inspired lens: 'normative, concerning the philosophical justifications for excluding some persons from particular social arrangements while admitting others; sociological, concerning the workings and maintenance of systems of inclusion and exclusion; and praxeological, concerning the impact of systems of inclusion and exclusion on human action' and the immanent potential for emancipatory political action.[69] The concern thus highlighted is how we might recognise and engage those who have been systematically excluded from dialogue and unable to voice their own interests or articulate how they may have been harmed by particular social policies or practices.

Linklater's 'thin universalism' posits that all individuals have a right to be consulted about decisions made outside their society which have adverse effects on them.[70] The relevant procedures of dialogue include the convention that 'no person and no moral position can be excluded from dialogue in advance, and the realisation that authentic dialogue requires a particular moral psychology'.[71] By matching his position so closely to Habermas's discourse ethics, he becomes vulnerable to Stephen Hopgood's charge that it 'presumes people are at least minimally liberal (other-regarding, egalitarian) in the first place'.[72] Recognising that a universal communication community is likely to be an impossible goal because a 'universal community, one that in principle includes all members of the species, must, by virtue of being a community, exclude or deny important differences amongst its members', Richard Shapcott has nonetheless argued that communicative models offer a better resolution than other frameworks to the tension between community, inclusion and difference identified within the cosmopolitan and communitarian debates.[73] Two fundamental problems with the conception of dialogic communities within the cosmopolitan project as advocated by Habermas and Linklater have been raised, however, arguing that it is 'potentially exclusionary of radical difference in at least two ways; in relation to the topics of conversation and to the conception of agency required for just conversation'.[74]

As suggested by the exegesis of Habermas's theory, dialogue should take a certain form.[75] The implementation of dialogue in accordance with discourse ethics requires that people must be willing to enter into dialogue and to be motivated by finding consensus; no position can be excluded in advance and people must be willing to be guided by the force of the better argument. Dialogue requires that there be no pre-determination of the outcome and that all members of the dialogue should be open to each other's perspectives and able to reflect upon their own embedded positions. Such dialogue implies that 'there is no certainty about who will learn from whom'.[76] These characteristics form what Habermas calls a 'post-conventional morality'; a term derived from Lawrence Kohlberg's stages of development which distinguish three levels of moral consciousness (pre-conventional, conventional and post-

The Habermasian project

conventional).[77] For Habermas, such a standpoint is necessary in order to learn how to conduct social life in a consensual manner. Pre-conventional and conventional forms of morality may have been consensual, but were often based on force or traditions. Post-conventional morality is concerned with consensus derived from ideal discursive verification and the construction of norms which are universal and valid for all, not just particular communities. These stages of development can be explained as follows:

> Pre-conventional morality exists when actors obey norms because they fear that non-compliance will be sanctioned by a higher authority; conventional norms are observed because actors are loyal to a specific social group; post-conventional morality occurs when actors stand back from authority structures and group membership and ask whether they are complying with principles which have *universal validity* ... Post-conventionalism demonstrates a capacity for ethical reflexivity in which agents recognise that moral codes are malleable social products rather than immutable conventions to which they must submit.[78]

This brings us to Shapcott's primary concern, which is that Habermas's conditions of universal dialogue restrict the role of agency unnecessarily. For Habermas, a post-conventional moral perspective requires a commitment to universal discourse. It is clear, however, that post-conventional ethics requires a particular reflective attitude towards social practices. This requires a particular conception of agency in order to be able to participate and suggests that only those who are able to 'conform to a specific ideal of reason' are able to participate in dialogue which, therefore, remains potentially exclusionary.[79] This excludes those who may conform to a pre-conventional or conventional consciousness and therefore favour traditional social practices and conceptions of the good life from participating in reasoned discussion. It also implies that those who inhabit conventional or pre-conventional consciousness are immature and need to be freed from such moralities in order to be able to engage in conversation, consequently endorsing an evolutionary, teleological and developmental account of human agency.[80] In response to the question of post-conventional morality, Habermas notes that in the failure to identify a shared good, the formal features of the shared situation of deliberation offers a way out of the 'modern dilemma, since the participants have lost their metaphysical guarantees and must so to speak derive their normative orientations from themselves alone'.[81] Recalling Shapcott's argument that justice also occurs at the level of identity and recognition, then in this context, the self–other relation is only equal insofar as all agents have developed the same consciousness.[82] There is clearly a sense of hierarchy implicit in Habermas's account of agency and this exclusion, or assimilation, is arguably aggravated by the goal of critical theory being emancipation, if emancipation has become not the goal but the prerequisite of dialogue.[83] By taking these objections into consideration the following account of communicative ethics seeks to place fewer limits on agency and topics of conversation.

Critics have raised another important objection concerning Habermas's emphasis on the principle (U) which, they argue, has greater implications for substantive content than Habermas acknowledges. Benhabib addresses the problem of the implications raised by (U) in a way which, she claims, allows us to avoid the charges of 'dogmatism and/or circularity'.[84] She emphasises the procedural aspects of discourse ethics which are evident from Habermas's insistence that content can only be determined by the participants, thus preventing the theoretical pre-selection of any specific institutional arrangement or political model. Consequently, Benhabib seeks to reformulate universalism as an 'interactive subjective procedure of argumentation' which encourages reversibility.[85] She puts forward two principles to support her formulation: first, the principle of universal moral respect, and secondly, the principle of egalitarian reciprocity. The former requires that we 'recognize the right of all beings capable of speech and action to be participants in the moral conversation', while the latter requires that within conversations everyone has the 'same symmetrical rights to various speech acts, to initiate new topics, to ask for reflection about the presuppositions of the conversation'.[86] The key to Benhabib's argument is the notion of respect for others which develops from processes of communicative socialisation. In order to defend her argument from claims of circularity or dogmatism, she argues that 'the presuppositions of the moral conversation can be questioned from within the conversation itself, they are placed within the purview of argumentation'.[87]

Although Habermas implies awareness of historical contingency, the notion of the universal normative 'ought' becomes problematic and homogenising. Benhabib concurs that Habermas has gone too far by 'insisting that the purpose of universalizability procedures in ethics must be the uncovering or discovering of some "general interest" to which all could consent'.[88] Instead she argues that (D) – which states that only those norms that meet, or could meet, with the approval of all concerned in their capacity as participants in a practical discourse can claim to be valid – is sufficient, in conjunction with those rules of argument governing discourse which she has summarised as the principles of universal moral respect and egalitarian reciprocity, to serve as the only universalisability test for a communicative ethics.[89] One of the key differences between Benhabib and Habermas is the role they attribute to consent. While for Habermas, (U) guarantees universality achieved by actual consent, Benhabib is unsatisfied by this prospect, arguing that the core intuition behind modern universalizability procedures is not that everybody could or would agree to the same set of principles, but that these principles have been adopted as a result of a procedure, whether of moral reasoning or of public debate, which we are ready to deem 'reasonable and fair.'[90]

Benhabib draws a distinction between universalisability as a procedure for testing maxims and for generating them. In so doing, she argues that communicative ethics is a powerful tool when considered as a 'procedure for testing the intersubjective validity of moral principles and norms of action', however, as 'a procedure for *generating* valid principles of action, the model of moral conversation is a necessary but insufficient test case that requires, in any given instance, adequate contextualization'.[91] This distinction maps onto the assessment in Part I of just-war informed criteria for the use of force as lacking a procedural capacity for critique of the way in which such substantive criteria have been decided. In other words, by whom and under what communicative conditions were these criteria established? Also neglected is consideration of the procedural legitimacy required for the application of substantive criteria to particular cases of the use of force. How are competing interpretations of just war criteria negotiated and how might we recognise coerced as opposed to voluntary consent regarding consensus on the legitimacy of military intervention?[92]

Those who adhere too closely to Habermas's principle (U) and its strong requirement of consensus face the hurdle of bringing critical theory close enough to the ground that it has critical purchase on empirical practice; it is easy to criticise the theory for its abstract nature when it finds that most, if not all, cases in practice fail to meet the rather high normative theoretical standards. This somewhat misses the point of the ideal speech situation, but it rightly calls for reflection on the role of universal consensus. Drawing on Benhabib's version of communicative ethics enables a firmer emphasis to be placed on the role of procedure as fairness and this becomes central to the communicative imperatives set out in the following chapter. It is unlikely that we either could or would want to specify the 'general interest'; however, discourse ethics, when focusing on process, offers the means to reveal the 'exclusion and silencing of *certain kinds* of interests'. At stake, therefore, is 'the uncovering of those partial interests which represent themselves as if they were general', thus exposing certain kinds of discourses which claim greater legitimacy than others.[93] Here the capacity of communicative ethics to contribute to conceptions of legitimacy becomes evident. The ability to reveal exclusion and coercion in linguistic, material and ideological forms is fundamental to a communicative ethics concerned in this instance with the justifications for the use of force.

Feminist critical theorists have highlighted another crucial critique which affects both who is included and the topic of conversation, arguing that gender bias and gender blindness are implicit in Habermas's discourse ethics. One central issue of contention is that the liberal private/public distinction goes unchallenged by his articulation of the lifeworld/system distinction and the role of the public sphere.[94] Additionally, his adoption of the 'rationalist' human subject central to Western philosophy retains the traditional binary logic which associates the 'feminine' with a lack of reason.[95] Carol Gilligan's critique of Kohlberg's account of moral development highlights the fact that men and women may often speak in different voices. Her argument is that associating the higher stages of moral consciousness with more abstract principles of justice privileges an 'objective' or impartial view of the public sphere which is free from the distorting influence of the particular or the private and grants superiority to abstract notions whilst paying little attention to the ethic of care and responsibility.[96]

The ethic of care, largely considered to be the domain of women, instead focuses on the development of individuals and family members. One of the central constitutive elements of the ethic of care is a 'highly developed hermeneutic grasp of personal character and social context – the very considerations which an abstract morality of justice deliberately ignores'.[97] Although Habermas places greater importance on the morality of justice because of its universal nature, and the consequent need to transcend the particular, this by itself, is insufficient. Instead, many feminists have argued that 'the morality of justice and the ethic of care and responsibility are complementary moralities: they should both feature prominently in a just society'.[98] Taking up this criticism, the preference for justice to the exclusion of an 'affective' dimension is restrictive and exclusive 'precisely because it rules out certain topics and concerns, which can justifiably be considered moral, from the conversation pre-discursively'.[99] Consequently, the content of what is considered acceptable dialogue has already been decided prior to any engagement with others.

Removing the emphasis from (U) enables this problem to be addressed since it is possible that conversation might be opened up with a broader focus that is more inclusive of difference and which seeks to engage with the other rather than form a universal consensus.[100] Iris Marion Young highlighted this potential when she discussed the transformation that the communicative process can produce in the opinions of participants and thus the potential to avoid either the exclusiveness or homogeneity of (U). If we assume that:

> communicative interaction means encountering differences of meaning, social position, or need that I do not share and identify with, then we can better describe how that interaction transforms my preferences ... each position is aware that it does not comprehend the perspective of the others differently located, in the sense that it cannot be assimilated into one's own.[101]

Echoing earlier arguments and developing the notion of 'different voices', Young claims that the tendency to restrict democratic deliberation to argument carries 'implicit cultural biases that can lead to exclusions in practice'.[102] The democratic assumption of consensus, moreover, may also have exclusionary consequences for minorities. She notes, in line with advocates of discourse ethics, that deliberative democracy promotes a 'conception of reason over power in politics'.[103] However, the deliberative model of communication which we are most familiar with and which is implicitly referred to in the literature is derived from Western institutional contexts such as scientific debate, national parliaments, intergovernmental institutions, courts and judicial processes, and so on. In other words, ruling institutions which have been predominantly male, white and upper class. Thus, Young's criticism is significant as she adds that the 'norms of deliberation are culturally specific and often operate as forms of power that silence or devalue the speech of some people'.[104] Some contexts privilege certain speaking styles over others; for example, contestatory, assertive and confrontational styles are privileged in parliaments and courts over tentative, informative, conciliatory, emotional, passionate or explorative styles. Consequently, Young is right when she remarks that such formal situations often privilege the right to speak or the authority of the well-educated white, middle-class man, rather than other groups in society whose voice may not conform to the established requirements and formal rules of speech. As a result, if other groups do speak, they may do so in a way which is classed as 'disruptive',[105] suggesting that the conditions necessary for an ideal speech situation are linguistic as well as social and material. These conditions are all relevant for any empirical analysis of communicative practices which looks for moments of distortion and illegitimacy.

A more sensitive approach to the ways in which communication can operate to exclude alternative forms of speech is particularly important for a communicative ethics when considering dialogue arising out of conflict situations where it is likely that anger, hurt and passionate concern may dominate communication, but do not necessarily make that communication any less valuable. The ethical-political possibilities resulting from interconnections between different levels of discourse relating to both an ethic of care and an ethic of justice are illustrated by Jean Bethke Elshtain's discussion of the case of the Mothers of the Plaza de Mayos in Argentina:

> The language [the Mothers] spoke was double: the language of a mother's loss and the language of human rights, moving back and forth from intensely particular, yet universally recognized, imperatives of love and terror, to what has become a universal and potent political discourse.[106]

In response to the recognition by critics of the limitations placed on agency and topics of dialogue by Habermas, communicative ethics as it is developed herein seeks to retain room for a variety of voices which extend to include those actors and discourses which are typically marginalised and lack recognition in international politics as a result of their use of affective dimensions of language, their status as an actor or their cultural contexts.

A further conversational nexus with discourse ethics is the philosophical hermeneutics of Hans Georg Gadamer. While there are points of similarity, Gadamer's approach provides an alternative model which allows a communicative ethics framework to avoid some of the assimilatory potential inherent in discourse ethics because it challenges the need for a 'strong' version of universal consensus.[107] Particular conceptions of hermeneutics are central to the work of both Gadamer and Habermas. Philosophical hermeneutics also conceives of understanding as a communicative act, 'between equal but differently situated agents, in which self and other achieve recognition through dialogue'.[108] The emphasis on understanding here, however, is not on the need for universal consensus, but rather on the experience of a new or different truth claim. This does not mean that we forget our own interpretation of meaning or content and/or our own ideas. Indeed, Gadamer argues that fundamental to hermeneutic reflection is the 'concrete historical positioning' of the interpreter and interpreted.[109] Gadamer perceives the interpreter to be embedded within 'tradition' and recognises that they bring to the activity of interpretation anticipations of its meaning which he calls 'prejudices'. He asks, however, that 'we remain open to the meaning of the other person or text'.[110]

Gadamer indicates that understanding is in fact interpretation and occurs through language; thus, he emphasises the primacy of dialogue.[111] All interpretation and understanding take place within the '"tradition" or horizon of consciousness constituted by the linguistic and historical tradition of the interpreter: the webs of meaning in which and through which we experience the world and which are the conditions of possibility of understanding'.[112] While philosophical hermeneutics begins from the premise of situated agents and particular norms, it does not limit understanding to the boundaries of a particular community. Gadamer stressed that 'understanding is always the fusion of these horizons supposedly existing by themselves', from which the prejudices of others are not simply obstacles to our understanding, but also a possible means towards it.[113] Habermas captures the concept when he argues that 'hermeneutics, then, accord[s] a higher position to acting and speaking than to knowing'.[114]

The purpose of a hermeneutic conversation 'is not the eradication of difference in agreement, but instead the understanding of identity and difference through what is common: language'.[115] While Habermas still indicates

The Habermasian project

that there should be universal consensus, for Gadamer, the 'truth is always particular, situated and in reference to some subject'.[116] Consequently, agreement on the scale implied by Habermas's principle (U), (i.e. only universalisable statements, therefore very few norms would be validated) cannot demonstrate the same sensitivity towards alterity, plurality, and understanding that hermeneutics offers. Similarly, if the *telos* of conversation for discourse ethics is consensus between post-conventional agents regarding universalisable principles, then for philosophical hermeneutics the purpose of conversation is that of hermeneutic understanding. An important consequence of the hermeneutic argument is that 'it can relieve the cosmopolitan project of the emancipatory task of seeking to create a realm of similarly constituted agents'.[117] If the ability to reason and reflect, to transform understanding in response to conversations with others, are properties of understanding which we possess as linguistically constituted agents, then Habermas's assignation of these qualities to post-conventional agents is shown to be unnecessarily restrictive for a communicative ethics applicable to the international sphere. By removing the requirement that dialogue can only address questions of 'right' and topics that can be universalised, there is a much broader and more inclusive conception of conversation and engagement between participants. The question raised, therefore, and explored in the following chapters, regards what dialogue might look like in the international sphere: does either universal consensus or hermeneutics offer an appropriate model?

The hermeneutic debate raises a number of pertinent elements for the development of a communicative ethics in relation to the legitimacy of decisions to use force. These concern potential alternatives concerning the end goal of dialogue and broadening the nature of the topics which may become subject to critical scrutiny. However, whilst hermeneutics of the kind described tempers some of the problems posed by Habermas's discourse ethics, his critique of hermeneutics is also relevant for a communicative ethics which seeks to retain the critical edge lacking in other accounts. Habermas notes, for example, the problem of 'linguistic idealism',[118] a reference to the neglect by hermeneutics of the fact that language is not just a means of communication with which to mediate and interpret our experiences, but also:

> a medium of domination and social power; it serves to legitimate relations of organized force. Insofar as the legitimations do not articulate the power relations whose institutionalization they make possible, insofar as these relations merely manifest themselves in the legitimations, language is also ideological.[119]

Habermas perceives three idealisations of ordinary language integral to a hermeneutic approach: firstly, it overestimates the consistency and comprehensibility it possesses; secondly, it assumes a greater potential for communication in a given context than is usually present; and thirdly, it assumes a degree of agreement (consensus) among speakers which is almost never present.[120] Habermas argues that these combine to prevent a sufficiently critical stance being taken and thus prevent the possibility of distinguishing between true communication and pseudo-communication or recognising systematically distorted communication. If, 'in the face of covert domination, social groups or whole societies have adapted to distorted forms of communication, hermeneutics would hence be in danger of preserving the status quo, rather than helping to achieve emancipation'.[121] What is required in such situations in order to retain the sensitivity towards understanding offered by hermeneutics, without falling prey to its 'blind spots', is a 'depth hermeneutic'. What this means is that the agent's self-interpretation and interpretation of others is placed in the context of social relations and agents are able to reflect upon this context. Social relations are considered to operate 'like a natural force upon [agents] (but behind their backs)', distorting their communicative actions.[122] The depth hermeneutic serves to make causes of distorted communicative visible and hold 'tradition' to account: it places the individual or a collective 'in a position to remove the source of the distortion, and so to give voice to the inhibited meanings'.[123] It is this critical capacity to recognise distortion which was previously identified as lacking in constructivist accounts of interpretive communities and argumentation in international politics.

For Habermas, we can only distinguish between a genuine and a false consensus if we presuppose the possibility of an ideal, normative standard in a theory of communicative competence; understanding needs to be linked to the idealising presuppositions of speech. In essence, discourse ethics is an 'ethics of suspicion'[124] concerning reliance on tradition for determining moral categories. Even traditions such as liberal democracies, which have provided a basis for the principles of political discourse, have to be looked at with suspicion. Certainly justifications for the use of force must be scrutinised carefully and an 'ethic of suspicion' is necessary for a critical interrogation of claims to legitimacy.

Conclusion

Despite the critiques of discourse ethics offered by hermeneutics, feminism and other forms of relativism, it is difficult to deny that some notion of normative rightness is still valued, particularly in the context of mass atrocity crimes and conflict. Normative legislative developments in international politics reflect our conviction that consensus on and judgement of some categories of action is both legitimate and desirable.[125] Habermas can help navigate such shifting sands because he emphasises the importance of intersubjectivity, reflexivity, ongoing moral conversation and the quality of argumentative practice. The equality of discourse ethics ensures that no one interpretation of events is privileged over any other except through the force of the better argument.[126] Engaging with the central concepts of the Habermasian project has established a dual understanding of dialogue as both normative grounds and the object of critique necessary for a communicative ethics. Key concepts such as the ideal speech situation, the distinction between strategic and communicative action, discourse ethics and the presuppositions of argumentation, facilitate the development of a communicative ethics with which to cast a critical and reflexive eye on the procedures and communicative practices through which claims to legitimacy are made for the use of force.

Addressing a series of critical interventions around discourse ethics has raised several concerns which must inform the development of a communicative ethics which can be applied at the international level. As has been suggested, the implications of (U) for consensus appear problematic because it requires converging understandings of the validity of moral norms. However, the feminist, cosmopolitan, and hermeneutic critiques raised in the course of this chapter offer a means to temper this interpretive process whilst at the same time retaining the 'ethic of suspicion' necessary for revealing communicative distortion as well as the emphasis on discourse as a procedural ethics. By shifting, as Benhabib does, the focus of discourse ethics away from an ideal of consensus towards deliberative procedure, the problematic distinction between justification and application is also ameliorated as it allows discourse ethics to overcome the restriction to questions of justice. Conceived as a procedure of discursive argumentation, questions of the good life can also be considered. Opening up questions of appropriate agency and communicative expression broadens the theoretical scope and application of a theory of communicative ethics without diminishing the reflexive requirements of participants. Communicative ethics is not, on this reading, attempting to generate moral norms, but to interrogate the intersubjective validity of claims to legitimacy.

Communicative ethics shifts the basis of our understanding of justice and encourages innovative practices for transforming conflict. Rather than being understood solely in distributive terms, justice should be understood in terms of the recognition of those who are marginalised or excluded from dialogue.[127] The effect of such an argument is to make us question the boundaries of inclusion and exclusion, how those are decided and by whom. Thus, justice and legitimacy are explicitly conceived of in communicative terms; injustice may be done through illegitimate exclusion or coercive communicative practices. Engaging in dialogue makes it much harder to dehumanise the enemy in a manner necessary to retain support for conflict and this is crucial for deliberative processes in international politics.[128] Once

Communicative ethics and the use of force

the notion that the language of force is the only option has been moved away from, it becomes much harder to justify the use of force to domestic publics. Such issues raise crucial questions for the structure and practice of international deliberative processes. By exploring a range of contributions to the debates surrounding discourse ethics, a number of thematic elements have begun to emerge which will be brought together in the following chapter in the form of an alternative communicative ethics framework which has at its core a series of 'communicative imperatives'.

NOTES

1 Fierke, *Diplomatic Interventions*, 18.
2 Habermas's writings are overwhelming in terms of their scope and volume. Whilst I focus on his work on discourse ethics, given its relevance to developing a communicative ethics in IR, I recognise that these concepts draw on other aspects of his philosophical and political thought which I cannot expand on here for reasons of space and cogency. For excellent discussions of Habermas's broader work, see T. McCarthy, *The Critical Theory of Jürgen Habermas* (Cambridge, MA: MIT Press, 1978); D. Held, *Introduction to Critical Theory: Horkheimer to Habermas* (Berkeley, University of California Press, 1980); White, *The Recent Work of Jürgen Habermas*; Benhabib and Dallmayr (eds), *The Communicative Ethics Controversy*; C. Calhoun (ed.), *Habermas and the Public Sphere* (Cambridge, MA: MIT Press, 1992); K. Baynes, *The Normative Grounds of Social Criticism: Kant, Rawls, Habermas* (Albany: State University of New York Press, 1992); J. Habermas and P. Dews, *Habermas: Autonomy and Solidarity*, 2nd edn (London: Verso, 1992); W. Outhwaite, *Habermas: A Critical Introduction* (Cambridge: Polity Press, 1994); D. Hoy and T. McCarthy, *Critical Theory* (Oxford: Blackwell Publishers, 1994); J. Bernstein, *Recovering Ethical Life: Jurgen Habermas and the Future of Critical Theory* (New York: Routledge, 1995); W. Rehg, *Insight and Solidarity: The Discourse Ethics of Jürgen Habermas* (California: University of California Press, 1997); P. Dews (ed.), *Habermas: A Critical Reader* (Oxford: Blackwell Publishers, 1999); Payrow Shabani, *Democracy, Power, and Legitimacy*.
3 D. Archibugi, *Debating Cosmopolitics* (London: Verso, 2003); D. Held and D. Archibugi (eds), *Cosmopolitan Democracy* (Cambridge: Polity Press, 1995); D. Held, *Models of Democracy*, 2nd edn (Cambridge: Polity Press, 1996); J. Dryzek, *Discursive Democracy: Politics, Policy and Political Science* (Cambridge: Cambrigde University Press, 1990); J. Dryzek, 'Handle with Care: The Deadly Hermeneutics of Deliberative Instrumentation', *Acta Politica*, 40:2 (2005), 197–211.
4 J. Fishkin, *The Dialogue of Justice: Toward A Self-Reflective Society* (New Haven: Yale University Press, 1992); J. Fishkin and R. Luskin, 'Experimenting with a Democratic Ideal: Deliberative Polling and Public Opinion', *Acta Politica*, 40:3 (2005), 284–98; D. Janssen and R. Kies, 'Online Forums and Deliberative Democracy', *Acta Politica*, 40:3 (2005), 317–35; K. Boréus, 'Discursive Discrimination: A Typology', *European Journal of Social Theory*, 9:3 (2006), 405–24; Hurrelmann, et al. (eds), *Legitimacy in an Age of Global Politics*.
5 V. Boon and N. Head, 'Critical Theory and the Language of Violence: Exploring the Issues', *Journal of Global Ethics*, 6:2 (2010), 79–87.
6 Payrow Shabani, *Democracy, Power, and Legitimacy*, 7. Habermas plans to '"reconstruct the possible condition of human understanding", which is the aim of communicative action. His theory, therefore, would take the form of a reconstructive science that

differs from ordinary sciences in being a blend of empirical scientific investigation and philosophical generalization aimed at uncovering the universal basis of human action' (Ibid., 32). It is worth noting that this is a particularly Habermasian interpretation of Adorno and Horkheimer to which not all critical theorists would subscribe. Thanks to Vivienne Matthies-Boon for pointing this out.
7 R. Wyn Jones, 'On Emancipation: Necessity, Capacity, and Concrete Utopias', in K. Booth (ed.), *Critical Security Studies and World Politics* (Boulder: Lynne Rienner Publishers, 2005), 224.
8 Forester (ed.), *Critical Theory and Public Life*, xi; M. Cooke, *Language and Reason: A Study of Habermas's Pragmatics* (Cambridge, MA: MIT Press, 1994), 8.
9 Forester, *Critical Theory and Public Life*, xi.
10 Habermas, *TCA*, vol. 2, 152.
11 Forester, *Critical Theory and Public Life*, xiii.
12 Habermas defines the lifeworld as 'represented by culturally transmitted and linguistically organized stock of interpretive patterns', *TCA*, vol. 2, 124.
13 Ibid., 182.
14 Ibid., 183–5. Habermas's system and lifeworld dualism has faced a number of critiques: see Payrow Shabani, *Democracy, Power, and Legitimacy*; A. Honneth, *The Critique of Power* (trans. Kenneth Baynes) (Cambridge, MA: MIT Press, 1991); T. McCarthy, *Ideals and Illusions* (Cambridge, MA: MIT Press, 1991). While Habermas initially presented the distinction between communicative and strategic action as directly correlating to illocutionary and perlocutionary acts, critics have questioned this move. Drawing on James Bohman's critique, Payrow Shabani concurs that they should instead be seen as 'an analytic distinction that allows overlapping areas between the two types of interaction' in order to maintain the theory's emancipatory character. Bohman argues: 'as emancipator, the social critic performs speech acts that are neither strictly perlocutions nor illocutions, but an important hybrid type that Habermas' "real distinction" disallows' (cited in Payrow Shabani, *Democracy, Power, and Legitimacy*, 36–7).
15 Habermas, *TCA*, vol. 2, 187.
16 Habermas, *TCA*, vol. 1, 356–73.
17 D. Rasmussen, *Reading Habermas* (Oxford: Blackwell, 1990), 38.
18 Cooke, *Language and Reason*, 22–6.
19 Fierke, *Changing Games*, 13, 171.
20 V. Boon, 'Jürgen Habermas and Islamic Fundamentalism: On the Limits of Discourse Ethics', *Journal of Global Ethics*, 6:2 (2010), 153–66.
21 Ibid., 153. See also O. Ramsbotham, *Transforming Violent Conflict: Radical Disagreement, Dialogue and Survival* (Abingdon: Routledge, 2010).
22 For example, Krasner, *Sovereignty: Organized Hypocrisy*; White, *The Recent Work of Jürgen Habermas*, 10–11.
23 Cooke, *Language and Reason*, Chapter 1.
24 Habermas later referred to this as an 'ideal' or 'universal' communication community although without making substantive conceptual changes. My usage of 'ideal speech situation' reflects its common use in the literature but makes no particular substantive theoretical claim beyond Habermas's own.
25 Also referred to as universal/formal pragmatics.
26 Bernstein, *Recovering Ethical Life*, 48.
27 Ibid. See Cooke, *Language and Reason*, 22–6. She indicates that within strategic action Habermas distinguishes between 'the *manifestly* and the *latently* strategic use of language and, as subdivisions of the latter, between the *conscious* and the *unconscious* latently strategic use of language' (22, original emphasis). The latently strategic use of

language maps onto the 'language of manoeuvre' identified within IR.
28 Habermas, *MCCA*, 203.
29 S. Benhabib, 'Communicative Ethics and Current Controversies in Practical Philosophy', in Benhabib and Dallmayr (eds), *The Communicative Ethics Controversy*, 336; White, *The Recent Work of Jürgen Habermas*, 49.
30 Outhwaite, *Habermas*, 40.
31 Habermas, *Theory and Practice*, 18.
32 Outhwaite, *Habermas*, 41, citing Habermas.
33 Bernstein, *Recovering Ethical Life*, 49.
34 Ibid., 50. See Habermas, *TCA*, vol. 1, 25.
35 S. Benhabib, *Critique, Norm and Utopia* (New York: Colombia University Press, 1986), 284.
36 Wyn Jones, 'On Emancipation', 224.
37 Habermas, *MCCA*, 90–1. See Fierke, *Changing Games*, 112. As Jackson asserts, 'Lying is behaviour which has been negatively appraised by reference to the standard of conduct of telling the truth', *The Global Covenant*, 69–70.
38 Habermas, *MCCA*, 65.
39 Ibid., 66.
40 Benhabib, *Critique, Norm and Utopia*, 285.
41 Ibid.
42 R. Blaug, *Democracy, Real and Ideal: Discourse Ethics and Radical Politics* (Albany: State University of New York Press, 1999), 11.
43 Benhabib, *Critique, Norm and Utopia*, 285.
44 Blaug, *Democracy, Real and Ideal*, 11. In the context of this book, it is preferable to see Habermas's pragmatic rules of fairness not as an individual right or entitlement to inclusion which its link with citizenship might suggest, but rather as focused on the conditions of legitimacy of the discourse: thus the onus is placed on the institutions of democracy/international community to find ways to include individuals if they and their justifications for action wish to be legitimate. See Blaug, 45–6.
45 Baynes, *The Normative Grounds of Social Criticism*, 114.
46 White, *The Recent Work of Jürgen Habermas*, 50.
47 Habermas, *MCCA*, 68.
48 Habermas and Dews, *Autonomy and Solidarity*, 251.
49 Bernstein, *Recovering Ethical Life*, 55.
50 Habermas, *MCCA*, 26.
51 J. Forester, 'The Policy Analysis – Critical Theory Affair: Wildavsky and Habermas as Bedfellows?', in Forester (ed.), *Critical Theory and Public Life*, 265.
52 Ibid.
53 Ibid., 267.
54 Habermas argues that 'facts, norms and subjective experiences have their *originary* locus in "their" corresponding worlds (objective, social or subjective)' (original emphasis) and Cooke clarifies this: 'When we adopt an objectivating attitude we relate, in the first instance, to the objective world of facts and existing states of affairs; when we adopt a norm-conformative attitude we relate, in the first instance, to the social world of normatively regulated interactions; when we adopt an expressive attitude we relate, in the first instance, to the subjective world of inner experience.' These worlds also relate to different types of validity claims (truth – 'It is raining outside'; right – 'Abortion is morally wrong'; and truthfulness – 'I have a headache'). Cooke, *Language and Reason*, 10–11.
55 A. Ferrara, *Justice and Judgement* (London: Sage Publications, 1999), 43. Eckersley

notes that more broadly Habermasian critical theory can be considered to have a meta-ethics and a proceduralist normative ethics, but, as a result of Habermas's distinction between the right and the good, not to have developed an applied ethics: 'As to meta-ethics, critical theorists maintain that a claim or norm is right or valid when it has received the unforced consent of the affected constituents after full and free deliberation from all conceivable vantage points. As to normative ethics, critical theory's overriding ethical goal is to promote emancipation, or to remove constraints on human autonomy, by means of ever more inclusive and less distorted dialogue. As to applied ethics, critical theorists can only offer evaluations about the degree to which particular conversations are "distorted" or free, or exclusive or inclusive, legitimate or illegitimate according to the regulative ideal of the discourse ethic. However, they cannot pronounce upon the good life, or offer advice on what should be done, because that would usurp the role of the relevant/affected social agents to work through these questions in practical discourses in particular contexts.' R. Eckersley, 'The Ethics of Critical Theory', in C. Reus-Smit and D. Snidal, *Oxford Handbook*, 347.
56 Ferrara, *Justice and Judgement*, 43.
57 Ibid.
58 Ibid.
59 However, McCarthy's point that 'The separation of formal procedure from substantive content is never absolute: we cannot agree on what is just without achieving some measure of agreement on what is good' is relevant for the argument that follows. McCarthy, *Ideals and Illusions*, 191–2.
60 Habermas, *MCCA*, 178.
61 C. Gilligan, *In a Different Voice: Psychological Theory and Women's Development* (Cambridge, MA: Harvard University Press, 1982).
62 Habermas *MCCA*, 179–80. In responding to critiques, Habermas has drawn on the principle of appropriateness found in the work of K. Günther, *The Sense of Appropriateness: Application Discourses in Morality and Law* (New York: SUNY, 1993).
63 A number of critics have noted the difficulties that Habermas's separation of justification from application raise. See A. Wellmer, *The Persistence of Modernity* (Cambridge, MA: MIT Press, 1991); J. Habermas, *Justification and Application: Remarks on Discourse Ethics* (Cambridge, MA: MIT Press, 1993); Blaug, *Democracy, Real and Ideal*; Payrow Shabani, *Democracy, Power, and Legitimacy*, Chapter 3: 'Discourse ethics decidedly does not embrace the contextual factors since they are assumed to be biased; instead, it is apt to settle the general issues of justice (morality) rationally. And since only few moral laws pass the filter of its U principle as the test of their validity, moral discourse is rendered of little use for our moral lives. Thus, given that the identity of the individual is formed within the context of ethical life, such minimal insight would not provide any meaningful answer to the problem of self-constitution and of self-realization of the modern subject' (72).
64 Habermas also argues that 'in modernity, the plurality of individual life-projects and collective life forms cannot be prejudged philosophically, because ways of living are handed over to the responsibility of socialized individuals themselves, and can only be assessed from the standpoint of a participant, the element which can convince *everyone* is narrowed down to the *procedure* of rational will-formation itself'. Habermas and Dews, *Autonomy and Solidarity*, 248.
65 Ibid., 248–9; Habermas, *TCA*, vol. 1, 73. This distinction is decided during discourse, not beforehand.
66 Habermas, cited in Payrow Shabani, *Democracy, Power, and Legitimacy*, 71.
67 R. Wolff, *In Defense of Anarchism* (New York: Harper & Row Publishers, 1970), 23–7.

68 Linklater, *The Transformation of Political Community*, 7.
69 Linklater, 'The Question of the Next Stage', 78. Praxeology can be defined as 'the method by which critical theory can highlight the unfulfilled promise of the Enlightenment and draw attention to the potential for more inclusive social arrangements that expand human autonomy', Eckersley, 'The Ethics of Critical Theory', 350.
70 Linklater, 'Dialogic Politics', 144.
71 R. Shapcott, 'Cosmopolitan Conversations: Justice Dialogue and the Cosmopolitan Project', *Global Society*, 16:3 (2002), 224.
72 S. Hopgood, 'Reading the Small Print in Global Civil Society: The Inexorable Hegemony of the Liberal Self', *Millennium: Journal of International Studies*, 29:1 (2000), 10.
73 Shapcott, 'Cosmopolitan Conversations', 223.
74 Ibid. The consensus required by the telos of (U) means that conversation is restricted primarily to the 'right'.
75 A. Linklater, 'Citizenship and Sovereignty in the Post-Westphalian State', *European Journal of International Relations*, 2:1 (1996), 86.
76 Ibid., 86.
77 Habermas, *TCA*, vol. 2, 174. For Kohlberg's specific stages of development see White, *The Recent Work of Jürgen Habermas*, 66–8. The three stages reflect different levels of reflexivity. However, by tying the stages of moral consciousness to varying stages of social integration, Habermas has also been criticised for drawing too close a parallel between individual and social learning processes. For an overview see P. Strydom, 'The Ontogenetic Fallacy: The Immanent Critique of Habermas' Developmental Logical Theory of Evolution', *Theory, Culture and Society*, 9:3 (1992), 65–93. Habermas defines post-conventional morality as follows: 'The concept of the capacity to act that develops at the post-conventional stage of interaction makes it clear that moral action is a case of normatively regulated action in which the actor is oriented toward reflectively tested claims to validity. Intrinsic to moral action is the claim that the settling of action conflicts is based on justified reasoning alone. Moral action is action guided by moral insight ... Only at the postconventional stage is the social world uncoupled from the stream of cultural givens' (*MCCA*, 162).
78 Shapcott, 'Cosmopolitan Conversations', 226–7, citing Linklater.
79 Linklater, 'Dialogic Politics', 227.
80 Shapcott, *Justice, Community and Dialogue*, 119.
81 J. Habermas, *The Inclusion of the Other*, ed. C. Cronin and P. De Grieff (Cambridge, MA: MIT Press, 1998), 41.
82 Shapcott, 'Cosmopolitan Conversations', 230. This preference for a post-conventional morality is reflected in Linklater's work as well. See Linklater, *Critical Theory and World Politics*; Jordaan, 'Dialogic Cosmopolitanism and Global Justice'.
83 Shapcott, 'Cosmopolitan Conversations', 231.
84 S. Benhabib, *Situating the Self* (Cambridge: Polity Press, 1992), 29.
85 Ibid., 28.
86 Ibid., 29.
87 Ibid., 32.
88 Ibid., 9.
89 Ibid., 37. The role of (U) is a controversial one. For a critical discussion see A. Abizadeh, 'In Defence of the Universalisation Principle in Discourse Ethics', *The Philosophical Forum*, 36:2 (2005), 193–211; J. G. Finlayson, 'Debate: What are "Universalizable Interests"?', *The Journal of Political Philosophy*, 8:4 (2000), 456–69; A. Heller, 'The Discourse Ethics of Habermas: Critique and Appraisal', *Thesis Eleven*, 10/11 (1985), 5–17; Cooke, *Language and Reason*, 153–4. Given that I am not attempting to

implement discourse ethics in IR, but am instead interested in seeing what critical tools Habermas has to offer for investigating the relationship between justification and claims to legitimacy surrounding the use of force, I am, for these purposes, close to Benhabib's position in this debate.
90 Benhabib, *Situating the Self*, 37.
91 Benhabib, 'Communicative Ethics and Current Controversies in Practical Philosophy', 341. Original emphasis.
92 Bjola makes a similar argument, *Legitimising the Use of Force in International Politics*, 35.
93 Benhabib, *Situating the Self*, 48.
94 Hutchings, 'Speaking and Hearing', 156; Fraser, 'What's Critical about Critical Theory?'.
95 Hutchings, 'Speaking and Hearing', 156.
96 Linklater, *The Transformation of Political Community*, 68.
97 Ibid., 68–9.
98 Ibid., 69.
99 Shapcott, 'Cosmopolitan Conversations', 229.
100 For an excellent general discussion see M. Pajnik, 'Feminist Reflections on Habermas's Communicative Action', *European Journal of Social Theory*, 9:3 (2006).
101 I. M. Young, 'Communication and the Other: Beyond Deliberative Democracy', in S. Benhabib (ed.), *Democracy and Difference: Contesting the Boundaries of the Political* (Princeton: Princeton University Press, 1996), 127.
102 Ibid., 122.
103 Ibid.
104 Ibid., 123. See also Crawford, *Argument and Change*, 416; N. Fraser, 'Rethinking the Public Sphere: A Contribution to the Critique of Actually Existing Democracy', in Calhoun (ed.), *Habermas and the Public Sphere*, 118–19.
105 Young, 'Communication and the Other', 124.
106 J. B. Elshtain, 'Antigone's Daughters Reconsidered: Continuing Reflections on Women, Politics and Power', in S. K. White (ed.), *Lifeworld and Politics: Between Modernity and Postmodernity* (Notre Dame: University of Notre Dame Press, 1989), 232.
107 See Hoy and McCarthy, *Critical Theory*, Chapter 6; N. H. Smith, *Strong Hermeneutics: Contingency and Moral Identity* (New York: Routledge, 1997); R. J. Bernstein, 'The Constellation of Hermeneutics, Critical Theory and Deconstruction', in R. J. Dostal, *The Cambridge Companion to Gadamer* (Cambridge: Cambridge University Press, 2002).
108 Shapcott, *Justice, Community and Dialogue*, 131.
109 Smith, *Strong Hermeneutics*, 26.
110 H.-G. Gadamer, *Truth and Method*, 2nd edn (New York: Continuum, 1991), 268.
111 Ibid. 307, 384.
112 Shapcott, *Justice, Community and Dialogue*, 136.
113 Gadamer, *Truth and Method*, 306.
114 Habermas, *MCCA*, 9.
115 Shapcott, 'Cosmopolitan Conversations', 236. See Hoy's argument on Gadamer's hermeneutical pluralism, Hoy and McCarthy, *Critical Theory*, 188–200.
116 Shapcott, *Justice, Community and Dialogue*, 141.
117 Shapcott, 'Cosmopolitan Conversations', 240.
118 Outhwaite, *Habermas*, 25; Smith, *Strong Hermeneutics*, 25–34.
119 Bernstein, *Recovering Ethical Life*, 45.
120 Ibid.
121 Haacke, 'Theory and Praxis in International Relations', 75; Habermas, *Theory and Practice*, 10: 'critical sociology guards itself against reducing the meaning complexes

objectified within social systems to the contents of cultural tradition. Critical of ideology, it asks what lies behind the consensus, presented as a fact, that supports the dominant tradition of the time, and does so with a view to the relations of power surreptitiously incorporated in the symbolic structures of the systems of speech and action.'

122 Haacke, 'Theory and Praxis in International Relations', 75.
123 Ibid.
124 Rasmussen, *Reading Habermas*, 62.
125 For example, the establishment of *ad hoc* international tribunals for Rwanda and Yugoslavia, the ratification of the International Criminal Court, the establishment of truth and reconciliation processes post-conflict, and the expanding understanding of the UN Security Council's mandate to protect 'international peace and security'.
126 Habermas, *TCA*, vol. 1, 100: 'A definition of the situation by another party that prima facie diverges from one's own presents a problem of a peculiar sort; for in cooperative processes of interpretation no participant has a monopoly on correct interpretation. For both parties the interpretive task consists in incorporating the other's interpretation of the situation into one's own in such a way that in the revised version "his" external world and "my" external world can – against the background of "our" lifeworld – be relativized in relation to "the" world, and the divergent situation definitions can be brought to coincide sufficiently.'
127 Shapcott, 'Cosmopolitan Conversations', 221–2.
128 K. M. Fierke, 'Constructing an Ethical Foreign Policy: Analysis and Practice From Below', in Smith and Light (eds) *Ethics and Foreign Policy*, 139–40. Fierke describes conversations with a Bosniac who also spoke of his preference for dialogue over force, and the likelihood of its greater long-term effectiveness.

5

The communicative imperatives

> Argumentation is designed to prevent some from simply suggesting or prescribing to others what is good for them ... the rules of discourse themselves have a normative quality, for they neutralize imbalances of power and provide for equal opportunities to realize one's interests.
>
> Jürgen Habermas[1]

Introduction

CENTRAL TO critical theory is not just an ability to interpret the social world, but to engage in a project of emancipation.[2] Communicative ethics provides a normative and critical orientation essential to interrogating claims to legitimacy in relation to the use of force. This dual focus on interpretation and emancipation requires a reflexive approach to the relationship between theory and practice. A critical assessment of democracy, for example, cannot simply be based on existing practices or institutions[3] as this offers no way to address the question of how legitimate government should be organised in the first place. Similarly, to assess claims to legitimacy for the use of force without the critical lens provided by communicative ethics is to fail to address the prior question: what is legitimacy and how is it constituted by our communicative practices? The communicative imperatives bring together the themes and concerns already identified in the relevant debates in both IR and critical theory, and as such, they operationalise a communicative ethics which can be applied to claims to legitimacy in relation to the use of force.

Justifications relating to the use of force concern moral-practical knowledge. In Habermas's terms, they can be contested under the validity claim of rightness.[4] Given that the case of Kosovo confronts us with conflicting interpretations of established norms we must find some way to assess the legitimacy of competing claims. Recalling that communicative ethics secures a dual understanding of dialogue as both *normative grounds* and *object of critique*, it appraises the communicative practices through which claims to legitimacy are voiced and reveals a series of conditions which limit the capacity of actors to engage freely and fairly in debate.

The framework set up in the first section of this chapter structures the empirical investigation which follows in Chapter 6 of the communicative practices which served to legitimate and justify the use of force in Kosovo. Recalling that the communicative imperatives are informed by an imperfect and analytical distinction between strategic and communicative rationalities in order to retain their critical orientation, they enable the operationalisation of communicative ethics. They can be considered as 'norms of evaluation internal to that political practice',[5] if the political practice in question is the claim to legitimacy. The aim of the imperatives is to reveal the effects of relations of power and domination on communicative practices within the international sphere despite institutional commitments to democratic norms of deliberation and equality.

The second section focuses on the relationship between theory and practice in order to cast light on the limits to theory intrinsic to discourse ethics. This serves to orient our thinking about the relationship between communicative practices and norms, justificatory processes and legitimacy, and strategic and communicative action in IR. The third section of the chapter argues that Hannah Arendt's concept of 'reflective judgement' is useful for responding to the concerns raised in the previous chapter over Habermas's distinction between discourses of justification and application.[6] Arendt's notion of judgement with its distinction between spectators and political actors also speaks to the dual purpose of the communicative imperatives as an instrument of critique and of emancipatory practice. The relationship between the contextual application of moral norms and the activity of judging is key to the critique levelled against criteria for the use of force for humanitarian purposes. These hold out the possibility of generating an international consensus on substantive questions regarding the use of force but cannot provide a means to mediate between competing interpretations of when the criteria have been met. Communicative ethics recognises that no set of substantive criteria can determine what must ultimately remain a political judgement made by actors. Instead, communicative ethics offers a procedural account of legitimacy which can be applied by participants and spectators alike to decision-making processes and which derives its emancipatory and critical power from an understanding of the conditions under which communication may be distorted.

Formulating the communicative imperatives[7]

The closest Habermas comes to drawing up any form of criteria for dialogue are the presuppositions of argumentation and Robert Alexy's subsequent formulation of pragmatic rules for discourse which Habermas has accepted.[8] These criteria, Alexy argues, should be treated as fallible and he adds that they may, in practical discourses, only be approximately satisfied. Moreover, he indicates their two-fold use is first, as an 'instrument of criticism of unjustifi-

The communicative imperatives

able limitations of the rights and opportunities of discourse-partners' and second, as 'a way of defining an ideal which can be approached through practice and organizational arrangements'.[9] It is precisely this dual approach of critique and normative development that underpins the development of the communicative imperatives.

The communicative imperatives bring together a range of theoretical interventions in debates on communicative ethics. Despite their name, they are only imperative in the sense that they retain a normative orientation; they are not equivalent to rules of conduct or institutionalised practices. Cognisant of the pitfalls of this kind of exercise, the qualities that form the communicative imperatives are not all-or-nothing, but will occur to different degrees in communicative practices. Thus, the evaluation of communicative practices is both reflective and qualitative. Intended to guide and inform our interpretation and critique of particular communicative practices, the imperatives mapped out here advance an innovative and coherent theoretical framework applicable to the contested legitimacy of decisions to use force. Below, I set out the communicative imperatives.[10]

1. Maximising inclusion
2. Minimising coercion
3. Expanding dialogue
4. Maximising diversity
5. Coherence
6. Reflexivity
7. Recognition

Maximising inclusion

- Who is consulted? (Communities of interests, communities of place, non-state actors.)
- To what extent do smaller actors have an equal effective opportunity to participate and to be heard?
- To what degree can any interested party participate with equal rights?
- To what degree do participants in the dialogue have the ability to initiate discourse on any issue pertinent to the discussion? Conversely, how fixed are the parameters of the dialogue?
- How are actors included? (e.g. as observers, participants, how often are they consulted?)
- Are the interests of absent actors represented and if so, how?

Inclusion is a central theme within debates across IR. As has already been shown, the concepts of 'good international citizenship' and the 'responsibility to protect' are crucially concerned with practices of inclusion and its correlate, exclusion, as they relate to humanitarian intervention. The notion of inclusion resonates with themes emerging from a multiplicity of debates, including those concerned with democratic theory and deliberative democracy at national, regional and international levels; those which deal with the nature of legitimacy; those on critical international relations theory; feminism; and more widely, in discussions of justice, recognition, citizenship, minority politics and harm in political theory. It is the imperative through which the others are framed, and as such is arguably the crux of a communicative ethics framework: practices of inclusion and exclusion are central to other judgements relating to practices of reflexivity, recognition, coercion, diversity and so on. Habermas's emphasis on the merits of arguments rather than the identities of the speakers – which lies at the heart of his notion of the public sphere – is a direct challenge to practices which seek to exclude particular groups or individuals on the basis of their identity or beliefs.[11] Furthermore, the justification offered by Habermas for the inclusion of 'all affected' relates to the shift from the Kantian monological standard of right to an intersubjective standard of right which is embedded in his discourse ethics. Transposed to the international sphere, this requires us to reflect upon the barriers to participation raised against particular actors.

Questions regarding who is included or excluded are not solely derived from theoretical debates, but also become evident through the experiences of real people and groups. Crucially, they emerge in the form of immanent claims to legitimacy made by various political actors. Such claims, as will be seen in the case of Kosovo, include explicit reference to the nature and extent of participation claimed for a particular negotiation or forum. In making these claims, political actors set up standards against which they may be judged: through 'reflection and critique', actors can become aware of their limitations as set against their own standards.[12] The presence of such immanent claims will be explored in the empirical analysis undertaken in Chapter 6. The potential for assessment of inclusive or exclusive practices to originate from immanent critique is important for retaining links to the critical theoretical tradition as this addresses the relationship between theory and practice by leaving room for the reflection of the participant. Practices of inclusion and exclusion became pivotal to the decision-making process surrounding the decision to intervene militarily in Kosovo and thus serve to shape evaluations of legitimacy. This speaks to the vital question of who should be included in dialogue concerning the use of force. Is it legitimate to exclude particular actors and, if so, under what conditions, and who decides?

The communicative imperatives

Minimising coercion

- To what extent is there evidence of effective persuasion?
- Are there signs of cooperative behaviour which transcend short-term self interest?
- Can we identify instances of systematic compulsion, threat, coercion (direct or indirect), ideology or manipulation within dialogue?
- To what degree is there an equal means of control over decision-making procedures, the agenda, and decisions?

Different forms of coercion and manipulation may prevent or control access to dialogue, to shaping agendas, and making decisions. Deriving from a strategic orientation to action, forms of coercion may be more or less overt. Some forms of coercion may be linguistic, others ideological or structural, while still others may be material. The threat of force exercised by NATO during the Kosovo conflict is a more obvious example of coercion than some. James Fishkin offers an example of practices which involve the systematic exclusion of some racial or ethnic group through discrimination. Empirically, it is unlikely that such a practice would satisfy the condition of consensus as this would require support from those excluded as well those included. But, it is possible that such a consensus might be achieved through repressive means. The repression necessary to maintain such a consensus would violate the requirements of liberty for a self-reflective society. If, however, the subordinate group remains quiescent, obviating any need for overt acts of repression by the dominant group, then clearly this also violates the conditions for legitimacy as it no longer gives 'unimpeded and effective voice to the interests across every significant cleavage in the society'.[13]

In her concept of discursive discrimination, Kristina Boréus extends the notion of coercion as exclusion through her distinction between the exclusion of voices and invisibility making.[14] The former occurs when a group of people is excluded from participating in debates which affect them. This type of exclusion is a matter of degree: the voices of a particular group may be totally absent from any manifestations of a particular discourse which fail to refer to or elicit their opinion or perception of their own interests; the opinions of the group may be referred to but no more; or, on a higher level of inclusion, representatives may take part in the debate on their own initiative and, as much as possible in public discourse, on their own terms.[15] The latter type, invisibility making, refers not to the voiced opinions of a group being excluded, but to the consistent exclusion within multiple discourses of 'references to and images of group members'.[16] When voices are silenced, forcibly or otherwise, the conditions for legitimacy are not present. Recognising the potential role of ideology and political manipulation, Fishkin argues, 'The fact that the practice might conceivably be so successful that it robs the subordinate group of any desire to voice its interests is only an indication of how dramatically our conditions are violated.'[17]

Evident in both Alexy's pragmatic rules for discourse and Benhabib's principle of egalitarian reciprocity is a concern for forms of coercion which, directly or indirectly, close down space for dialogue by preventing discussion of particular topics or by limiting the scope for reflection on the presuppositions of the conversation and thereby exercising unjustified control over the agenda and the decision-making process. From a normative perspective, communicative ethics looks for the degree to which communicative practices are unconstrained and for evidence of persuasion and argumentative rationality rather than coercion or strategic self-interest.

Expanding dialogue

- If there is a failure to reach agreement, what happens? Do states enter into a different sort of communicative interaction where those norms and truth claims which are contested and problematic are treated as hypotheses requiring justification and defence? Or do states retreat to a more strategic orientation?
- To what degree are alternatives to strategic action discussed?
- To what extent is strategic action acknowledged and justified?
- When are communicative options exhausted? When have we reached the justification of force as last resort?

The focus here lies with the distinction which has recurred throughout the book between strategic and communicative action. Strategic rationality remains a dominant approach in social science and is embraced by, among others, rational choice theorists. Strategic rationality reflects a means–ends rationality, whereby objects and other individuals are related to instrumentally in terms of their relation to the goal.[18] Consequently, in strategic action 'one actor seeks to *influence* the behaviour of another by means of the threat of sanctions or the prospect of gratification in order to *cause* the interaction to continue as the first actor desires'.[19] Habermas's preoccupation has been to demonstrate the inadequacy of strategic rationality as an exclusive mode of reasoning and the threat it poses to the potential flourishing of human beings.[20] His shift in focus to the concept of communicative action sought to demonstrate a sense of rationality which cannot be reduced to strategic dimensions. Habermas writes:

> In contexts of communicative action, we call someone rational not only if he is able to put forward an assertion and, when criticized, to provide grounds for it by pointing to appropriate evidence, but also if he is following an established norm and is able when criticized, to justify his action by explicating the given situation in the light of legitimate expectations.[21]

The communicative imperatives

Whilst the distinction between strategic and communicative action is a valuable analytic one, it is not, in reality, so easy to label actors' orientations as either strategic or communicative. I have retained the distinction which is integral to Habermas's ideal speech situation because it offers a degree of critical leverage concerning communicative practices. Like the ideal speech situation, these distinctions cannot be mapped directly onto practice; instead they help, as Ricardo Blaug argues, to 'train our eyes'.[22] This tension between the ideal and the real becomes unavoidable when we move to the empirical realm. Further uncertainty was revealed in Chapter 3 through the idea of the 'language of manoeuvre' whereby language is used to mask particular interests or strategic positions. A willingness to engage in dialogue leaves unanswered the question to what degree *both* communicative and strategic orientations may be present in the practices of individual actors.

The justification of last resort, so central to the claims raised to justify the use of force in Kosovo, embodies this tension between rationalities. As discussed in Chapter 2, there was extensive disagreement among Council members over whether dialogue had been exhausted and the use of military force was the only option to stop the humanitarian crisis. It is difficult to ascertain whether states on either side of the fence of 'last resort' were acting *either* strategically *or* communicatively in the Habermasian sense of the term. At one level, the fact that actors feel the need to give a justification for their actions to their peers in the Security Council demonstrates that language and justification are critically important. It may also lead to the Skinnerian conclusion that this 'need to legitimate' constrains actors in their actions. However, this recourse to justification does not make it easier for other participants or spectators to evaluate the nature of their communicative practices. Recognising the potential presence of *both* orientations, we still want to be able to exercise a degree of critical leverage – derived in part from the validity claims intrinsic to Habermas's conception of genuine communication – over the communicative practices adopted. This is secured by applying the communicative imperatives to interrogate the communicative practices adopted by actors through which claims to legitimacy are voiced.

Maximising diversity

- To what degree do public sphere opinion-forming media (e.g. the media) reflect and support official government policy as opposed to serving as an independent vehicle for discourse and the expression of differences?
- To what degree are dominant discourses reinforced through the use of interpretive communities (legal or humanitarian)?
- To what extent are there noticeable polarisations of identity?
- Which is given preference in dialogue: hermeneutic understanding or universal consensus?

Communicative ethics and the use of force

The importance of diversity relates to the need for an active, functioning public sphere, whereby a plurality of opinions and voices can be heard. This speaks to Habermas's concern over the nature of critical public debate as the principle of the public sphere.[23] The public sphere is intended to be 'a site for the production and circulation of discourses that can in principle be critical of the state'.[24] More recently, Habermas has written that 'Mediated political communication in the public sphere can facilitate deliberative legitimation processes in complex societies only if a self-regulating media system gains independence from its social environments.'[25] This raises questions concerning the role that the media played in the public debate over intervention in Kosovo.

The imperative picks up on patterns of behaviour whereby particular discourses or voices become dominant and, in relation to the other imperatives of inclusion, coercion, and recognition, seeks to reveal and understand these dynamics and their implications for enabling or constraining particular courses of action or justification. It is relevant for the critique of the justification of last resort in relation to Kosovo because it indicates how dominant discourses such as humanitarianism or international law may be drawn upon to enable or constrain particular justifications. As is the case with other strategic positions, this is not to say that last resort cannot be justified and may not be judged as the morally right outcome by a legitimate communicative process, but that we must be aware of the potential effect of such dominant discourses on the justificatory process.

The tension apparent in the structures of international society between the possibility for a hermeneutic understanding and the need for consensus reflects the theoretical debates surrounding Habermas's principle (U) and hermeneutics. It indicates both the challenges posed by the organising principles underpinning international society and the potential for alternative principles to emerge. While communicative ethics encourages interpretive reason, which Michael Saward defines as 'the acceptance of the inevitability of pluralism and "the undecidability and inconclusiveness of all interpretation"', order (and action) within international society calls for legislative reason which involves the 'philosopher's untrammelled "licence to judge" and to impose'.[26] It is, after all, consensus which is most frequently sought after in fora such as the Security Council. At stake here are concerns which ask what kind of consensus or agreement is appropriate to justify the use of force? How should disagreement among states be managed? While the pragmatic demands of international politics should not be ignored, the communicative imperatives seek to highlight and cultivate alternative ways of thinking about political engagement. Central to their purpose is a desire to avoid falling into the reifying trap of necessity as sufficient justification.

The communicative imperatives

Coherence

- Are the same norms always offered in argument or do evolving norms gain acceptance?
- To what extent is there coherence between the actions of states and their words?
- To what extent do actors present consistent arguments?
- Are arguments presented consistent with both the validity claims they raise and the norms which shape them?
- Are norms and exceptions to norms applied coherently?

The relationship between legitimacy and coherence is one of mutual dependence. Institutions which fail to apply their own rules consistently or coherently erode their legitimacy. Thus, the introduction of inconsistent and unjustified application of rules not only undermines the credibility and legitimacy of the institution, but also the perceived legitimacy of the rule itself.[27] Thomas Franck introduced a distinction between consistency and coherence, arguing that 'consistency requires that "likes be treated alike" while coherence requires that distinctions in the treatment of "likes" be *justifiable in principled terms*'.[28] In a book concerned with the legitimacy of the language of justification, however, there is a need to supplement this definition of consistency and coherence. Two, related, aspects of coherence suggest themselves.

The first, as outlined above, relates to the degree to which justifications for the application of rules and norms to a particular situation correspond to the justifications for the application of rules and norms to other similar situations and, if they do not, how persuasive an argument is made to uphold such differing treatment.[29] This reflects a broader concern with issues such as the coherent application of the principle of self-determination or the use of force for humanitarian purposes across a number of different cases. In order to persuade others of a coherent interpretation and application of a rule, then states must present rational justifications for a particular course of action. However, this should be supplemented by the means to analyse the validity claims raised by states when offering justifications for their positions and actions. Thus, Franck's argument benefits from explicit attention to a more internal understanding of coherence which relates to the nature of communicative practices, and the degree to which they are accepted intersubjectively free from coercion. This requirement of coherence is implied by Habermas's formal-pragmatic rules. Here, coherence also refers to the consistency between actors' words and their actions and the degree of sincerity, comprehensibility, and truth present within communicative practices. This will be seen over Kosovo in the manner in which states accepted or challenged particular validity claims and the degree to which their words were matched by their actions.

Reflexivity

- To what degree is there evidence of reflexivity concerning the construction of negotiations?
- To what degree do actors acknowledge error or fallibility?
- How far do states recognise or acknowledge their own explicit or implicit historical involvement in conflict environments?
- Are compromises reached? If so, to what degree are the relevant trade-offs acknowledged and discursively redeemed?

Reflexive practice is embedded in critical theoretical approaches, not least in the self-conscious relationship between theory and practice.[30] Reflexivity is the 'process by which people [and groups] observe themselves engage in their own interactions'.[31] Accepting that the Security Council is a central forum for deliberation for many divisive issues in world politics, it is crucial that an ability to recognise aspects of illegitimacy within its decision-making procedures is available. This requires a process of reflection about the nature of legitimacy and the quality of the communicative practices whereby legitimacy is claimed. Thus, reflexivity refers to an awareness of the procedures in place within institutions or particular negotiations which guide decision-making processes, of the implications of such procedures for a variety of actors, and of the character of actors' own communicative practices. It also requires an awareness of the trade-offs – which acknowledges both theoretically and empirically the unavoidable presence of strategic action in international politics – taking place when compromises are reached and how these may affect individual actors.

Through the development of communicative ethics a relationship has been identified between assessing the legitimacy of justifications for the use of force and the ability to be reflexive or to recognise fallibility. A legitimate communicative practice or consensus can only remain legitimate if two factors are present: first, there should exist a continuing openness to criticism, and secondly, the possibility of further debate leading to a new consensus or practice. In light of the critiques of Habermas set out in Chapter 4, it is worth reiterating that this notion of consensus need only be procedural. It may, for example, be a consensus specifying agreement on how to disagree, but also, given those disagreements, how each side must be given an appropriate hearing to resolve disputes.[32] Such procedures for managing disagreement exist to a degree in the Security Council, although states tend not to prioritise reflexivity regarding the relationship between legitimacy and the communicative practices through which they engage in decision-making processes.

Recognition

- To what degree are certain values/identities publicly set up as the 'right'?
- To what extent do actors seek to understand other perspectives beyond their own viewpoint?
- To what extent do participants in dialogue acknowledge their situated positions?
- To what extent do different types of voice/speech receive equal opportunities to participate and be heard?

Acknowledgement of the perspectives of others' and one's own situated position is necessary for the reciprocal recognition central to the formulation of communicative ethics.[33] A strong link also exists between coercion and its implications for discrimination and exclusion, and the importance of recognition. Boréus acknowledges this link when she argues that underrepresentation, inherent in the notion of invisibility making, constitutes unfavourable treatment and has social and political implications. This is because of a 'strong social and psychological need to be seen: it is a kind of recognition and confirmation. To be made invisible can be seen as unfavourable treatment, since it frustrates that need.'[34]

In his seminal work on recognition, Axel Honneth provides further theoretical justification of its importance to justice and morality.[35] Acknowledging that justice requires more than merely the fair distribution of material goods, claims concerning recognition, inclusion, exclusion and harm imply normative judgements about the legitimacy of social arrangements. Honneth's work on recognition is important for two main reasons. First, it reinforces the case for a communicative ethics which is sensitive to difference. Second, it allows us to develop a clearer understanding of inclusion and exclusion and the implications of this for the individual which is relevant for practices of exclusion in the international sphere. If human self-realisation is the end for recognition, then self-realisation is enabled by three conditions, or patterns of recognition: self-confidence, self-respect, and self-esteem, other-wise referred to as love ('relations of love and friendship'), rights ('legally institutionalized relations of universal respect for the autonomy and dignity of persons'), and solidarity ('networks of solidarity and shared values within which the particular worth of the individual members of a community can be acknowledged') respectively.[36] These aspects of a positive relation-to-self are gained through the experience of recognition which can only be acquired through interaction with others. If denied this recognition due to exclusion from social groups, legal rights or status, then the individual faces a form of coercion which prevents recognition or identity-formation. Should a person (or groups of persons) be 'systematically denied certain rights ... this would imply that he or she is not being accorded the same degree of moral responsibility as other members of society'.[37]

The link between recognition and potential harm is taken up in Linklater's harm principle intrinsic to his later concept of good international citizenship and cosmopolitan harm conventions. Linklater observes that 'indifference harms the self-respect of the vulnerable by forcing them to conclude that they have no claims against communities which can alleviate their misery without much cost to themselves'.[38] Denial and the resulting hurt or harm rests, however, as indeed does mutual esteem, on the perceived existence of a shared, or intersubjective, interpretation of normative expectations and values within a society which amount to recognition and enable self-realisation. This intersubjective awareness of values and moral expectations is arrived at through a communicative process. The absence of these conditions can cause 'harm' when it is understood in material and psychological terms for both individuals and groups. Narratives of recognition are integral to experiences of exclusion, marginalisation, and control over the agenda.[39] Consequently, what kinds of actors receive recognition in the international sphere? What impact does 'indifference' or a legal lack of recognition have on actors within conflict situations and, by extension, on conflict resolution processes? If key actors in conflict resolution processes are not granted recognition what impact, if any, does this have on the legitimacy of justifications for the use of force in cases such as Kosovo? These factors are all pertinent to an evaluation of the claims to legitimacy for the use of force in Kosovo.

On using the communicative imperatives: problems between theory and practice

There is a long roll-call of theorists who have lamented the apparent disjuncture between Habermasian theory and practice. The difficulties of constructing a Habermasian politics and the dangers of conflating the distinction (which Habermas insists upon) between normative grounds for legitimation and institutional design are well documented.[40] It is, nonetheless, inevitable that questions of ideal democratic practices, institutional arrangements and substantive political goods arise despite an awareness of the pitfalls of too literal a translation or transposition from theory to practice, or what Albrecht Wellmer has called a 'short-cut'.[41]

The communicative imperatives reflect the practical intentions of critical theory in three ways. First, the framework identifies a set of issues and structures which operate as mechanisms of repression and domination.[42] The issues identified in this context centre on the character of communicative practices and the legitimacy of justificatory processes, while the structural factors relate to the regulative role and composition of the UN Security Council, the structure of the state and the international system, ideology, and institutions of sovereignty and international law. The communicative imperatives which serve as the practical face of a communicative ethics approach offer insights into the presence and function of these mechanisms.

Second, this has an educative role as it reveals illegitimate practice to social actors, specifically, those actors whose interests are affected by decisions taken within a community or society. Critical theory is not used by an expert in order to impose policy and so manipulate social conditions to reach a particular pre-determined goal, but rather 'to enlighten the social actors so that, coming to see themselves and their social situation in a new way, they themselves can decide to alter the conditions which they find repressive'.[43] Third, the framework offers a means of social change or emancipation in the tradition of critical theory through the possibility of acting as a catalyst for change which remains situated and dialogic. Such change cannot be implemented as a set of external or abstract laws, or imposed, as the nature of critical theory demands that it is interpretive and intersubjective. For this reason, critical social theory 'is not divorced from social practice in the sense of being set over and against it as a blueprint to be followed: here, the objects of the theory actually become subjects of it, which is to say, they help to fashion it by their own choices and actions, and by their responses to it'.[44] This is an important conceptual and methodological perspective because a static blueprint does not allow for communication or reflexivity which in critical theory remains an intersubjective and continuous process. Fay strongly defends the intrinsic and constitutive link between critical theory and practice, calling for recognition of the 'self-conscious integration of theory and practice' as critical theory's central core[45] and it is in this sense that the communicative imperatives seek to be understood. Echoing earlier debates, it is through this self-conscious position that communicative ethics draws together the critical and sociological aspects of Habermasian critical theory.

Any normative theoretical approach incurs the danger of becoming prescriptive when attempts are made to apply it in practice. E. H. Carr captured the utopian dilemma when he recognised that idealist principles will always become tainted with self-interest and power when they become embedded in political practice and institutions. They will, therefore, once again need to be subjected to realist critique.[46] Once an ideal has been institutionalised it ceases to be an ideal and instead becomes the expression of vested interests. While Carr suggested this is due to the impossibility of ultimately reconciling power and morality, Blaug has argued that the difficulties faced by the application of theory to practice are related to the 'profound ambivalence regarding the relation of meta-theory to substantive political questions'.[47] Blaug suggests that critical theorists are faced with a problem that is inherent in any theoretical account which attempts to address the issue of universalist ethics. He writes,

Wanting to provide images of emancipation yet at the same time fearing the coercive power of utopianism, they are left to squeeze themselves into the middle ground, where their knowledge of the consequences of utopianism prevents them from acting and where their awareness of the suffering in the world only serves to make them miserable.[48]

In response to charges that critical theory in general, and Habermas in particular, run the risk of moving into authoritarian territory, Fay argues for the distinction between the instrumentalist potential in critical theory and the instrumentalism intrinsic to positivist models of social science. The relationship between critical theory and practice should be placed within an intersubjective communicative model which goes a long way to remove the authoritarian strains visible in other models: 'according to the critical model there must exist a constant critical interchange between the policy expert and the actors who will be affected by his decisions'.[49] Not only must they be consulted in the first instance, but they must continue to be consulted, as policy effectiveness can only be judged by the social actors concerned.[50] This brings to the fore the concepts of reflexivity and fallibility which are part of the communicative imperatives.

The distinction between procedure and substantive content that Habermas makes explicit in order to limit the use of theory and prevent its use in a more prescriptive and authoritarian manner also resonates throughout the communicative imperatives. The transformation of consciousness necessary for social change cannot be dictated from above in a vanguardist fashion, but must originate with the participants. Any move to alter structural constraints, institutional composition or institutional practices must develop with the approval of the participants themselves. The framework can only offer guidelines which might allow communicative practices to be engaged in in a manner approximating Habermas's ideal notion of speech. The latter cannot be imposed, only offered as a regulative ideal with the intention of removing certain of the injustices and unfair procedures revealed by a close inspection of existing practice.

The messy practicalities of real politics indicate that finding a situation which maps perfectly onto Habermas's theoretical model is very unlikely. Instead, we must find procedurally acceptable trade-offs which allow us to act without losing all normative grounding. The significance of the need for an awareness of such trade offs is perhaps clearest when we consider the questions raised by the imperative of inclusion. Following Habermas, participation in deliberation should extend to all those who are affected. In practice, this is rarely, if ever, reflected in actual dialogue. Instead, we must ask how we can conceive procedures within international deliberations to be as fair as possible and remain as close as possible to the deliberative core of the normative ideal. If the necessity of trading off levels of inclusion for practical purposes such as efficiency is accepted, then the question is *how* those exclusions are defended and *who* has decided who should be excluded. This is a question that remains essential for a communicative dimension of legitimacy in international politics and reiterates key issues not only about the kinds of actors who may or may not be included in conflict resolution processes but how their exclusion might be justified and discursively redeemed.

Judgement beckons? From justification to application

In tandem with the theoretical difficulties of Habermas's universalism are the problems incurred in the moment of application. The previous discussion on the relationship between theory and practice demonstrates the need for an awareness of how the communicative imperatives might be applied to practice. Hegel's powerful critique of Kantian universalism raises difficulties for any framework which takes its inspiration from Habermas's theory of communicative action, given the universalist and formal nature of discourse ethics and the debate this has generated over the distinction between justification and application.[51] Central to the debate is how a general law may be applied to a particular situation. The ability to determine the appropriate application of a universal law implies that 'some sort of judging faculty is required'.[52] In light of this, Habermas has offered a distinction between Kantian morality and his own.[53] He recognises that

> Practical reason cannot bring itself into force merely through foundational discourses alone. In the process of grounding norms practical reason expresses itself in the principle of universalization, whereas in the application of norms it appears in the form of a principle of appropriateness.[54]

However, Habermas does not make a substantial leap towards relativism with this acknowledgement, as he argues that even in discourses of application, 'we must rely on grounds which are valid not only for you or me, but in principle for everyone'.[55] A procedure which requires sensitivity to context does not need to be 'itself context-dependent and lead to context-dependent results'.[56] By limiting himself to a procedural ethics, Habermas deliberately maintains a space for dialogue between participants which is the only way to determine content.[57]

Habermas has argued that the discourse of justification should be perceived as separate from that of the discourse of application and that both are needed in order to apply norms to actual contexts. This separation has been criticised on the grounds that situations requiring the exercise of moral sense confront everyone who must then decide how best to act.[58] Habermas's strong emphasis on consensus and universalisability renders judgement determinant and impartial, thus failing to recognise real differences between individuals.[59] Further criticism of Habermas's conception of judgement concerns the apparent difficulty of achieving consensus in collective deliberation either as a result of the increasing plurality of value-perspectives or because of the cognitive demands made on participants.[60] Blaug refers to the difficulties of meeting the requirements of (U), particularly when confronted with conflicting norms and the need to justify exceptions, as 'cognitive overload'.[61] Although abandoning (U) threatens to withdraw critical leverage, it still leaves us with the validity of the process and the ideal of procedural fairness. Benhabib argues that rejecting (U) enables a consideration of the validity of moral judgement in terms of the presuppositions of fairness. By retaining the inescapable presuppositions of argumentation, she argues, a cognitive aspect of judgement is retained and thus validity can be communicatively defended: the crux of communicative ethics.[62]

The kind of judgement appropriate to a communicative ethics is, it is suggested, Hannah Arendt's reflective judgement and its correlate requirement of 'enlarged thinking'. Reflective judgement was one of two forms of judgement developed by Kant, with the other being determinate. Determinate judgement examines when and how universal principles are applicable to any set of particulars (the source of Hegel's critique of Kant), whereas the former, developed as part of Kant's work on aesthetics, looks for the universal within the particular and demands that we think for ourselves. Arendt's interpretation and use of reflective judgement diverges from Kant's own. Kant's restriction of judgement to the aesthetic sphere was insufficient for Arendt who saw judgement as relevant to political action because she argued that both aesthetic and moral validity are expressed through reflective as opposed to determinant judgement. They cannot produce universal or final, abstract truth claims.[63] In Kant's doctrine, Arendt discovered a 'procedure for ascertaining intersubjective validity in the public realm. This kind of intersubjective validity clearly transcended the expression of simple preference while falling short of the a priori and certain validity demanded by Kantian reason.'[64] Intersubjective validity, according to Arendt, means the idea that common consent must be won or 'wooed' and is not simply provided by a shared background of understandings. In Arendt's words, which are worth quoting at length, this enlarged way of thinking is defined as follows:

> I form an opinion by considering a given issue from different viewpoints, by making present to my mind the standpoints of those who are absent; that is, I represent them. This process of representation does not blindly adopt the actual views of those who stand somewhere else, and hence look upon the world from a different perspective; this is a question neither of empathy, as though I tried to be or to feel like somebody else, nor of counting noses and joining a majority but of being and thinking in my own identity where actually I am not. The more people's standpoints I have present in my mind while I am pondering a given issue, and the

better I can imagine how I would feel and think if I were in their place, the stronger will be my capacity for representative thinking and the more valid my final conclusions, my opinion.[65]

Representative thinking, as Arendt describes it above, as the basis for judgement indicates the need for related capacities, namely, imagination – imagining what it would be like to be somewhere else – and the consequent requirement for the exercise of imagination, disinterestedness, in other words 'the liberation from one's own private interests'.[66] Habermas implicitly touches upon these concepts to some degree in the discourse ethical requirements contained in (U) and (D).[67] Like discourse ethics, representative thinking can only be done in the public sphere where opinions can be exchanged and reformed, and other standpoints examined. While Habermas's concept of justice implies that moral motivation is drawn from reason rather than from moral feelings, he nevertheless acknowledges the role of moral feelings in constituting moral phenomena as 'feelings provide the basis for our *perception* of something as a moral issue'.[68] Moral feelings also provide the basis for the judgement of individual cases (application of moral norms), as they 'build the experiential basis for our first intuitive judgements', for example, 'pain and the sense of injury for our reproaches against another person who has harmed us'.[69] Lastly, they serve to aid in the grounding of moral norms through discourse as:

> Empathy ... the capacity to transport oneself by means of feeling across cultural distance into alien and *prima facie* incomprehensible life conditions, patterns of reaction, and interpretive perspectives – is an emotional precondition for the ideal taking over of roles, which requires each person to adopt the standpoint of all the others.[70]

This shift in the understanding of judgement might be viewed as the move from Kant's precept, 'Act in such a way that the maxim of your actions can always be a universal law of nature' to Arendt's reformulation, 'Act in such a way that the maxim of your actions takes into account the perspective of everyone else in such a way that you would be in a position to "woo their consent".'[71] This shifts the balance closer to a hermeneutic and context-sensitive approach central to communicative ethics. In other words, consent is still required, but it is no longer the consent required by Habermas's (U).

It is important to be aware of who is doing the judging. Agency remains ambivalent in Arendt's writings: judgement belongs to both the political actor and the spectator at times.[72] The judgement of political actors is a function of representative thinking, whereas the latter is exercised retrospectively by the spectator who 'does not leave the world of appearances but retires from active involvement in it to a privileged position in order to contemplate the whole'.[73] Both models share the faculties of communicability, imagination, intersubjectivity and representative thought and so Arendt's ambivalence serves us well. This dual aspect of judgement appears most clearly in Arendt's writings on Eichmann. First of all, she identifies Eichmann's own inability to think or to judge, to tell right from wrong. Second, she asks 'How should we judge the meaning of Eichmann from a vantage point temporally and spatially removed from the events in question?'[74] This duality of judgement pervades IR as well, both as the very real concern of the political actor and the responsibility of the spectator as 'storyteller', analyst, historian or journalist.[75] This resonates with the dual purposes of a communicative ethics framework which is intended as both an instrument of critique and potentially able to inform political action. The difficulties faced by participants in concrete contexts indicate the indeterminacy of abstract principles[76] and the need for an understanding of judgement in order to engage in the complex evaluations, trade-offs and comparisons present in everyday contexts. Nowhere is this more evident than in the complex demands placed on states and their political representatives in the international sphere. The disagreement over the right way to respond to the conflict in Kosovo demonstrated the indeterminacy of international law; the response of the international community to the conflict indicated the difficulties of maintaining coherent and consistent policies; and the nature of the conflict required careful evaluations of validity claims, moral and legal evaluations of the role of the combatants and their justifications for fighting, and judgements concerning the appropriate forms of dialogue, negotiation, and diplomacy to end the violence. As Benhabib notes, 'both moral sagacity and strategic-political savvy would be involved in the application of communicative ethics to life contexts'.[77]

It is widely acknowledged that decision-making procedures and institutional arrangements must be examined for their relative fairness. This is crucial for communicative ethics as such procedures must be as fair as we can make them. The communicative imperatives constitute a recognition of this relationship between legitimacy and fairness. This, as Blaug argues, is the same as saying 'they should be as fair as we are here and now able to see. Such judgements are reflective, for they inspect particulars for their exemplification of the ideal of communicative fairness.'[78] However, this actual judgement by participants of validity or comparative validity is akin to recognising 'family resemblances between fair and unfair procedures'[79] rather than a direct comparison with Habermas's ideal of undistorted communication which would inevitably indicate a failure to meet the required standards. It is an appropriate means with which to approach a conflict such as Kosovo where the way in which the problem is described is 'both crucial and contentious'[80] and where we confront what appear to be conflicting interpretations of established norms and must find some way to assess the legitimacy of competing claims. The empirical analysis of the deliberations surrounding Kosovo, therefore, is undertaken in the spirit of reflective judgement. Whilst this particular analysis is undertaken from the critical perspective of the spectator, in Arendt's terms, there is nothing within the communicative imperatives or the accompanying approach to judgement which prevents political actors engaging in similar exercises of critique or judgement.

Conclusion

The discussion of the relationship between theory and practice and the limits to theory demonstrate that communicative ethics cannot remove the reality of structural factors which impose power inequalities on actors in international politics and impact upon communicative capacities and practices. It can, however, enable the recognition of power differences and also potentially reduce such differentials through being able to challenge claims to legitimacy and the validity claims they raise.[81] Suggesting that reflective judgement is appropriate for a communicative ethics recognises the need for both actors and spectators to engage in political judgement. Thus, when mediated through the lens of reflective judgement, the communicative imperatives offer some guidance to those participants engaged in political action. Similarly, a communicative ethics approach can inform the *ex post* evaluation of existing practices by spectators.[82]

Habermas is well aware of the limitations of theory; while he confirms that his theory can offer a valid, normative, ground for social criticism, he is also clear that the theoretical principles which constitute discourse ethics are insufficient, by themselves, to determine which outcomes are morally right or wrong. At its core, the communicative imperatives are no more able to determine, without the input of participants, which outcomes may be morally right or wrong because that is not their purpose. Instead, a communicative ethics approach seeks to establish that legitimate justifications for the use of force have, *per force*, a communicative component, as well as the legal and moral elements which more frequently frame debates on the legitimacy of military action. It cannot establish whether or not the military intervention in Kosovo was morally right or wrong: that remains a matter for the moral and political judgement of participants and spectators. When applied by a lone spectator, the communicative imperatives can only evaluate the nature of the communicative practices which were central to the claim that the use of force in the case of Kosovo was legitimate. In so doing, they can reveal moments of distortion in communicative practices which may undermine the claim to legitimacy. The ability to identify different forms of constraints on practical discourse offers access to a powerful account of legitimacy. Having interpreted Habermas's model of discourse as a principle of legitimacy rather than a concrete institutional design, it is clear that practical political dialogues and

Communicative ethics and the use of force

debates take place under a variety of conditions and constraints. The framework developed from Habermasian ideas offers possible criteria for deciding which constraints are legitimate in international politics and which are not.[83] Such a theoretical perspective seeks to foster real spaces for deliberation and negotiation which offer political alternatives to strategic action in situations of conflict which are precluded by the traditional paradigms of IR. With this in mind I turn to the justifications for the use of force in Kosovo to explore what the critical interpretive power of the communicative imperatives can reveal about communicative practices and consequent claims to legitimacy.

NOTES

1 J. Habermas, 'Discourse Ethics: Notes on a Program of Philosophical Justification', *MCCA*, 48.
2 S. O'Neill, 'Struggles Against Injustice: Contemporary Critical Theory and Political Violence', *Journal of Global Ethics*, 6:2 (2010), 127.
3 D. Beetham, *Auditing Democracy in Britain* (London: The Charter 88 Trust, 1993), 6.
4 Habermas, *TCA*, vol. 1, 334.
5 Fishkin, *The Dialogue of Justice*, 123.
6 See Benhabib on the relationship between communicative ethics and reflective judgement in 'Afterword: Communicative Ethics and Current Controversies in Practical Philosophy', in Benhabib and Dallmayr (eds), *The Communicative Ethics Controversy*, 360–4.
7 Other approaches which consider the quality of argumentation have been articulated by Fishkin, *The Dialogue of Justice*, 124; Janssen and Kies, 'Online Forums and Deliberative Democracy'; Risse, 'Let's Argue!', 18–19; Bjola, *Legitimising the Use of Force in International Politics*.
8 Habermas, *MCCA*, 88; R. Alexy, *A Theory of Legal Argumentation* (trans. Ruth Adler and Neil MacCormick) (Oxford: Clarendon Press, 1989), 193. These rules correspond to the conditions identified by Habermas for the 'ideal speech situation': 1. Every subject with the competence to speak and act is allowed to take part in a discourse. 2. a. Everyone is allowed to question any assertion whatever. b. Everyone is allowed to introduce any assertion whatever into the discourse. c. Everyone is allowed to express his attitudes, desires, and needs. 3. No speaker may be prevented, by internal or external coercion, from exercising his rights as laid down in [1] and [2]. Alexy's following rules reflect the validity claims of truth [1.1], sincerity [1.2], consistency of the speaker [1.3], and communality of linguistic usage [1.4]: 1.1 No speaker may contradict himself; 1.2 Each speaker may only assert what he himself believes; 1.3 Every speaker who applies predicate F to object A must be prepared to apply F to all other objects resembling A in all relevant aspects; 1.4 Different speakers may not use the same expression with different meanings. See R. Alexy, 'A Theory of Practical Discourse', in Benhabib and Dallmayr (eds), *The Communicative Ethics Controversy*, 163–4.
9 Alexy, *A Theory of Legal Argumentation*, 194. Original emphasis.
10 I am indebted to Ricardo Blaug for coining this term.
11 See Calhoun (ed.), *Habermas and the Public Sphere*.
12 Held, *Introduction to Critical Theory*, 185.
13 Fishkin, *The Dialogue of Justice*, 134.
14 Boréus, 'Discursive Discrimination'. She defines discursive discrimination as discrimina-

tion carried out through the use of language and distinguishes between four main forms: 1) negative other-presentation; 2) exclusion; 3) proposals pointing towards non-linguistic unfavourable treatment; and 4) discriminatory objectification (405–9, 413).
15 Ibid., 414.
16 Ibid., 415. Citing Jane Mansbridge, Nancy Fraser makes a similar point when she acknowledges that 'Even the language people use as they reason together usually favours one way of seeing things and discourages others. Subordinate groups sometimes cannot find the right voice or words to express their thoughts, and when they do, they discover they are not heard.' Although not formal exclusions, these forms of silencing extend beyond gender relations to include class, ethnicity and other unequal social relations. In so doing, she draws attention to the fact that deliberation can mask subtle forms of coercion and domination. Fraser, 'Rethinking the Public Sphere', 119.
17 Fishkin, *The Dialogue of Justice*, 134.
18 White, *The recent work of Jürgen Habermas*, 10. White adds that most rational choice theorists do not require the assumption of self-interested motivation. There is no necessary reason why other motivational assumptions, including moral ones, cannot also be employed (10–11).
19 Habermas, *MCCA*, 58. Original emphasis.
20 See White, *The Recent Work of Jürgen Habermas*, Chapter 2; Habermas, *Knowledge and Human Interests*; T. Adorno and M. Horkheimer, *Dialectic of Enlightenment* (London: Verso, 1979).
21 Habermas, cited in White, *The Recent Work of Jürgen Habermas*, 28.
22 Blaug, *Democracy: Real and Ideal*, 111.
23 Calhoun (ed.), *Habermas and the Public Sphere*, 21.
24 Fraser, 'Rethinking the Public Sphere', 110.
25 J. Habermas, 'Political Communication in Media Society: Does Democracy Still Enjoy an Epistemic Dimension? The Impact of Normative Theory on Empirical Research', *Communication Theory*, 16 (2006) 411–12.
26 M. Saward, 'Enacting Democracy', *Political Studies*, 51 (2003), 161.
27 Franck, *The Power of Legitimacy Among Nations*, 142.
28 Ibid., 144. Original emphasis. The latter fits with Franck's argument concerning mitigation in international law to address the issue of uses of force that are illegal but justifiable. Mitigating circumstances, as in the case of Kosovo, breach the gap between the law and a common sense of moral justice (Franck, *Recourse to Force*, 177–91). Franck's definition of coherence – that *principled justifications should be offered* when like cases are treated inconsistently – rebuts Michael Ignatieff's critique of the relationship between consistency and legitimacy. Ignatieff argues: 'perfect consistency is a test of legitimacy that political action can never meet, and hence the prerequisite of consistency serves (even if it does not intend to) either as a justification for doing nothing or as a condemnation of any intervention actually undertaken'. M. Ignatieff, 'Human Rights, Power and the State', in S. Chesterman, M. Ignatieff and R. Thakur (eds), *Making States Work* (Tokyo: United Nations University Press, 2005), 60. Thanks to Nick Wheeler for bringing this to my attention.
29 Franck, *The Power of Legitimacy Among Nations*, 153.
30 For example, J. Habermas, 'Some Clarifications of the Concept of Communicative Rationality', in M. Cooke (ed.), *On the Pragmatics of Communication* (Cambridge, MA: MIT Press, 2000), 310.
31 J. Rothman, *From Confrontation to Cooperation: Resolving Ethnic and Regional Conflict* (London: Sage, 1992), 59.

32 Fishkin, *The Dialogue of Justice*, 127.
33 This can be seen in Benhabib's 'interactive universalism' (*Situating the Self*), in Habermas's 'ideal role taking' (*Justification and Application*, 52), and in Gadamerian hermeneutics (*Truth and Method*).
34 Boréus, 'Discursive Discrimination', 415.
35 A. Honneth, *The Struggle for Recognition: The Moral Grammar of Social Conflicts* (trans. Joel Anderson) (Cambridge: Polity Press, 1995).
36 Ibid., xii.
37 Ibid., 133; C. Taylor, 'The Politics of Recognition', in C. Taylor and A. Gutman (eds), *Multiculturalism* (Princeton: Princeton University Press, 1994).
38 Linklater and Suganami, *The English School*, 252–3.
39 For a discussion of the narrative of recognition in the context of the Oslo Peace Accords, see Lloyd Jones, *Cosmopolitan Mediation?*, 130–40.
40 Blaug, *Democracy: Real and Ideal*, J. S. Dryzek, 'Discursive Designs: Critical Theory and Political Institutions', *American Journal of Political Science*, 31:3 (1987), 656–79; J. S. Dryzek, *Discursive Democracy*; A. Wellmer: 'Practical Philosophy and the Theory of Society: On the Problem of the Normative Foundations of a Critical Social Science', in Benhabib and Dallmayr (eds), *The Communicative Ethics Controversy*; Benhabib, *Situating the Self*; Fraser, 'Rethinking the Public Sphere'.
41 Cited in Blaug, *Democracy: Real and Ideal*, 65. The idea of a short-cut is the attempt to 'overextend theory, to move too quickly from normative to empirical matters and thus to be excessively utopian in one's institutional designs'.
42 B. Fay, *Social Theory and Political Practice* (London: George Allen & Unwin Ltd, 1975), 104.
43 Ibid., 103. See also J. Habermas, 'An Avantgardistic Instinct for Relevances: The Role of the Intellectual and the European Cause', in Habermas, *Europe: The Faltering Project*; B. Fay, 'How People Change Themselves', in T. Ball (ed.), *Political Theory and Praxis: New Perspectives* (Minneapolis: University of Minnesota Press, 1977); B. Manin, 'On Legitimacy and Political Deliberation', *Political Theory*, 15:3 (1987), 354.
44 Fay, *Social Theory and Political Practice*, 109; Blaug, *Democracy: Real and Ideal*, 36. Blaug argues that the practical intentions of Habermas's theory should be conceived along 'critical-hermeneutic lines': 'Normative theory should help us understand our social world, to penetrate beyond its mere appearances and reveal its hidden structures. Theory should change minds, train eyes, exert a pressure on our intuitions, and help us reclaim our individual and collective authorship of the social world; thus moving us closer to living the lives we wish to live.'
45 Fay, *Social Theory and Political Practice*, 109.
46 Carr, *The Twenty Years' Crisis*, 118.
47 R. Blaug, 'Between Fear and Disappointment: Critical, Empirical and Political Uses of Habermas', *Political Studies*, 45:1 (1997), 112. It is worth noting that some IR theorists have engaged with Habermasian theory with a practical intent. For example, M. Hoffman, 'Third-Party Mediation and Conflict Resolution in the Post-Cold War World', in J. Baylis and N. Rengger (eds), *Dilemmas of World Politics: International Issues in a Changing World* (Oxford: Clarendon Press, 1992) and Lloyd Jones, *Cosmopolitan Mediation?*.
48 Blaug, 'Between Fear and Disappointment'.
49 Fay, *Social Theory and Political Practice*, 106.
50 Ibid., 106–7.
51 Habermas, *MCCA*, 195–6.
52 Blaug, *Democracy: Real and Ideal*, 13.

53 Habermas and Dews, *Autonomy and Solidarity*, 251.
54 Ibid.
55 Ibid., 267.
56 Ibid.
57 Ibid., 167–8. Blaug, *Democracy: Real and Ideal*, 16: 'Where Hegel criticized Kant for his abstraction, indeterminacy in regard to outcomes, inability to generate morality, and for the insufficiency of the moral law alone, Habermas accepts his theory be limited to a procedural test and asserts the importance of processes of socialization in the generation of norms and in the practical discourses to test their validity'.
58 Günther, *The Sense of Appropriateness*, 51, citing Wellmer: 'Only in cases where we are concerned with authoritatively given norms, as in law, can we meaningfully distinguish between justification and application; whereas in morality, which does not have norm-giving authority, everyone is directly confronted with the situation and must act with moral sense, so that moral discourse and moral judgement belong together here'. See also Rehg, *Insight and Solidarity*, Chapter 4.
59 Blaug, *Democracy: Real and Ideal*, 89–90.
60 Ibid., 92.
61 Ibid. Refers to two meanings of 'cognitive': 1) the ability of the human intellect to process information, and, 2) the ability to rationally defend one's arguments.
62 Blaug, *Democracy: Real and Ideal*, 102–3.
63 Some of these ideas are further explored in N. Head, 'Bringing Reflective Judgement into International Relations: Exploring the Rwandan Genocide', *Journal of Global Ethics*, 6:2 (2010), 191–204. For further discussion on the role of reflective judgement in practice, see R. Fine, 'Cosmopolitanism and Violence: Difficulties of Judgement', *British Journal of Sociology*, 57:1 (2006), 49–67; R. Fine, 'Judgement and the Reification of the Faculties: A Reconstructive Reading of Arendt's Life of the Mind', *Philosophy and Social Criticism*, 34:1–2 (2008), 157–76; B. Garsten, 'The Elusiveness of Arendtian Judgement', *Social Research*, 74:4 (2007), 1071–108. While reflective judgement draws on the 'force of the example', Crawford indicates that the concepts of analogy and metaphor play much the same role in helping individuals to make sense of and evaluate highly complex phenomena, *Argument and Change in World Politics*, Chapter 2.
64 Benhabib, *Situating the Self*, 132, citing Arendt.
65 R. Beiner (ed.), 'Hannah Arendt on Judging', in H. Arendt, *Lectures on Kant's Political Philosophy* (Sussex: The Harvester Press Limited, 1982) 107, citing Arendt.
66 Beiner, 'Hannah Arendt on Judging', 107, citing Arendt.
67 It should be noted that Arendt did not agree with Habermas's theory of communicative action and this debate is reflected in Habermas's essay: 'Hannah Arendt's Communications Concept of Power', in L. Hinchman and S. Hinchman (eds), *Hannah Arendt: Critical Essays* (Albany, NY: State University of New York, 1977).
68 Habermas and Dews, *Autonomy and Solidarity*, 251.
69 Ibid., 269.
70 Ibid. This is different from the version of hermeneutic understanding elaborated in Chapter 4.
71 Benhabib, *Situating the Self*, 136.
72 M. Passerin d'Entrèves, 'Arendt's Theory of Judgement', in D. Villa (ed.), *The Cambridge Companion to Hannah Arendt* (Cambridge: Cambridge University Press, 2000), 252.
73 Arendt in M. Passerin d'Entrèves, *The Political Philosophy of Hannah Arendt* (London: Routledge, 1994), 131.
74 Arendt, *Lectures on Kant's Political Philosophy*, 100.

75 Head, 'Bringing Reflective Judgement into IR', 195.
76 See Franck, *The Power of Legitimacy Among Nations*, for a discussion on the nature of indeterminacy in international law and its implications for legitimacy.
77 Cited in Blaug, *Democracy: Real and Ideal*, 80.
78 Ibid., 111. See also A. Ferrara, '"Political" Cosmopolitanism and Judgement', *European Journal of Social Theory*, 10:1 (2007), 53–66.
79 Blaug, *Democracy: Real and Ideal*, 111.
80 Ibid.
81 Crawford, *Argument and Change in World Politics*, 417. Although we do not need discourse ethics to recognise the power differentials that exist around the permanent five in the Security Council, it does allow us to theoretically ground the subsequent critique and attempt to reduce such power differentials.
82 Blaug, *Democracy: Real and Ideal*, 74–8.
83 S. White, 'Reason and Authority in Habermas: A Critique of the Critics', *The American Political Science Review*, 74:4 (1980), 1010.

6

Applying the communicative imperatives: debating Kosovo

I've B52 bombers in one hand and U2 surveillance spy planes in the other.
General Michael Short[1]

Introduction

THE STORY OF Kosovo established in Chapter 2 identified a number of ways in which opportunities for dialogue over the rising levels of conflict prior to 1998 were closed down, as well as indicating the conventional narratives of the debates within the Security Council and NATO justifications for the use of force. We now revisit Kosovo in order to reinterpret the story through the framework of communicative ethics developed in Chapter 5. The interpretive power of the communicative imperatives is brought to bear on the communicative practices surrounding the decision to intervene militarily in order to deliver both detailed critical purchase on the empirics and the accompanying *ex post* evaluation of existing practices which a communicative ethics promises. The focus is the deliberations which took place over the Kosovo conflict within the UN Security Council (March 1998–June 1999), during the Holbrooke negotiations in October 1998, and at the Rambouillet negotiations in February 1999 immediately prior to the use of force.

The development of the communicative imperatives articulated in Chapter 5 offers an understanding of process that can be used to interrogate communicative practices and reveal moments of illegitimacy conceived as unjustified exclusion, coercion, lack of reflexivity or recognition, incoherence and so on. The following empirical analysis reveals how a communicative ethics can inform analysis of real communicative practices. Of equal importance, standards for legitimate communication are also revealed immanently within the language appealed to by the actors themselves. Adopting a broader temporal and historical perspective, the communicative imperatives reveal missed opportunities for dialogue and dominant narratives which shaped and constrained the available choices in response to the Kosovo conflict. The degree of controversy over the public justifications for the use of force indicates the need for further analysis of the communicative practices which underpinned claims to the legitimacy of military intervention. The analysis which emerges unsettles conventional interpretations of the military intervention in 1999 through its contestation of the degree to which the communicative practices surrounding the decision to intervene were legitimate. Crucially, it challenges the enabling justification of last resort and highlights key moments of illegitimate dialogue (*contra* the claims of the respective actors) which paved the way for the use of force.

Communicative practices and the imperatives applied to the Kosovo debates: what can they tell us about unfair procedure?

Maximising inclusion

Practices which exclude groups or individuals who have a claim to be included in deliberations require justification because it is frequently as a consequence of exclusionary practices that other harms are inflicted. As indicated in Chapter 5, the argument against unjustified exclusion rests on a number of grounds, not least the reason for which Habermas's communicative ethics differs fundamentally from the Kantian categorical imperative for deciding the standard of right. As Kantian ethics remains a monological process, universal laws could be willed in a manner which excludes consultation with those most affected. For Habermas, the standard of right is 'derived from the intersubjective structure of discursive communication in which anyone affected by a proposed norm has the opportunity to participate; to exclude someone thus affected is to render one's normative validity claim immediately suspect'.[2] This challenges the dominance of strategically oriented agreements that protect particular interests and requires not only participation in a practical discourse, but also the recognition of individuals or groups when validity claims, such as truth or normative rightness, are decided which affect them. The questions intended to facilitate the operation of the communicative imperative of inclusion are designed to reveal moments of illegitimacy related to the 'who' and the 'how' of inclusion.

Beginning with the 'who' of inclusion, the proceedings within the Security Council and the negotiations with Milošević and, later on, the Kosovo Liberation Army (KLA) were driven largely by the Contact Group. Similarly, the resolutions agreed upon in the Council between March 1998 and June 1999 reflect, to a large extent, the demands and statements of the Group. Four of the six Contact Group countries are, needless to say, permanent members of the Security Council and have the right of veto over decisions taken within this forum. As will be shown, the combination of their permanent status within the Council and their membership of the Contact Group granted these countries a greater ability to participate and influence the framing of the resolutions than other states. This signifies that some actors were granted a degree

Applying the communicative imperatives

of access to dialogue unavailable to others.³ It also reveals a preference for consultation within a particular community of interest such as that composed of established, Western, and sovereign powers.⁴ This preference is further reinforced by such procedures for participation in the Security Council as we find, for example, in the meeting at which Resolution 1160 (31 March 1998) was voted on under Chapter VII of the Charter. As per UN practice, the resolution stated that interested countries who were not members of the Security Council had a right to participate in the discussion but not to vote and, usually, only to speak after the vote had taken place.⁵ This issue highlights the implications of the procedural rules of the UN Charter for equality and inclusion. However, while it remains a structural factor which denies to some actors the opportunity for effective participation, it is nevertheless a procedural rule to which members of the UN have given their consent.

The exclusion of either elected Kosovar representatives or the KLA raises questions concerning the legitimacy of the decisions taken within the Security Council. This builds on the exclusion of elected Kosovar representatives from negotiations over the former Yugoslavia throughout the 1990s. Exclusion from the Security Council was particularly important given the opportunities afforded to the FRY (via both written and spoken statements) and the Republic of Serbia (via submitted statements) to participate and be heard. This is despite the fact that, given the dissolution of the SFRY, the FRY had no seat at the UN. It was, however, permitted to maintain the permanent mission of the SFRY to the UN and officials were accredited as representatives of the SFRY mission, which enabled them to circulate documents, participate in the work of UN committees and attend Security Council meetings as observers.⁶ This reinforces the privileged status of sovereign powers; due to Kosovo's lack of statehood, elected Kosovar representatives were denied equal opportunity to speak and be heard, despite the degree to which decisions taken would affect their interests and their *future* ability to participate. Acknowledging that the exclusion which takes place as a result of the preference granted to statehood occurs repeatedly, the imperative of inclusion nevertheless draws attention to the way in which the rules of international society contribute to the marginalisation of particular voices which, in the case of Kosovo, contributed in turn to an exacerbation of the conflict.

There was no real attempt to justify the exclusion of such a key actor as the Kosovars from the dialogue, although if pressed, it is likely that the Contact Group would have defended its actions on two counts. First, by arguing that it was talking to the Kosovo Albanians, albeit not within the Council, and second, that it is not accepted policy to talk to terrorists, which is how the KLA were defined both by Serbia and the international community. However, there are three responses to this account. First, it does not acknowledge the exclusion of Kosovar representatives from earlier negotiations during the 1990s. Second, as established in Chapter 2, the rise of the KLA has to be situated in the context of Kosovo Albanian politics during the 1990s, and the international community's broader policies of engagement in the Balkans and its consequent marginalisation of the Kosovo issue. Third, the Contact Group did eventually talk to the KLA, first behind the scenes as they recognised the likelihood of prolonged conflict if no agreement could be reached, and then later at Rambouillet in an attempt to secure an agreement.

Prior to Rambouillet there was also a distinction in the treatment of and validity granted to Ibrahim Rugova (as Kosovo's elected President) and the KLA, as official, high-level talks were only held with Rugova. Although this seems a legitimate distinction at first glance, between an elected representative and a non-elected armed group, this distorts the reality of Kosovar politics and, rightly or wrongly, served to exclude the KLA from talks. The misunderstanding of Kosovar politics here is crucial as a better understanding and recognition of the actors involved would have indicated that no agreement emerging from negotiations solely with Rugova would have met with acceptance in Kosovo and therefore ended the conflict. Isa Blumi makes a similar point when she argues that 'Kosova's problem grew out of control because Western policies relied on individuals who were alienated from their own populations, rather than engage the components of conflict.'[7] Although US mediators increasingly understood the power of the KLA, it was not until 1999 at Rambouillet that they were drawn into any kind of multilateral dialogue. Meetings between the KLA and US mediators prior to Rambouillet were largely carried out with the aim of persuading the KLA to accept Rugova's leadership in return for participation in talks.[8] This issue was addressed in an OSCE report which stated that:

> Representatives of the KLA believe that the political parties should accept the existence and importance of the armed organization and that none of the parties represents the KLA. Neither do they recognize the leadership of Ibrahim Rugova. The KLA further rules out the possibility of declaring a ceasefire should the talks resume without them being accepted as one of the negotiating parties.[9]

The KLA – which had, it should be remembered, significant grassroots support – recognised the need for their inclusion in talks, to be able to participate equally and be recognised to the extent that claims being decided would affect them. This is not necessarily to attribute to them a more reflexive approach to communication, as they were clearly willing to use force to achieve their strategic objective, namely independence for Kosovo.

There were also pertinent issues concerning inclusion and participation at a local level within the groups constructed by Rugova to participate in dialogue at a regional or international level, which went unmentioned at the level of international dialogue. According to an International Crisis Group

Applying the communicative imperatives

(ICG) report, the group of fifteen individuals organised by Rugova in spring 1998 to participate in talks included a number of prominent and diverse ethnic Albanian opinion-makers. According to testimony given to the ICG, however, Rugova did not intend to consult with or listen to anyone from that group. Members complained that 'meetings were often humiliating and, worse still, unproductive'.[10] Not only were the conditions for fair communication questionable at an international level, but they were also not present at the local level, a factor which greatly compounded the complexity of political and communicative distortion.

There were a number of key moments during the decision-making process which speak clearly to the imperative of inclusion. A meeting took place among the Contact Group on 8 October 1998 in a VIP lounge at Heathrow Airport. It was a crucial meeting in two respects. First, it played a significant role in determining a shift in policy towards permitting the use of military force, and secondly, it contributed towards shaping the balance between strategic and communicative action within relevant communicative practices. The meeting brought together former British Secretary of State for Foreign Affairs, the late Robin Cook; Hubert Védrine, his French counterpart; Klaus Kinkel, the German foreign minister; Madeleine Albright, US Secretary of State; Richard Holbrooke, US special envoy; Igor Ivanov, the Russian foreign minister; representatives of the OSCE; the Austrians in their capacity as current EU chairmen; and other ministers and aides. The decision was taken to reduce the number of people present by including only foreign ministers and a few other key actors.[11] The issue debated was the use of force and the necessity – or not – for a new UN resolution. Not only was this clearly an exclusionary meeting – consulting only key (Western/Contact Group) figures firmly closed the door to other interested parties and located control over the decision-making procedures and the agenda firmly in the hands of the Contact Group – but neither the interests of the Kosovars nor Serbs were directly represented and there was little indication of reflexivity concerning whether or not this was an appropriate forum in which to decide such a crucial question regarding the use of force. As it was not a public meeting, it is difficult to ascertain exactly what was said, although Judah reports that:

> Ivanov said: 'If you take it to the UN, we'll veto it. If you don't we'll just denounce you.' Kinkel says he wants to take it to the Security Council, as do the British and French. Madeleine and [Holbrooke] say: 'That's insane!' So, Kinkel says: 'Let's have another stab at it.' But Ivanov says: 'Fine, we'll veto it.' And Kinkel asks again and Ivanov says: 'I just told you Klaus, we'll veto it . . .' He says: 'If you don't we'll just make a lot of noise . . .'[12]

Even if the decision to exclude relevant parties had been justified in terms of efficiency, as suggested by the notion of trade-offs raised in Chapter 5, the outcome successfully prevented further public dialogue as, crucially, no draft resolution was tabled in the Security Council on the use of force. The US did not feel they needed a Security Council resolution to act and other states believed that it would be substantially harder to intervene if a draft resolution had been defeated in the Council. Consequently, this meeting enabled strategic action to dominate by closing down opportunities for dialogue and shifting to a policy on the use of force which remained unjustified in a public forum such as the Security Council or, under the Uniting for Peace resolution, the General Assembly.

Another key moment which reflects an absence of the understanding of the need to include all relevant parties emerged in the form of the Holbrooke agreement signed in October 1998 between Richard Holbrooke and Milošević and endorsed by the Security Council in Resolution 1203. The KLA were not party to the negotiations and therefore did not consider themselves to be bound by the agreement.[13] This act of exclusion was to have significant consequences for the success of the agreement, a factor seemingly ignored by its architects and certainly not represented as problematic. The agreement temporarily secured the withdrawal of Serb forces which the KLA took advantage of to deploy their own forces. This action ensured the escalation of violence as the Serbs retaliated.[14] The action by the Kosovars needs to be set against their exclusion from the Holbrooke agreement and their perception that the basic principles of the agreement failed to recognise their political grievances – a key requirement for conflict transformation – whilst reaffirming conventional norms of territorial integrity and sovereignty in relation to the FRY.[15]

While the negotiations instigated by Albright at Rambouillet in February 1999 were the most substantive of those held over Kosovo, there were significant differences between the attitudes of the parties towards engaging in dialogue conducive to compromise. While the Kosovo delegation submitted detailed comments on the formal documents presented to it, eleven days passed before the Serb/Yugoslav delegation submitted any written comments. During this time, Kosovar submissions did not receive any feedback. US Ambassador Christopher Hill's visit to Milošević in Belgrade, considered by the Kosovars as having been responsible for breaking the Yugoslav/Serb silence, indicates a greater opportunity afforded to the Serbs to participate and influence outcomes, as well as giving lie to the statement concerning the status of the participants in the Serbian delegation.[16]

Following the Yugoslav/Serb submission, a revised draft was produced by the international negotiators which not only reintroduced the issue of the legal status of Kosovo (a key condition for the Kosovars to come to Rambouillet was that Kosovo's legal status would not be determined), but also introduced a number of proposals responding to Milošević's demands. These

Applying the communicative imperatives

included a second chamber which further entrenched the concept of national communities, and a veto mechanism for all national communities which would effectively have paralysed legislative action in Kosovo.[17] In the attempt to ensure that the Serbs would sign, it has been argued that significant compromises and attention were granted to the Serb delegation, thus skewing the effective opportunity of the Kosovo Albanians to guide the development of the settlement and distorting the legitimacy of the deliberations.[18] In response, the Kosovo delegation questioned the fairness of a process which apparently rewarded the Serbs for their obstruction of the talks.[19]

The revised draft was submitted to the parties, who were invited to consider it the final version: in other words, initiating further discussion would not be welcomed.[20] The Kosovo delegation considered this new draft, substantially different in key aspects and favourable to the Serbs, as unacceptable and as evidence of exclusionary practices. The delegation declared that

> If the consent of the delegation of Kosova is sought, the unilateral changes imposed, apparently as a result of talks outside of the Conference, must be reversed. There cannot be a process of obtaining concessions from the Kosova delegation first, through the process of regular proximity talks which this delegation has constructively supported from the first day of the conference, and of then imposing a second set of unacceptable concessions as a result of separate negotiations between the Contact Group and Belgrade in which the Kosova delegation has no involvement.[21]

The concerns over the legitimacy of the decision-making process identified by communicative ethics are clearly mirrored in the response of the Kosovar delegation.

Following the failure of the negotiations at Rambouillet, later decisions taken concerning the basis for a political settlement lay largely with the G-8 countries.[22] The talks which finally ended the war were based on two elements: the G-8 principles and the trilateral talks of former Finnish President and UN Special Envoy Martti Ahtisaari (EU), Russian Envoy Viktor Chernomyrdin, and Deputy Secretary of State Strobe Talbott (US), with Milošević. However, rather than negotiations on an acceptable agreement for Serbs and Kosovars, the trilateral talks were focused on trying to find an agreement acceptable to the US, Russia, and Milošević. The UN role was more or less limited to passing Resolution 1244. The UN was deliberately marginalised by the Americans for fear that its inclusion would weaken NATO's position in negotiations.[23] There was no inclusion of Kosovar representatives within any of these fora; they were excluded from the UN, the G-8 and the trilateral talks.

Although looking through the lens of communicative ethics cannot ascertain that the KLA, for example, should have been included in dialogue, it can demonstrate that their unjustified exclusion had implications for the legitimacy of decisions taken which concerned them. The significant exclusions identified posed barriers to competent participation, and in turn, affected the quality of intersubjective relations. Exclusionary practices not only challenged the legitimacy of the agreements being negotiated, but also contributed to the perpetuation and escalation of the conflict in ways which point towards factors to be considered in future conflicts.

Minimising coercion

If we accept the grounds for the communicative imperative of inclusion, then it is only a small step to accepting that included parties should be able to participate free from a variety of coercive actions and constraints which may be linguistic, ideological or structural as well as material/military. Constraints identified in this section include the presence of preconditions for dialogue, the threat of force and coercive diplomacy, the refusal to consider alternative proposals for negotiation and the control over the agenda and decision-making process displayed by the Contact Group and its representatives.

To begin with constraints originating from the Serbian side, evidence from an OSCE report suggests that the Serbian Government's decision in April 1998 to hold a referendum on the question of accepting or rejecting 'the participation of foreign representatives in the settlement of the problem of Kosovo and Metohija' was a diversionary and inflammatory tactic, favouring rhetoric rather than a genuine attempt at communicative engagement.[24] An EU report indicates that the FRY were deliberately failing to meet the requirements put in place by Resolution 1160 concerning participation and representation in the negotiations in order to hinder progress on a political settlement of the conflict whilst outwardly seeming to be willing to engage in communicative action and thus blaming the Kosovars for the failure of dialogue to actually take place.[25] The requirement on beginning a dialogue contained in Resolution 1160 was explicitly directed at the government of the FRY. In reality, any such invitation was consistently issued by the Serbian Government with the inclusion of a sole Federal representative, which did not meet the Security Council requirement. This statement of intent on the part of the FRY/Serbia to initiate genuine dialogue was not matched by its increasing levels of violence against Kosovars and thereby constitutes an example of manipulation or strategic action. Moreover, the EU report notes that, 'although the Serbian authorities have insisted that the dialogue can take place without preconditions, the stipulation that a solution must be found within the Republic of Serbia (rather than leaving this question open) amounts to the establishment of a precondition'.[26]

A related issue under scrutiny is the terms in which the need for dialogue was presented by the international community. At the same time as clearly delineating the boundaries of inclusion, the UN resolutions called for all parties to enter 'without preconditions' into a meaningful dialogue on political status issues. Other calls included demanding the initiation of 'genuine dialogue between the Serb authorities and the ethnic Albanians',[27] as well as the need for the Kosovo Albanian team to be 'fully representative of their community in order to speak authoritatively'.[28] Such calls for inclusive dialogue denote immanent claims to inclusion as they constitute a benchmark against which to evaluate communicative practices and thereby offer potentially emancipatory or democratising tendencies. The Contact Group statement agreed at a meeting in Bonn on 25 March 1998 called for both sides to enter into an 'unconditional dialogue',[29] 'without preconditions'[30] and without a 'pre-determined outcome'.[31] Yet, at the same time, and consistent with pluralist norms of sovereignty and territorial integrity, the Contact Group formulated what must amount to a kind of prejudgement. This is a form of coercion because it amounts to a determination of the outcome without recourse to practical dialogue by the relevant participants. The Contact Group indicated that,

> Without prejudging what the result may be, we base the principles for a solution to the Kosovo problem on the territorial integrity of the Federal Republic of Yugoslavia and on OSCE standards, the Helsinki principles, and the Charter of the United Nations. Such a solution must also take into account the rights of the Kosovar Albanians and all those who live in Kosovo.[32]

The United Kingdom emphasised the point made by the Contact Group and other states by declaring that it 'does not support separatism or independence in Kosovo'.[33] The German statement also served to emphasise the consensus on this point, stating that it was necessary

> to enter without preconditions into a meaningful dialogue, including on political status issues. Without prejudging what the result may be, the resolution supports an enhanced status for Kosovo within the Federal Republic of Yugoslavia, with a substantially greater degree of autonomy and meaningful self-administration. Such a solution would by no means impair the sovereignty or the territorial integrity of the Federal Republic of Yugoslavia.[34]

Such preconditions and judgements are a form of constraint on dialogue and can be identified as such on the international community's own terms. The communicative practices in which these judgements are voiced do not attempt to 'persuade' others of the normative rightness of their arguments, but, instead, draw on the norms of international law and humanitarianism to state that this position must indeed be the solution. These validity claims of rightness – derived from both pluralist and solidarist principles of international society – are crucially not redeemed through argumentation in practical discourse. In sum, they reveal situated preferences for an end solution, without due respect for the deliberative process, implying procedural and substantive forms of communicative distortion. Although not openly voiced by many, the issue of preconditions was recognised by some non-governmental actors, including the European Action Council for Peace in the Balkans, which stated:

> The international community should not burden the process by promoting the option it prefers – enhanced autonomy – since this option is rejected by both sides. The parties themselves should define the permanent status of Kosovo. International promotion of any specific option will also hamper the principle of 'no preconditions' in negotiations. Thus, the international community should *aim to start the process, not define the final outcome.*[35]

Similar pre-conditions underpinned Rambouillet as the fundamental principles on which the talks were based were present in all key communications issued by Contact Group states.[36] Despite Robin Cook's representation of the framework document as being one which had enjoyed widespread consultation by all relevant parties as a result of Hill's shuttle diplomacy over several months, unmentioned is that both sides had already rejected the Hill draft and elements of the basic approach which underpinned it.[37] In this light, it seems difficult to perceive any negotiation or settlement based on the Hill document without seeing it as an exercise in coercion.

Discussed already in terms of its exclusionary foundations, the Holbrooke agreement must now be considered as an agreement reached on the basis of coercion. To the dissatisfaction of Russia and China, the agreement was reached in the context of the NAC having agreed on October 13 to authorise air strikes if Serb security forces were not withdrawn from Kosovo within 96 hours.[38] The absence of discussion of alternative positions such as had been voiced by the Kosovars in response to Hill's plan in September indicates a form of silencing. Such alternatives refer to the informal understanding reached between the parties about a three-year stabilisation and normalisation period to allow for the re-establishment of democratic institutions, after which period new approaches could be envisaged. The plan avoided the issue of the status of Kosovo and focused on 'a pragmatic assignment of powers to different levels of administration'.[39] Public power was not to be located in Kosovar institutions, however, but in individual communes and national communities (based on ethnicity) which was considered highly undesirable by the Kosovars. However, while Kosovar representatives were formulating their response to the initial draft, the Holbrooke agreement was concluded. This document, unlike the Hill document, included a specific provision concerning the territorial integrity and sovereignty of the FRY and was reached unilaterally with Milošević.[40] The Holbrooke agreement demonstrates that Serbian cooperation in signing the agreement did not indicate a commitment which transcended their short-term interests. Signing was a means to an end; it allowed them to prevent the imposition of sanctions or the use of force by the international community without requiring that they make any major concessions to the Kosovo Albanians.[41] This was evidenced by the FRY's decision to renege on their commitment in the Holbrooke agreement to conclude a political settlement by November 2.

The shift to coercive diplomacy and strategic action became fully evident when the summons issued by the Contact Group to bring the parties to Rambouillet was backed by the threat of force. NATO maintained this threat throughout the negotiations at Rambouillet. An NAC statement issued on 30 January 1999 states that 'it stands ready to act and rules out no option to ensure full respect by both sides in Kosovo for the requirements of the international community ... by compelling compliance with the demands of the international community'.[42] Despite acquiescing to the summons issued by the Contact Group, Russia argued in the Security Council following the commencement of NATO's military campaign that the threat of force had been detrimental to negotiations and warned of the 'harmful consequences of this action ... for the prospects of a settlement of the Kosovo situation and for safeguarding security in the Balkans'.[43] Russia's position raises wider questions about strategic action in terms of the relationship between threats of force and the successful outcome of negotiations.

Despite, or perhaps because of, the threat of force, Marc Weller argues that the negotiations at Rambouillet were 'actually conducted in a way which made very significant concessions to Yugoslavia, in order to obtain consent relatively freely given'.[44] The position for the Kosovar delegation was somewhat different. Far more damaging to the Kosovar cause than the threat of military strikes was the threat of political disengagement if they refused to sign at Rambouillet. The threat of force amounted to an indirect threat rather than overt military strikes against the KLA. The presence of political coercion as well as military, was a double-edged sword for the KLA. As the weaker party, participation at Rambouillet was necessary, yet potentially might have produced an agreement inconsistent with Kosovar demands and thus unenforceable in reality.[45] The strategic bargain was made quite clear by Albright: without Kosovar agreement, NATO would not be in a position to act. Her spokesperson, James Rubin, stated that,

> if one is to apply the military pressure on the Serbs that is necessary to get them to agree or that is the only way to get them to agree, then we need to work from the Kosovo Albanian yes, in order for Secretary General Solana to draw the appropriate conclusions. And so I think she explained very forcefully that reality.[46]

The dominance of the Contact Group during the negotiations process leading up to the decision to use force in both the Security Council and at Rambouillet indicates that there was not equal access to or control over the decision-making procedures, the agenda, and decisions. The Contact Group statement on 29 January 1999 set in progress the Rambouillet Conference. However, the statement outlining the construction of the talks indicates that control over the procedures, agenda, and final decisions lay with the Contact Group rather than the UN or the parties themselves.[47] Weller's summary of the procedural rules supports this:

> The rules of the conference provided for the tabling of detailed elements of a settlement based on the Non-negotiable principles. The Contact Group drafts would stand, unless either party could persuade its negotiators that a change would be required in order to better implement a specific provision, or if both sides agreed on a change. The inequality in formulating the Non-negotiable principles would therefore be directly injected into the conference proceedings through drafts based upon them, which could not be easily deviated from.[48]

Furthermore, the Contact Group indicated that the framework already set out 'meets the legitimate aspirations of the Kosovo Albanians', thus determining effectively what may or may not be considered as a legitimate aspiration.[49] Again, subtle control over the agenda emerges as other aspirations that the Kosovo Albanians may have had were ruled out prior to negotiation as unacceptable or illegitimate in the face of preferences voiced by dominant states within the international community.

Overall, the application of direct or indirect coercion did not succeed in delivering a successful peace agreement prior to NATO's military action in March and again raises the question of the degree to which the justification of last resort was warranted. The presence of preconditions, the threat of force or political disengagement, and unequal control of the agenda all point towards the closing down of opportunities for dialogue. It was frequently those participants who had the ability to initiate dialogue on issues central to the discussion who had most control over the decisions. Consequently, participants with less influence, such as non-Contact Group members of the Security Council, or those who were unable to participate at all, commonly found that it was difficult to challenge the parameters of dialogue. Thus, a focus on the communicative practices highlights a series of constraints and coercion in the nature and structure of the Contact Group's approach to Kosovo.

Expanding dialogue

The consistent emphasis placed by states on the need for dialogue contrasts significantly with the actions actually taken to promote democratic dialogue and the eventual resort to military force by the international community. The Contact Group statement of 12 June 1998 notes that 'Ministers repeated that no solution to the problems of Kosovo can be found through violence.'[50] The Contact Group continued to condemn Belgrade's 'massive and disproportionate use of force' and insisted that the 'Kosovo Albanian leadership [must] make clear its rejection of violence and acts of terrorism'.[51] It is not then, the use of force *per se* which is being condemned here, but rather the use of force by those party to the conflict. In a solidarist vein, it does not rule out the possibility of a legitimate use of force by a third party in order to protect or defend particular responsibilities, rights or values. By condemning the violent methods adopted by the KLA on behalf of the Kosovo Albanian community, however, the Contact Group failed to reflect upon its own role in the development of the crisis, or the conditions under which the KLA developed. It also placed Rugova in a position uncongenial to further dialogue as it required him either to abandon his political aim in order to retain the favour of the international community (which would have made his position untenable domestically), or to reject the perspective of the international community and to support the KLA. This was not a position calculated to aid the establishment of effective and legitimate dialogue that might end the violence.

An area of particular interpretive contention in the debates over the course of action taken at Rambouillet centres on the controversial military implementation agreement[52] which gave NATO unimpeded military access to FRY territory. When questioned about flexibility concerning the implementation agreement and whether there might be a middle ground whereby the force could be composed in a way more conducive to agreement, Albright's spokesperson, James Rubin, made it very clear, at least publicly, that this would not be the case – the construction of the implementation agreement was not up for discussion.[53] The late briefing on the implementation agreement and the lack of opportunity for negotiation purportedly prevented the parties from being able to discuss the way the agreement would be implemented in practice with NATO representatives and others. Weller argues convincingly that this presented a number of obstacles to the signing of an agreement and precipitated the use of force which might have been avoidable had another approach been adopted:

> As the annex provided for the demilitarisation of the KLA, it could not have come as a surprise to the negotiators that some reassurances as to the implications of this concept would have to be given to a delegation which was effectively dominated by the KLA and a political party close to it [LBD, the United Democratic Movement]. Similarly, the negotiators lost the opportunity to explain certain provisions to the FRY/Serb side, which were later presented as evidence of entirely unacceptable demands of the part of the Contact Group, or rather NATO.[54]

By contrast, and suggesting greater flexibility on this issue, Ivo Daalder and Michael O'Hanlon have suggested that had the Serbs accepted the political aspects of the agreement, then NATO would have revised the implementation agreement to make it acceptable.[55] Despite a lack of clarity over the status of the military annex, it is clear that the late introduction of these provisions led to the need for the March talks in Paris to focus on the implementation agreement in order to prevent the talks breaking down altogether as significant elements had not been discussed at Rambouillet. This demonstrates a lack of reflexivity concerning the best possible construction of the talks, both practically and procedurally, as well as a failure to recognise the key interests of the parties.

There is a great deal of documentary material which indicates the uncontested presence of strategic communication by various actors. The imperatives remind us that when truth claims are contested, actors can call for their justification and defence. This can reveal the distortion of the communicative process through the resort to the strategic use of language on the part of particular actors. For example, while the Secretary-General's report of 5 August 1998 notes 'the sharp escalation of violence and the reported use of excessive force by [FRY] security forces against civilians as part of the government operations against the KLA',[56] the Serb representative insists that this approach 'conceals the true nature of the hostilities: the terrorist attacks of Albanian separatists'.[57] The operations of the Serbian security forces are seen as being 'in accordance with their legal authority, aimed at protecting citizens and their property'.[58] The Serbian interpretation justifies the continued oppression of the Kosovars and permits them to claim continuing sovereignty over Kosovo. This interpretation and the rhetoric which supports it distort the reality of continuing actions on the ground. The governments of Serbia and the FRY claim to be 'determined to solve the problems in Kosovo and Metohija peacefully, through dialogue and with respect for the integrity of Serbia and the Federal Republic of Yugoslavia and with full guarantees of equal human rights to all citizens and ethnic communities living in the province'.[59] China's position is similarly contentious as it declares in September 1998 that it

> appreciate[s] the position of the Government of the Federal Republic of Yugoslavia regarding settling the Kosovo issue through unconditional dialogue. The situation in the Kosovo region is now stabilizing. There is no large-scale armed conflict, still less any escalation of the conflict.[60]

Not only does this contradict findings in the Secretary-General's reports of 4 September 1998[61] and 3 October 1998,[62] but it also demonstrates an apparent willingness to take the FRY's words at face value rather than critically assessing them against the reality on the ground. China's position concerning minority rights and territorial integrity may have been motivated by strategic self-interest and a desire to avoid setting a precedent which might later be applied against it. Nonetheless, the statements made by China and the Secretary-General were contradictory and raised validity claims of sincerity and truth. As such, these specific claims should have been subject to argumentation and public contestation by other member states in order to establish a clearer sense of the communicative or strategic orientation to language contained in China's statements and, if the latter, to expose the weakness of the argument in the Council.

Instead, what the transcripts of the Security Council meetings show is that there was little or no deliberation among Council members concerning the veracity of the situation on the ground in Kosovo. We do not observe a more general shift towards a different form of communicative interaction where truth and rightness claims are treated as hypotheses requiring justification and defence. While these conflicting validity claims are raised in debate there is little direct engagement with them; a process which would, in Habermasian terms, shift the discourse to another level in order to reach consensus on their validity. In other words, why are the Serbian and Chinese truth claims not directly and publicly contested and rebutted in order to limit their ability to legitimately offer particular arguments?

An important exception to this lack of contestation was the rejection of the Russian draft resolution on 26 March 1999 which called for the cessation of NATO air strikes.[63] A number of states, notably Slovenia, challenged the truth and rightness validity claims raised by Russia and its supporters and appeared to engage in argumentative reasoning in response to the draft resolution, noting discrepancies, inconsistencies, and unconvincing reasons offered by the draft's supporters. However, theoretical issues concerning the distinction between strategic and communicative action are revisited in two ways by this empirical discussion. First, it is difficult to untangle the degree to which particular communicative practices may be said to be communicative or strategic in orientation given our inability to be certain of the motives of actors. Second, the complexities of determining empirical examples of different categories of strategic action become clearer. As already noted, strategic action encompasses both overt and concealed uses of language. The difficulty in identifying the correct form empirically again emerges from the challenge posed by knowing the real motivation of another actor. What does become clear is that we must consider the possibility not just that Russia was acting strategically, but that it may have genuinely opposed the intervention, believing that the threshold of last resort had not been reached. Even so, what may have been principled reasons offered by Russia and others were not persuasive enough given the humanitarian urgency presented by the ongoing reality on the ground in Kosovo, the repeated refusal of Milošević to sign up to a peace agreement, and the earlier factual inaccuracies invoked which served

Communicative ethics and the use of force

to weaken the validity of their arguments. However, while appearing to be an example of communicative action, it is also plausible that states supporting NATO's military action had strategic concerns in play as well, given the need to ensure the defeat of the Russian draft. Having begun military action, they were unlikely to be willing to be persuaded by Russia's arguments on the dubious legality and effectiveness of unilateral military action for achieving their humanitarian goals or a lasting political settlement in Kosovo, or their concerns over the consequences for the authority of the UN and international law.

Communicative ethics cannot safely navigate these waters and it is not intended to; we cannot – as spectators – satisfactorily settle the debate concerning the respective communicative orientations of the actors concerned. The task of communicative ethics is not to identify pure empirical examples of the analytical distinction between strategic and communicative action. Just as this distinction is criticised in theory, so it cannot be entirely untangled in practice. Instead, the value of a communicative ethics framework is that it allows an interrogation of the communicative practices through which particular claims to legitimacy are made, which in turn may reveal degrees of communicative distortion, including degrees of strategic action which remain unjustified. Such difficulties with the transition from the ideal to the real do not obscure the point that the debate over the draft resolution was not as straightforward as it is often presented and, crucially, that the wider process concerning the decision to intervene militarily was infused with unredeemed exclusionary, strategic, and coercive factors on all sides. The distinction between critical and sociological approaches to analysing communicative practices is reflected here. While constructivists also recognise the work that argumentation does, they do not, as is the case with communicative ethics, evaluate the wider legitimacy of the decision-making process.

A relevant question – central to disagreement in the Council over the use of force in Kosovo – is when can we say that all diplomatic options have been exhausted and we have reached the position of last resort? The justification of last resort which framed the debate surrounding the decision to intervene militarily – and manifested through the failure of the negotiations at Rambouillet – was iterated by a number of states in the Council meeting of 24 March 1999. The argument that diplomatic efforts had been exhausted served as a key enabling factor in the shift to the use of force. This point emerged clearly in Slovenia's statement that 'all diplomatic means have been exhausted and military action in the Federal Republic of Yugoslavia has become inevitable'.[64] It was mirrored by the representative of the Netherlands who stated that the 'present state of affairs should convince every delegation that with regard to the problem of Kosovo, the diplomatic means of finding a solution are now exhausted'.[65] There were, nonetheless, a number of dissent-

Applying the communicative imperatives

ing voices (e.g. Russia, Namibia, China, India) who rejected framing the issue as one of last resort. The Russian Federation declared that, 'NATO's decision to use military force is particularly unacceptable from any point of view because the potential of political and diplomatic methods to yield a settlement in Kosovo has certainly not been exhausted'.[66] Russia's belief that more could have been done after the negotiations at Rambouillet to prevent the use of force underpinned its rejection of the justification of last resort[67] and serves as a timely reminder of the controversial nature of this justification and the need to reflect upon its use within the wider framework of communicative ethics. The question as to whether the threshold criteria – such as last resort – have indeed been met in particular cases can only be answered through practical discourse between actors. Here again just war-informed criteria do not have the tools at their disposal to analyse the decision-making process for evidence of exclusion and coercion which might affect the subsequent legitimacy of such processes.

From the perspective of orientation towards strategic or communicative action, Russia's statement in the Council on 24 March 1999 is interesting because it rejects the argument that

> NATO's actions became inevitable because one or two of the permanent members of the Security Council had blocked action in the Council. That is simply not correct, for one simple reason: no proposals on this topic were introduced in the Security Council by anyone. There was never any draft resolution; there were no informal discussions, not even in the corridors – at least not with one permanent member of the Security Council, namely, Russia.[68]

Removing this decision from the purview of the Security Council not only limits the scope for inclusion and transparency of the decision-making process, but it also begs the question as to whether or not states would have voted in the same way had a resolution been tabled by NATO states as they did when presented with the *fait accompli* of military action. In sum, as the scope for communicative action seemed to narrow, the trajectory of the negotiations became increasingly strategic.

Maximising diversity[69]

The following analysis illustrates ways in which the potential for the expression of political diversity necessary for a free and frank public debate about the legitimacy of the use of force were closed down by particular patterns of communicative practices. The extent to which the media represents an independent vehicle for discourse and the expression of differences within an intervening state remains important. Furthermore, its role in terms of agenda-setting and the framing or priming of issues is a central aspect of a communicative ethics approach.[70] The power of the media is located in the selection and processing of 'politically relevant content' and thus they 'intervene in both the formation of public opinions and the distribution of influential interests'.[71] Habermas identifies the presence of power relations which act to constrain the ability of the media to form an independent and self-regulating system. His claim that structural distortion is evident in the contemporary nature of the media has been a long-running theme throughout his work.

As regards the independence of the media and in terms of critical purchase, Habermas distinguishes between an 'incomplete differentiation of the media system from its environments on the one hand and, on the other, a temporary interference with the independence of a media system that has already reached the level of self-regulation'.[72] Despite the seemingly more minor nature of temporary interference, to illustrate his point Habermas draws upon the manipulation of the American public by the US government's communications management before and after the Iraq war in 2003. What is important is not the framing of 9/11 by President Bush as the trigger for a 'war on terrorism', but the 'absence of any counterframing. A responsible press would have provided the popular media with more reliable news and alternative interpretations.'[73] Accounts of the intervention in Kosovo which have focused on the role of the media bear witness to the significance of this imperative.[74] Marina Blagojević draws attention to the need to apply this critical logic not just to the Western media and their role in creating favourable conditions for NATO's intervention, but also to the role of the media in Serbia and Kosovo over an extended period of time. Connections are drawn between the presentation of information through a particular interpretive framework – the construction of national identity – and ethnic and political conflict.[75]

The preference for consensus rather than hermeneutic understanding appears to be intrinsic to international structures and practice. Consent or consensus is given preference in contemporary practice because it is understood to be a necessary prelude for action. In the struggle to create such consensus, we see a polarisation between pluralist and solidarist constructions of international society reflected by those states lining up behind a 'humanitarian' identity as a justification for the use of force, and those preferring to be identified with the more conventional precepts of international order. Former British Prime Minister Tony Blair's speech in the House of Commons immediately prior to the start of the bombing demonstrates clearly the moral discourse which secured consensus on the nature of humanitarian need as well as being used to legitimate the intervention:

Applying the communicative imperatives

> We must act: to save thousands of innocent men, women and children from humanitarian catastrophe, from death, barbarism and ethnic cleansing by a brutal dictatorship; to save the stability of the Balkan region, where we know chaos can engulf all of Europe.[76]

Costa Rica's statement in October 1998, bearing interesting echoes of Habermas's own reflections on Kosovo, demonstrates the legitimating function of humanitarian language:

> What we have here is a moral and ethical imperative for the international community. Inasmuch as this moral objective leaves no room for doubt, and in that an international presence in Kosovo would take on a high moral character, Costa Rica would never fail to lend its support to a multilateral action aimed at such a noble purpose ... we would like to state some of our misgivings, which are of a legal nature ... A goal such as this one, which is ethically and morally unquestionable, deserves to be achieved by means of international law.[77]

In the search for consensus, there are clear references to humanitarian and Balkanisation discourses. The language used by the US and British leaders, among others, became increasingly polarised prior to NATO's intervention as Albright and others attempted to create a more or less unambiguous picture of good and evil; the innocent Kosovars and the evil, brutal Serbian dictator. Blair described the bombing as a 'battle between good and evil; between civilisation and barbarity; between democracy and dictatorship'.[78] When the language of humanitarianism is used, it requires the construction of an 'other' and this was reflected in NATO's representation of the situation as a 'clear-cut case of a brutal repressor tormenting defenceless victims'.[79] Such language serves to facilitate the exercise of force against the 'other'. Drawing a distinction between friend and enemy 'rules out or sidelines dialogue in favour of a stark and ineluctable antithesis'.[80] Consensus better suits this construction than hermeneutics which attempts to break down such barriers and enable understanding of multiple narratives and the perspective of the 'other'. Given the location of control over the agenda, the varying forms of exclusion and coercion, the use of proximity talks and the dissatisfaction of both Serbs and Kosovars with the text at Rambouillet, it is difficult to see how any real understanding of the 'other's' position might have developed. Such dominant narratives closed down alternative avenues for non-violent engagement and different kinds of communicative practices, thereby limiting the plurality of voices able to effectively intervene in the debate.

Coherence

Exploring the degree of consistency and coherence between actors' statements and their actions is relevant for interrogating claims to sincerity, truth, and their consequent communicative or strategic orientation. There were a number of positions articulated by different actors over which consensus and consistency were maintained. The FRY was consistent in the arguments it presented on at least three points:

1) The right of the FRY to oppose terrorism[81]
2) The rejection of attempts to internationalise Kosovo[82]
3) The rejection of independence for Kosovo[83]

There was also consensus among the Contact Group and among other members of the Security Council concerning several positions:

1) The situation is a threat to international peace and security[84]
2) The territorial integrity of the FRY must be respected[85]
3) Further violence might lead to the destabilisation of the region (including mass refugee flows)
4) The situation presents a humanitarian tragedy, as evidenced by a mounting death toll; the unacceptability of human rights violations, and references to previous humanitarian tragedies in the Balkans – the 'never again' syndrome.

The FRY/Serb position, although rhetorically consistent, reveals a certain incoherence when we try to reconcile actions and words. They referred constantly to the need to engage in positive dialogue. Further, they maintained that all citizens in Serbia (and Kosovo) are equal, irrespective of nationality/ethnicity; that all national minorities enjoy full cultural autonomy; that the government of Serbia distinguishes between terrorists (legitimate targets) and members of national minorities; and that the government seeks to promote a tolerant, multi-ethnic and democratic state. Yet these positions are fundamentally at odds with their actions in Kosovo. For example, the FRY representative stated that:

> Under the constitution and laws, all of them are granted the same civil and human rights: to their language, culture, media and religion; to elect and to be elected; and to participate in genuine political processes, from self-rule to republican and federal parliaments.[86]

This should be contrasted with Turkey's statement in the same Council meeting on 31 March 1998:

> The dangers inherent in the situation in Kosovo have been visible since at least 1989, when the acquired rights of autonomy and self-administration of the people of Kosovo were suddenly abrogated. Moreover, the economic hardships and deprivation faced by the people of Kosovo following the disintegration of the Socialist

Federal Republic of Yugoslavia put unbearable strain on their endurance. The restrictions on the right of education also added fuel to the feeling of deep resentment, as, over the years, children have been deprived of adequate education.[87]

Furthermore, the FRY claimed, somewhat surprisingly, that, 'There are no armed conflicts in Kosovo and Metohija.'[88] This creates severe problems with the validity claims of truth and sincerity raised by the FRY. Even if we accept that it is not sufficient to make a direct comparison between statements and reality but, as Habermas argues, that truth must be defined in terms of a 'projected consensus',[89] justifiable doubts are raised given the limited consensus as to the reality of the situation. This brings into question sincerity claims, as the gap between other information sources, the consensus of the international community over the situation in Kosovo, and the claims of the FRY jeopardise our belief that the FRY representative is being honest with us. Consequently, this returns us to issues raised by the imperative of expanding dialogue; our lack of faith in the speaker's sincerity should leave us with two options: to move to a discourse form of communication where the aim is 'systematically to examine and test problematic truth and normative claims in their own right',[90] or to adopt a strategic and instrumental attitude. However, the Security Council does neither of these. Prior to the decision to use force in March, the FRY's claims went largely unchallenged and states continued to try to broker a settlement without recognising the degree to which communication had been distorted.

Juxtaposing two situations demonstrates how easy it is to misconstrue both actions and words, especially when their coherence and consistency can be questioned. First, Rugova met Kofi Annan on 2 June 1998 and was assured that the international community would not leave the situation as it was in Kosovo, although he was given no clear indication as to what this might mean for the future of the Kosovars.[91] Contrast this with Judah's record of a conversation with a KLA commander at a checkpoint in Kosovo who is reported as saying that they were not interested in talks:

> When asked whether or not he should be [interested in talks] as the Americans insisted that Kosovo could not be independent, he replied with impeccable logic: 'And they said that none of the six republics of former Yugoslavia could be independent either'. 'They'll come round.'[92]

Given the overall level of inconsistency between the actions and words of the international community during the 1990s towards the former Yugoslavia, it is not surprising that it was widely believed among Kosovo Albanians that attitudes towards Kosovo's status would also change. Recalling that the inconsistent application of a rule does not automatically render it incoherent, such inconsistency must be explained satisfactorily with reference to a principled justification concerning the distinction granted a particular case. In this light, the disagreement voiced over Kosovo's status in relation to the other constituent parts of the FRY following the relevant decisions of the Badinter Commission suggests reasonable concern regarding the coherent application of the norm of self-determination across the Balkans.[93]

Despite the defeat of the Russian draft resolution, there was little suggestion that substantial agreement existed concerning an evolving norm of humanitarian intervention which presupposes a right to intervene militarily without the authorisation of the Security Council.[94] In the case of Kosovo, reasons were given by key Western members of the Council for military intervention as a permissible exception to the bedrock rule restricting the use of force in the UN Charter. But, in order to remain coherent, similar situations in the future which are not treated alike must be justified in principled terms which others can accept.[95] It is not, therefore, simply that arguments matter in international politics, but that legitimacy has a temporal element which requires consistent or coherent justifications for the (non-) use of force over a period of time. Although there was consistency in the arguments presented by the Serbs and the international community within the Council, much of which centred on the need for dialogue, the application of the communicative imperatives reveals a lack of coherence between the stated aim of dialogue without preconditions and the dialogue that was in fact initiated. In conclusion, the coherence element of communicative ethics demonstrates the complexity of establishing legitimate communicative practices and the lasting implications for resolving conflict of the signals which are communicated by our (in)actions and (in)consistencies to other parties.

Reflexivity

The procedural construction of the dialogue demanded by the international community between the Serbs and Kosovars has received little overt attention. It remains important, however, as a means by which the educational orientation of critical theory with practical intent is manifested. In other words, how might dialogue be constructed differently? In the OSCE report of 20 April 1998, we can observe the way in which establishing preconditions also impacts upon the procedural construction of talks:

> A delegation from Belgrade travelled to Pristina on several occasions declaring a readiness to begin a dialogue. The Kosovar Albanians declined to participate because there was *no agreement on a framework and procedure* for the talks. Moreover, this invitation for dialogue was issued by the Serbian Government in their Pristina offices and with the requirement that the question of the status of Kosovo be discussed only in the framework of the Republic of Serbia. This has been interpreted by the Albanian side as a precondition. At the same time, the request of the Kosovar Albanians and the international community to allow

Applying the communicative imperatives

participation of an outside representative or representatives has been rejected by Belgrade.[96]

As discussed under the imperative of inclusion, there were disagreements and power struggles within the conflicting parties which affected the negotiations. Just as the relations among the Kosovar leadership (political and military) were not as black and white as they were supposed by the international community, neither were those of the Serbs. While Rugova showed little desire to share power locally and by so doing open up input on procedural and substantive aspects of dialogue, there were, conversely, some Serbs who remained capable of reflexivity concerning their position towards dialogue. One such was Artemije, the Serb Orthodox Bishop of Prizren and Raška, who made a statement which is extraordinary in light of the perceptions of dialogue held by other actors involved:

> After the massacre in Drenica, the chances of a dialogue as a way of resolving the problem have been missed. Now what remains is what the gentlemen in Belgrade have chosen – the loss of Kosovo, just like that of Krajina, in war ... War would give the international community an excuse to get involved and in that case the Serbian army and police would be forced to withdraw as occupation forces ... We do not need mediators, people who impose solutions, but representatives who would listen to both sides in the Serbian-Albanian dialogue and inform the international community. They would not be an obstacle but are necessary. Serbia is not capable of offering a healthy dialogue without someone from outside.[97]

Although the Holbrooke agreement, endorsed in Resolution 1203, has already been mentioned in connection with other communicative imperatives, it is worth reiterating that the negotiators showed little reflexivity regarding the procedural need for trade-offs to maintain the legitimacy of the discourse. Such trade-offs are not impossible, but their validity lies in the manner of their justification. There was no public attempt to discursively redeem the procedural shortcomings of the negotiations by engaging the affected parties in order to justify and defend their exclusion. Such trade-offs cannot impede the ability of participants to engage in and arrive at future political judgements. The exclusion of the Kosovo Albanians from these negotiations without their agreement arguably affected their ability to make relevant political judgements and potentially affected their future ability to preserve the necessary conditions for their participation.

Similarly, the use of proximity talks at Rambouillet may have been a more likely means through which to arrive at an agreement in the short term, but not necessarily a more effective means of achieving peace, as it offered the parties no chance to explore contested understandings of events or to understand the perceived legitimacy of the actions of the other. Consequently, the enforcement of the settlement was likely to be more difficult, as the agreement was founded on a threat of force and coercion. The following comment made by one of the negotiators, Christopher Hill, illustrates some of the difficulties surrounding proximity talks:

> What happens is you get comments from one side, you go in another room and you get comments from the other side. You try to incorporate the more sensible of the comments, and then you bring out a new draft and, lo and behold, they look and they say, 'Where did this come from?' Well, it obviously came from the other side and they don't like that. And then they say, 'Well, what happened to our idea?' and you say 'Sorry, the other side couldn't allow that in there and neither could we.'[98]

What such talks are unable to do is address the underlying sentiments of hostility between the parties and thereby transform the nature of the relationship.

There appears to have been little questioning of procedural decisions by Western states, who declared that 'We consider that the Contact Group approach and the documents being tabled to the parties, provide the basis for the interim political settlement.'[99] This lack of reflexivity, on the one hand, can be contrasted with the awareness, on the other, of the international community's prior involvement in the Balkans. Although it was the desire to avoid a repetition of the Bosnian war which served to motivate and justify military intervention in Kosovo, there is little explicit reference to or reflexivity concerning earlier refusals to address the problems in Kosovo. In other words, the missed opportunities for dialogue identified in the 1990s do not guide the communicative practices of the international community in 1998–99.

When the justification of last resort, so central to enabling the use of force, is considered through a framework which points to missed opportunities for non-violent engagement, then the absence of reflexivity on the part of states becomes marked. The justification of last resort serves to narrow the focal point down to the moment of crisis, at which point the only options on the foreign policy table are 'to intervene or not to intervene'. The dilemma is perceived to be between military force or moral bankruptcy, and this dilemma prevents the cultivation of alternative resources for thinking about conflict and humanitarian crises. Once again, communicative ethics challenges states to reflect upon the consequences of their communicative practices both for the legitimacy of their positions and in terms of conflict transformation. It is by generating greater reflexivity concerning the constraints on public discourse that a critical theoretical perspective retains an emancipatory element.

Applying the communicative imperatives

Recognition

Earlier we asked: What impact does a lack of political or legal recognition have on actors within conflict situations and, by extension, on conflict resolution processes? What forms of harm result from exclusion, misrecognition, or indifference in such circumstances? Some of the consequences of such actions have, at the very least, been implicit in the analysis of communicative distortion presented through the other imperatives. Here, it is argued explicitly that recognition of actors and their situated, particular, perspectives is important for a conflict such as Kosovo. What we in fact saw, however, in response to a diversity of conflicting political and ideological aims, were particular values and identities set up as the 'right'. These primarily derived from discourses of international law, statehood, humanitarianism and human rights, principles of sovereignty and non-intervention. It is partly as a consequence of these dominant discourses that other exclusions and constraints identified were placed on dialogue where some voices had a greater opportunity to be heard than others.

One such example is that, almost unanimously, member states of the Security Council referred to the role of the KLA within the conflict as an example of terrorism, in line with the position taken by the FRY/Serbia. It is only in the statement of Slovenia that we see a more nuanced discussion of this concept and whether it is accurate to apply it to the conflict in Kosovo.[100] Slovenia refers to

> the danger of political misuse of the word 'terrorism'. There is a clear need to avoid the trap set by those who use the label of terrorism for reasons of political convenience and without proper factual foundation ... there are forms of struggle that, albeit undesirable, are not terrorism and ought not to be labelled as such.[101]

The refusal of the Council to question the labelling of KLA operations as 'terrorism' not only strengthened the position of the Yugoslav authorities, but also, given the indication that it would not be recognised as a legitimate actor, removed any incentive the KLA might have had to reconsider its activities or limit its targets to military objectives. Such an approach failed to understand the complexity of the situation in Kosovo, the circumstances surrounding the rise of the KLA, and the relationship between the KLA and FRY/Serb forces, who, incidentally, were not publicly accused of state-sponsored terrorism despite the numerous incidents of violence against Kosovar civilians and the issue of ethnic cleansing. When the military actions of FRY/Serb forces against ethnic Albanian villages were condemned in the Council it was in the language of 'large scale police actions'.[102] The labelling of the KLA as terrorists began early on when on 23 February 1998, Robert Gelbard, US special envoy to the region, visited Priština, criticising the violence of the Serbian police and then attacking the KLA: 'We condemn very strongly terrorist actions in Kosovo. The UÇK [KLA] is, without any questions, a terrorist group.'[103] This was a turning point: 'If the KLA were a terrorist group and the representative of the most powerful nation on earth said so, then there could be no objection to the Serbian police moving in to finish it off. No doubt unintentionally, the US had appeared to give Milošević a green light to act.'[104] Albright compounded this perception when, on 9 March 1998, she declared that 'The authorities in Serbia will try to blur the picture by claiming their actions are a legitimate response to a terrorist threat. We do not deny that they face such a threat.'[105] The naming of the KLA as terrorists in this fashion demonstrated a lack of understanding of both the dynamics of the conflict and the consequences that such recognition would have on the levels of violence.[106] As such, it is evident that the act of recognition serves to constitute power relations which favour some but disadvantage others.

The public statements of the FRY in relation to the conflict shed light on the extent to which actors sought to understand perspectives beyond their own viewpoint – an important element of the imperative of recognition. Such statements demonstrate clearly the difference not only between the way that the Serbs perceived the conflict in Kosovo and its perception by other actors, but also an intrinsic difference between the way that the Serbs and Kosovars perceived their own history. As discussed earlier, Kosovo is undisputedly, in the minds of both Serbs and Kosovars, important symbolic territory and plays a significant role in the construction of their respective identities. Only the Serb perception is portrayed within the Security Council debates due to the absence of a Kosovar voice; the FRY/Serbia representative in the UN states that:

> Kosovo and Metohija is a Serbian province that has always been, and is today, an integral part of the Republic of Serbia. That territory has never been part of any other State. It is the cradle of the Serbian State, one of the oldest European States, the birthplace of Serbian culture and civilization.[107]

This contrasts with a view that is representative of many Kosovars and is voiced by one of the most famous contemporary Albanian authors, Ismail Kadaré. He writes that 'It is the distortion of history which has fomented this crime in the Balkans',[108] and declares:

> No serious historian, no reliable historical source indicates that the Serbs were the first inhabitants of Kosovo, and the Albanians the latecomers. It is exactly the opposite: the Albanians have always been there, the Slavs only arrived afterwards.[109]

Neither Serbs nor Kosovars demonstrate a significant attempt within limited dialogues to understand the perspectives of the other, nor indicate awareness of their own explicit or implicit involvement in the political construction of

Applying the communicative imperatives

this conflict.[110] The position adopted by the international community did not help to break down barriers between identities or opposing perspectives. Whether a dialogue informed by the principles of communicative ethics and sensitive to the transformative nature of such dialogue might have enabled Serbs and Kosovars to enter into such a communicative engagement remains an important counterfactual question. Nonetheless, the fact that these issues were not even raised points to the need for a significant shift towards embracing communicative ethics in the mindset of actors within the international community.

Conclusion

The 'burden of persuasion'[111] lies heavy on states when they claim legitimacy for the use of force for humanitarian purposes. The constraints and exclusions identified hitherto reveal the need for a greater recognition of the critical role of communicative ethics in order to uphold such a burden. In the case of Kosovo, these constraints centred on the following: the exclusion of key participants, which was not redeemed through argumentation to justify this exclusion; Western states' control over the agenda and hence the parameters of the dialogue; the use of dominant narratives to support justifications which consequently enabled the closing down of alternative voices or opportunities for dialogue; a failure to shift to justificatory discourse regarding contested validity claims; inconsistencies between the actions and words of states; an absence of procedural reflexivity; and the privileging of certain actors and positions over others without offering justifications, not least through the setting of preconditions. When the extent to which parties engaged in argumentative reasoning or effective persuasion is examined, it becomes clear that all parties, despite claims to the contrary, prejudged the outcome of any dialogue on the issue of Kosovo's status. Judgements of illegitimate practices extend to the Security Council, the Holbrooke negotiations, and the negotiations at Rambouillet which were demonstrably not as 'fair, just and balanced' as the US declared.[112]

The communicative imperatives applied in this chapter do not seek to demonstrate exactly how speech may be made legitimate, but rather to illuminate the inequalities and illegitimacy of communicative practices which purport to be justified and legitimate. It is not a question of passing moral judgement on the specific decisions of states concerning the use of force for humanitarian purposes in Kosovo, but rather of demonstrating their shortcomings in terms of legitimacy by virtue of identifying relevant constraints on communicative practices. In this light, the contribution of communicative ethics is clearly recognisable as offering a means by which some of these constraints and exclusions may be recognised and removed by participants, although not a blueprint for an ideal speech situation. In practical discourse, the burden is on those who wish to be recognised as legitimate actors to ensure that relevant constraints and exclusions are addressed.

It is necessary, as indicated in Chapter 5, to develop an awareness of the limitations encountered when applying the communicative imperatives to a concrete situation. While all intersubjective interactions are highly complex and influenced by a significant number of material and ideational factors, the copious number of potentially affective conditions and motivations at the international level place obstacles in the path of anyone hoping to offer a final and all-encompassing account of decision-making processes. The shift from theory to practice is not without hindrances; we encounter a number of challenges when seeking to bring Habermasian critical theory onto empirical ground. However, through an attention to particular communicative practices, the imperatives can highlight moments of illegitimacy, despite the claims of the actors concerned. This indicates a capacity for communicative ethics to develop a critical and evaluative stance towards justifications for the use of force beyond existing constructivist and critical branches of the 'communicative turn' in IR.

Communicative ethics clearly contributes an additional requisite dimension to the question of legitimacy which extends beyond the moral and legal questions so often asked regarding the intervention in Kosovo. Whilst providing explanatory insights into the (il)legitimacy of particular communicative practices, the imperatives simultaneously reveal ways in which future conflict resolution processes could be transformed through a willingness among political actors to take into consideration a range of procedural elements. Communicative ethics also invites engagement with a multiplicity of perspectives including non-state actors, the absence of which in the case of Kosovo coloured the evaluation of the claims to legitimacy. Coupled with the missed opportunities for dialogue mapped out in Chapter 2, the critique of the communicative practices established through a communicative ethics approach suggests alternative non-violent paths which *might* have been taken by actors within the international community over an extended period of time.

NOTES

1 General Michael Short speaking to Milošević during the Holbrooke negotiations. Cited in Judah, *Kosovo*, 185.
2 White, 'Reason and Authority in Habermas', 1015.
3 It is worth reiterating the way in which I use the term 'dialogue' here. I am defining it as what happens when people talk to each other in negotiations, Council meetings, private meetings, etc. In this sense, it is not necessarily normative (or synonymous with discourse ethics). However, just as Habermas's distinction between strategic and communicative action is problematic in practice, so this difficulty extends to the term

'dialogue'. I use 'dialogue' to refer to communicative practices which may be more or less communicative/strategic in orientation. Communicative ethics refers to the normative approach embedded in the book.
4 Labelling the Russian Federation in this way may be a point of contention, but for the purposes of noting the relations and locations of power in this context it is sufficient.
5 S/PV.3868, 31 March 1998.
6 S. Murphy, 'Contemporary Practice of the United States Relating to International Law', *American Journal of International Law*, 94:4 (2000), 677–8.
7 I. Blumi, 'A Story of Mitigated Ambitions: Kosova's Tortuous Path to Its Postwar Future', *Alternatives: Turkish Journal of International Relations*, 1:4 (2002), 3.
8 International Crisis Group, 'Kosovo's Long Hot Summer: Briefing on Military, Humanitarian and Political Developments in Kosovo', Report No. 41 (September 1998), 13.
9 S/1998/712, 5 August 1998.
10 ICG, 'Kosovo's Long Hot Summer', 11–12.
11 Judah, *Kosovo*, 183.
12 Ibid. In an attempt to explain Russia's behaviour at this private meeting, Bellamy points towards Yeltsin's anger and upset at Milošević's almost immediate betrayal of the agreement they had signed on 16 June 1998. *Kosovo and International Society*, 90–3.
13 To ask whether there would have been an agreement if the KLA had been represented is a counterfactual. Whilst we cannot establish this, a good argument can be made that their exclusion was problematic.
14 IICK, *The Kosovo Report*, 78–9.
15 'The leader [Rugova] of the Albanian community in Kosovo ... voiced disappointment that no representatives of the Albanian community from Kosovo had been a party to the negotiations.' S/1998/1068, 12 November 1998.
16 Press Briefing by the three negotiatiors, Rambouillet, 9 February 1999, Weller, *The Crisis in Kosovo*, 428. Ambassador Petritsch: 'Both sides have sent politically competent people in regard to the negotiating process-experts. So I believe both sides have sent their best people.' Whilst the Kosovar delegation read like a 'who's who' of Kosovar politics, this contrasted heavily with the composition of the Serbian delegation which included no one of real stature – Milošević, who made the real decisions, was not there. See Judah, *Kosovo*, 200–1. Weller narrates chasing after Hill on his way to the airport in an attempt to prevent the trip given the message it sent to the Kosovars.
17 Weller, *The Crisis in Kosovo*, 403. See Interim Agreement for Peace and Self-Government in Kosovo, 2nd Draft, 18 February, 1999, Weller, *The Crisis in Kosovo*, 434–41.
18 Weller, 'The Rambouillet Conference on Kosovo', 250.
19 Letter from Delegation of Kosova to Contact Group Negotiators, Rambouillet, 17 February 1999, Weller, *The Crisis in Kosovo*, 433.
20 Press Briefing by the Contact Group Negotiators, 18 February 1999, Weller, *The Crisis in Kosovo*, 441.
21 Kosova Delegation Statement on New Proposal for a Settlement, 18 February 1999, Weller, *The Crisis in Kosovo*, 444–5.
22 The G-8 countries are Russia, the UK, the USA, France, Italy, Germany, Canada, and Japan.
23 J. Norris, *Collision Course: NATO, Russia, and Kosovo* (Westport: Praeger Publishers, 2005), 86.
24 S/1998/361, Annex II, 30 April 1998.

25 S/1998/361, Annex I. See FRY/Serbian statements of 13 and 14 March 1998, Weller, *The Crisis in Kosovo*, 351
26 S/1998/361, Secretary-General's report, Annex 1.
27 S/1998/223, 11 March 1998.
28 S/1998/657, 9 July 1998.
29 S/1998/272, 27 March 1998.
30 S/1998/223.
31 S/1998/272. See also S.PV/3868, 31 March 1998. In the context of advocating dialogue it is worth bearing in mind a point raised by Gambia in the Security Council meeting: 'The use of force, more often than not, further exacerbates a problem and produces compliance based on a fragile foundation.' S/PV.3868, 14.
32 S/1998/272.
33 S.PV/3868, 12.
34 S.PV/3868, 20.
35 Troebst, *Conflict in Kosovo*, 92–3, citing: European Action Council for Peace in the Balkans and the Public International Law and Policy Group of the Carnegie Endowment for International Peace, *Kosovo: From Crisis to a Permanent Solution* (Amsterdam: Washington, DC, 1 November 1997), 14. Emphasis added.
36 Contact Group Non-negotiable Principles/Basic Elements, 30 January 1999, Weller, *The Crisis in Kosovo*, 417. To recap, these include: peaceful solution through dialogue; interim agreement; a mechanism for a final settlement after an interim period of three years; territorial integrity of the FRY; international involvement and full cooperation by the parties on implementation; high degree of self-governance in Kosovo; establishment of national community structures.
37 Response of Kosova to Views Adopted by the Contact Group, 30 January 1999, Weller, *The Crisis in Kosovo*, 417.
38 IICK, *The Kosovo Report*, 76; C. Guicherd, 'International Law and the War in Kosovo', *Survival*, 41:2 (1999), 26.
39 See Weller, *The Crisis in Kosovo*, 349–50.
40 Ibid.
41 I. Daalder and M. O'Hanlon, *Winning Ugly: NATO's War to Save Kosovo* (Washington, DC: The Brookings Institute Press, 2000), 47–50.
42 Statement by the NAC on Kosovo, 30 January 1999, Weller, *The Crisis in Kosovo*, 416. Article 2(4) of the UN Charter prohibits not only the use of force, but also the threat of the use of force.
43 S/PV.3988, 24 March 1999.
44 Weller, *The Crisis in Kosovo*, 398.
45 Weller, *The Crisis in Kosovo*.
46 James Rubin, Press Briefing on the Kosovo peace talks, Rambouillet, 21 February 1999, Weller, *The Crisis in Kosovo*, 451–2.
47 S/1999/96, 29 January 1999.
48 Weller, *The Crisis in Kosovo*, 400.
49 S/1999/96.
50 S/1998/567, 24 June 1998.
51 S/1998/567.
52 Zolo, *Invoking Humanity*, 30; J. Pilger, 'Revealed: The Amazing Nato Plan, Tabled at Rambouillet, to Occupy Yugoslavia', *New Statesman*, 17 May 1999; Bellamy 'Lessons Unlearned', 48; R. Miller: 'Respectable Oppressors, Hypocritical Liberators: Morality, Intervention, and Reality', in Chatterjee and Scheid (eds), *Ethics and Foreign Intervention*, 242.

53 Department of State Spokesman Briefing on Kosovo peace talks, Rambouillet, 20 February 1999, and James Rubin, US Press Briefing, Rambouillet, 20 February 1999, Weller, *The Crisis in Kosovo*, 447–8.
54 Weller, *The Crisis in Kosovo*, 403; Bellamy, *Kosovo and International Society*, 138. There is little consensus about the relative importance of the military implementation agreement. Daalder and O'Hanlon argue that these provisions were not decisive for Milošević (although they do not mention the potential impact they had on the Kosovar delegation) and would have been up for discussion had they been objected to (*Winning Ugly*, 14).
55 Daalder and O'Hanlon, *Winning Ugly*. Bellamy concurs with this noting that in fact the Europeans formally offered the renegotiation of the implementation agreement to the Serbs without consulting the Kosovars. *Kosovo and International Society*, 145.
56 S/1998/712.
57 S/1998/757, 13 August 1998.
58 S/1998/757.
59 Ibid.
60 S/PV.3930, 23 September 1998.
61 S/1998/834, 4 September 1998: the report refers to increasing numbers of refugees and internally displaced people, continuing human rights abuses, inadequate security conditions for returnees and the continuing destruction of homes.
62 S/1998/912, 3 October 1998: 'During the reporting period, fighting in Kosovo continued unabated ... In the week following the adoption, on 23 September 1998, of resolution 1199 (1998), the forces in fact intensified their operations, launching another offensive in the Drenica region and in the Suva Reka-Stimlje-Urosevac triangle. Those operations have reportedly resulted in the displacement of some 20,000 additional people ... Fighting continued on 28 and 29 September, contrary to the statement of the Serbian Prime Minister, Mr Marjanovic, on 28 September, that anti-insurgency operations in Kosovo had been completed and that peace reigned in Kosovo.'
63 S/PV.3989, 26 March 1999.
64 S/PV.3988, 6. See also the UK's statement: 'when diplomacy has failed, do we react just with further words? ... Every means short of force has been tried to avert this situation. In these circumstances, and as an exceptional measure on grounds of overwhelming humanitarian necessity, military intervention is legally justifiable' (11–12).
65 S/PV.3988, 8.
66 S/PV.3988, 3.
67 Wheeler, 'Legitimating Humanitarian Intervention', 556.
68 S/PV.3988, 13. It should be noted that there were informal discussions in October 1998.
69 The relevant elements of this communicative imperative can only be broadly sketched because an in-depth examination of the media coverage of Kosovo and the intervention is beyond the scope of the book.
70 Habermas, 'Political Communication in Media Society'.
71 Ibid., 419.
72 Ibid., 420.
73 Ibid., 421.
74 Herring, 'From Rambouillet to the Kosovo Accords', 239–40. Critical discussion of these issues can be found in a range of literature, including, D. K. Thussu, 'Legitimizing "Humanitarian Intervention"? CNN, NATO and the Kosovo Crisis', *European Journal of Communication*, 15:3 (2000), 345–61; P. Hammond and E. Herman (eds), *Degraded*

Capability: The Media and the Kosovo Crisis (London, Pluto Press, 2000); P. Goff, (ed.), *The Kosovo News and Propaganda War* (Vienna: International Press Institute, 1999); Indymedia and Media Lens (e.g. www.indymedia.org.uk/en/2004/03/288316.html, accessed 30 November 2010). A common critical view is that the media machine constructed by NATO to sell the war presented it in a highly distorted fashion, ensuring that the press briefings presented the 'bombing campaign in a sanitised, euphemistic fashion, as if there could be no civilian blood spilt or fear induced . . . It is difficult not to conclude that the alliance used stories – which it knew were not adequately corroborated and were often coming from sources with a vested interest in intensifying the conflict – to justify the bombings to an unconvinced public' (Goff, *The Kosovo News*, 15).

75 M. Blagojević, 'War on Kosovo: A Victory for the Media?' in Bieber and Daskalovski (eds), *Understanding the War in Kosovo*, 166–83. Mechanisms referred to include: reduction and simplification of the explanation; counting on ignorance; the power of victimisation; producing stereotypes; prejudices and hatred; factual distortion; the destruction of meaning; hierarchisation of the victims; omission of certain topics from discussion which might complicate or bring different perspectives to understanding the conflict; the destruction of empathy; and construction of a new moralism.

76 Statement by the Prime Minister, Tony Blair, in the House of Commons, Tuesday, 23 March 1999, Weller, *The Crisis in Kosovo*, 495.

77 S/PV.3937, 24 October 1998. There are many examples of such language in the Security Council meetings on 24 March, 1999, S/PV.3988; 14 May 1999, S/PV.4003.

78 *Sunday Telegraph*, 4 April 1999. See P. Hammond, 'Reporting "Humanitarian" Warfare: Propaganda, Moralism and NATO's Kosovo War', *Journalism Studies*, 1:3 (2000).

79 Goff, *The Kosovo News*, 17.

80 F. Dallmayr, 'Conversation Across Boundaries: Political Theory and Global Diversity', *Millennium: Journal of International Studies*, 30:2 (2001), 4.

81 S/1998/229, 12 March 1998. See also S/1998/240, 16 March 1998: 'the recent actions of police forces of the Republic of Serbia in Kosovo and Metohija have been carried out exclusively in the function of combating terrorism'; S/1998/285, 30 March 1998.

82 S/1998/285.

83 S/1998/250, 18 March 1998; S/1998/361, Annex 1, 30 April 1998.

84 S/1998/246, 17 March 1998.

85 The Contact Group made their position concerning the sovereignty of the FRY abundantly clear: 'No one should misunderstand our position on the core issue involved. We support neither independence nor the maintenance of the status quo' (S/1998/223, Contact Group statement, London, 9 March 1998). See Press Conference by Richard Holbrooke and William Walker, 29 October 1998, Weller, *The Crisis in Kosovo*, 295; S/1998/272.

86 S/PV.3868, 31 March 1998, 15.

87 Ibid., 21.

88 Ibid., 17.

89 Outhwaite, *Habermas*, 41.

90 Bernstein, *Recovering Ethical Life*, 49.

91 S/1998/470, 4 June 1998.

92 Judah, *Kosovo*, 156.

93 See Chapter 2.

94 S/PV.3988; S/PV.3989; H. Walker, 'The Case of Kosovo', *Civil Wars*, 7:1 (2005), 28–70. This question in relation to Kosovo is, by itself, the subject of a voluminous

literature and will not be discussed further here. For example, see Guicherd, 'International Law'; Charney, 'Anticipatory Humanitarian Intervention in Kosovo'; Falk, 'Kosovo, World Order'.
95 This is a position echoed by Slovenia in the Council meeting on 26 March 1999 which rejected the Russian draft resolution. Slovenia's representative recognised that 'the requirement of consistency in the interpretation and application of the principles and norms of the United Nations Charter demands at least some indication as to the specific justification for the approach proposed by the draft resolution in the present case. Such indication is sadly lacking and, as I mentioned before, cannot be replaced by the strong words we see in the draft resolution.' S/PV.3989.
96 S/1998/361, Annex II. Emphasis added.
97 Judah, *Kosovo*, 160. Bishop Artemije's views are decidedly Serbian as to his position concerning Kosovo's status, but it is his pro-talks approach that is important in this context. Artemije's position is represented in the same way in the ICG's, 'Kosovo Spring', 33.
98 Press Briefing by the Contact Group Negotiators, 18 February 1999.
99 Chairman's conclusions, Contact Group Meeting, Paris, 14 February 1999, Weller, *The Crisis in Kosovo*, 431.
100 S/PV.3868.
101 S/PV.3868.
102 Weller, *The Crisis in Kosovo*, 221.
103 Judah, *Kosovo*, 138.
104 Ibid. Other Balkan observers concur with this interpretation such as Caplan, 'International Diplomacy', 753–4; Daalder and O'Hanlon, *Winning Ugly*; Howard Clark; and Marc Weller.
105 Statement by Madeleine Albright at the Contact Group Ministerial meeting on Kosovo, London, 9 March, 1998: http://secretary.state.gov/www/statements/1998/980309.html. Use of this quotation is not intended to support the violent methods adopted by the KLA, but to draw attention to the power relations constituted by particular forms of recognition.
106 Troebst, *Conflict in Kosovo*, 104.
107 S/PV.3868, 15.
108 Preface, I. Rugova, *La Question du Kosovo: Entretiens realises par Marie-Francoise Allain et Xavier Galmiche* (Paris: Fayard, 1994), 18. All translations are the author's own. 'C'est en défigurant l'Histoire que l'on a fomenté ce crime dans les Balkans.'
109 Ibid. 'Aucun historien sérieux, aucune source historique fiable n'admet que les Serbes aient été les premiers occupants du Kosovo, et les Albanais des adventices. C'est exactement le contraire: les Albanais ont toujours été là, les Slaves ne sont arrives qu'ensuite.'
110 See Kostovicova, *Kosovo: The Politics of Identity and Space*; Clark, *Civil Resistance in Kosovo*; Mertus, *Kosovo: How Myths and Truths Started a War*.
111 Falk, 'Humanitarian Wars', 330.
112 S/PV.3988, 4.

7

Conclusion

> Dialogue did not fail in Kosovo. Dialogue had just never been properly tried.
> Steinar Bryn[1]

Legitimacy matters ...

In an international political realm in which power is all too often perceived as the dominant factor, why do questions of legitimacy and justification matter when actors use force? *Justifying Violence* has sought to answer this question by showing through an analysis of the Kosovo conflict how state and non-state actors recognised the need to justify their use of violence to both domestic and international audiences. Thus, as constructivists argue, even in the absence of enforcement mechanisms, states almost always recognise the need to justify their actions, though how successful they are in securing legitimation of these claims varies depending on how far they depart from established norms, and the play of power and interests in particular cases. Despite the strengths of constructivist approaches, especially those which recognise the centrality of language, I have argued that they do not capture the understanding of legitimacy provided by a communicative ethics framework. The latter goes beyond constructivist approaches by providing a set of tools – the communicative imperatives – for interrogating the communicative practices of actors. Communicative ethics derives its critical and emancipatory power through an understanding of the conditions under which communication may be distorted and thus secures critical purchase over the empirical practices through which states and other actors make claims to legitimacy.

The IICK's declaration that NATO's intervention in Kosovo was 'illegal but legitimate' has been the foil against which the argument has been developed that it is vital to move beyond understanding legitimacy in only legal and moral terms. Instead, any discussion of legitimacy claims – and this is never more important than in relation to decisions to use force – must include a critical communicative dimension. Drawing on Habermasian critical theory, I have developed an innovative conception of communicative ethics which can be operationalised through the communicative imperatives set out in Chapter 5 to interrogate past, present, and future claims to

Conclusion

legitimacy in relation to decisions on the use of force. The communicative imperatives offer a means with which to investigate the immanent and normative claims to legitimacy of particular communicative practices and this translates into a nuanced account of communicative distortion in international politics. Specifically, the book has applied this communicative ethics framework to NATO's intervention in Kosovo and, in so doing, revealed a series of communicative practices both within the Council and in other fora such as the ECCY, the Badinter Commission, and the Holbrooke negotiations, characterised by moments of exclusion, coercion, incoherence, or a lack of reflexivity or recognition.

Exclusion operated as a crucial factor in shaping the course of events over Kosovo in the 1990s and this has contributed significantly to the undermining of claims to legitimacy of NATO's intervention. Exclusion – and its converse, inclusion – also serves to highlight most clearly ways in which diplomatic interventions could have been conducted differently and alternative non-violent forms of engagement adopted. The case shows that developing more inclusionary practices calls for consideration of the structural barriers to participation at the international level faced by non-state actors. It also calls for reflection upon the way in which states and their representatives construct negotiations and peace processes with a particular focus on the *how* of such processes; in other words, their procedural legitimacy. While the threat of force remains the clearest sign of coercion and strategic action, the analysis in Chapters 2 and 6 demonstrates the degree to which coercion can take the form of a subtle process of marginalisation of ideas and actors, one which raises concerns over the efficacy and legitimacy of dialogue aimed at ending conflict.

Re-reading Kosovo through the lens of the communicative imperatives has revealed the lack of coherence in the policies pursued by the international community towards the Balkans and Kosovo during the 1990s. The lack of coherence in policy terms can not only be identified in the mismatch between the words and actions of states, but in the fundamental dilemma faced by the international community over Kosovo in trying to satisfy two incompatible positions. No political solution was likely to be reached while the international community simultaneously supported the sovereignty and territorial integrity of the FRY and the human and political rights of the Kosovars.[2] This, in part, was a reflection of the tension among members of the international community between pluralist and solidarist values and the different sets of international norms they entailed. Any solution when framed as an either/or situation required that the international community acknowledged support for the claim of one side over another. Given that by 1998, this involved either support for the KLA or for Milošević, both emerged as deeply problematic, if not equally unappetising, alternatives.

The latter dilemma sharpens our awareness of alternative paths of non-violent engagement. The analysis highlights the missed opportunities for securing a peaceful settlement of the conflict which were lost through the lack of support given to the non-violent resistance movement during the 1990s. What the case clearly shows is the need for greater awareness on the part of key actors of the problematic nature and consequences of particular communicative practices. If actors using violence want their claims to legitimacy validated and subsequent actions to be perceived as legitimate by a wider audience, then communicative ethics provides critical guidance as to how they might engage in dialogue through offering a series of normative and procedural suggestions which would crucially expand inclusiveness and reduce (though not eliminate) the role of strategic action. This concern over the quality and nature of the communicative practices regarding Kosovo in 1998–99 is heightened when placed in the wider context of the international community's approach to the conflict throughout the 1990s. Indeed, central to the communicative ethics framework developed in the book is recognition of a temporal dimension to claims of legitimacy as such an approach leads us to look for moments when opportunities for dialogue in conflict situations were closed down. These critical insights into the relationship between legitimacy and communicative practices in the case of Kosovo raise crucial questions for policy-makers and scholars alike to reflect on when considering justifications for the use of force.

The engagement with the debates over communicative ethics in critical theory, where these concepts originated, and in IR, to which they have been translated, has been, and at times remains, an uncomfortable journey. By drawing on the theoretical resources of each field of enquiry, the concept and boundaries of communicative ethics has broadened, deepened, and taken, perhaps, some unlikely turns. Nonetheless, the theoretical framework which has emerged – embodied in the communicative imperatives – has, it is suggested, enriched the theoretical and empirical purposes to which Habermas's work has been adopted in IR. It also poses a number of important questions to the existing theoretical approaches in IR which have been engaged with in the course of the book, namely, the concepts of 'good international citizenship' and 'responsibility to protect', the constructivism of Johnstone and others who take the role of language seriously, and the critical theoretical approach broached by Bjola's notion of deliberative legitimacy.

It is in the work of English school theorists that we have seen rich developments in the sphere of theorising legitimacy with regard to the use of force for humanitarian purposes. Advocates of the broad concept of good international citizenship have articulated varying positions regarding the relative emphasis accorded to principles of order and justice in international society which, broadly speaking, align with the spectrum of pluralism and solidarism.

Conclusion

Recognising the tension contained within the UN Charter between protecting human rights on the one hand, and upholding the principles of non-intervention and sovereignty on the other, good international citizenship theorising and associated concepts like the responsibility to protect have sought to find innovative procedural ways in which state responsibilities could be re-framed so as to ensure that crimes such as genocide, ethnic cleansing, and mass human rights violations would not be met with inaction by the international community. At the heart of these procedural innovations has been the role of the Security Council, and in particular, the difficulties of agreeing on whether any exit should be permitted from the strict procedural rules of the Charter and the ever-present threat of the veto held by the permanent members of the Council.[3]

Building on such insights regarding the need to act legitimately in cases of mass human rights violations, while recognising the potential obstacles within the structures of the Security Council and UN Charter, the ICISS report, *The Responsibility to Protect*, published in 2001 and strongly influenced by NATO's intervention in Kosovo, shifted the focus of the debate further still. The responsibility to protect doctrine proposed a series of threshold and precautionary criteria under which action to prevent conflict and protect individuals could be taken legitimately. Not wishing to detract from or minimise the responsibilities of sovereign authority, the responsibility to protect established a hierarchy of responsibilities to try and ensure that where states failed to act, regional or international mechanisms or bodies could step in to fill the gap.

At the heart of many pluralist objections to interventions such as NATO's in Kosovo was the absence of explicit Security Council authorisation. Solidarists might reply that in the face of the impending humanitarian catastrophe in Kosovo, NATO had little choice but to circumvent the rules of the Charter given Russia and China's threat to use the veto. NATO states chose to act outside the Council rather than risk doing so after having had a draft resolution, which would have provided this authority, defeated by a Russian and Chinese veto. Had NATO acted in the face of a Russian and Chinese veto, this would have left it even more exposed in terms of its claims to legitimacy.

What we see emerge in the writings of those who incline towards the solidarist end of the spectrum are procedural suggestions regarding the role of the veto within the Council and the force of moral arguments whereby the use of force for humanitarian purposes may be countenanced through progressive challenges to legalist positions.[4] While Linklater has argued that good international citizens should perhaps challenge the 'legitimacy of the veto by irresponsible powers that are prepared to block international action to prevent human rights violations', the ICISS went further still and proposed a 'code of conduct' to be adopted by the Permanent Five regarding limitations on exercise of the veto.[5] Cognisant of the challenge posed to the rules and norms of international society by any future unauthorised military interventions resulting from action being blocked in the Council by the veto, the ICISS proposed new procedural criteria regarding the notion of right authority. This is primarily, although not exclusively, located within the body of the Security Council whereupon the permanent members of the Council are enjoined to withhold the use of their veto powers in 'matters where their vital state interests are not involved, to obstruct the passage of resolutions authorizing military intervention for human protection purposes for which there is otherwise majority support'.[6] The ICISS, along with similar frameworks discussed in Chapter 2, all of which are informed by the *jus ad bellum* concerns of the just war tradition, include procedural mechanisms setting out how to resolve disagreements wherein the Security Council is unable or unwilling to act.

Whilst the recommendations for how to proceed (procedural legitimacy) in cases where the Security Council is unable to agree on the use of force contribute importantly to the debate over the legitimacy of the use of force in international politics, it is the contention of this book that there are two fundamental limitations with approaches of this kind. First, the argument for limits on the veto suggested by exponents of good international citizenship like Linklater, and the arguments of the ICISS, ignore the critical communicative dimension of legitimacy. Put differently, what these frameworks lack are different kinds of procedural criteria, namely, those that can examine the legitimacy of the communicative process through which such procedural and substantive criteria for deciding when intervention is permissible are agreed upon. Framed in this way, the challenge of procedural legitimacy in relation to the use of force goes beyond questions (important though they are) about limits on the veto to encompass issues which all too often remain hidden in debates over 'right authority' concerning levels of inclusion, the absence of coercion, and reflexive dialogue.

Second, a communicative ethics framework would contend that the question as to whether the substantive criteria governing the use of force – this book has focused crucially on the criterion of last resort – have been met in particular cases can only be answered through practical discourse free from constraints between the relevant actors. Here the contention is that the responsibility to protect and other similar frameworks with *jus ad bellum* criteria do not have the tools to analyse specific decision-making processes for evidence of relevant constraints, such as exclusion and coercion, which might affect their subsequent legitimacy. When procedural legitimacy is embedded in the critical theoretical approach of communicative ethics, a reflexive and evaluative 'check' on actors (and the rules they establish) is always available, providing forms of critique which open up the potential for the removal of constraints which shape and are shaped by relations of power and domination.

While communicative ethics and advocates of good international citizenship and the responsibility to protect could share common ground – albeit with different conceptual starting points regarding the meaning to be accorded to procedural legitimacy – in suggesting that had NATO tabled a resolution in the Security Council seeking authorisation for military action the situation might have unfolded differently, for communicative ethics the story does not end there. Even had this been the case and even had such a resolution been adopted (most likely still justified by the claim of last resort), the communicative practices within the Council debate would remain a legitimate focus of communicative ethics given the possibility that consensus might be established through coercion. Moreover, communicative ethics would still be able to challenge the claim of last resort given the foreclosure of alternative non-violent paths by the international community and the presence of other constraints on dialogue. It is out of this debate over the meaning to be ascribed to procedural legitimacy that the central arguments concerning the claim of last resort emerge. NATO's justification for the use of force drew heavily on the claim of last resort, with the Alliance arguing that all other credible non-violent options had been exhausted. As Michael Walzer cogently asserts, however, 'it is not so easy to reach the "last resort". To get there, one must indeed try everything (which is a lot of things) and not just once.'[7] The difficulty of making a good case for last resort is evident given the disagreement among Security Council members as to whether this criterion had been met in the case of Kosovo. While Russia was adamant that all diplomatic and political options had not been exhausted, the five NATO states on the Council argued otherwise. These positions were reflected in the debate over the draft resolution tabled by Russia on 26 March 1999 immediately following the commencement of NATO's bombing campaign. Two key arguments become evident once the disagreements between Russia and NATO are looked at through the prism of communicative ethics.

First, as seen in the discussion of strategic and communicative rationalities in Chapter 6, it is not possible to ascertain, with any certainty, the motives informing the positions adopted by states in the Council in response to the draft resolution. Multiple interpretations are plausible concerning the degree to which communicative and/or strategic orientations were adopted by Russia or NATO states. This clearly highlights the limitation imposed upon the empirical application of Habermas's analytical distinction between strategic and communicative action, and this point will be returned to below.

The second argument, and directly relevant to NATO's claim of last resort, derives from the point made earlier that applying a communicative ethics framework leads to recognition of a temporal dimension to questions of legitimacy. It was noted above that the analysis of Kosovo in the book has identified a series of missed opportunities for dialogue which, cumulatively, served to undermine the argument that all credible options had indeed been exhausted. Consequently, NATO's claim of last resort – fiercely contested by Russia and China – failed to acknowledge this temporal dimension. What communicative ethics does is help write back into history the missed opportunities for dialogue and non-violent political engagement. In so doing, it challenges those actors and spectators who want to reduce the debate over legitimacy to a judgement concerning the moral or legal merits of NATO's use of force against the FRY. The temporal dimension of communicative ethics opens our eyes to the longer-term relationship between legitimacy and communicative practices which exists outside of the immediate period of humanitarian emergency and which cannot simply be subsumed within those moments of crisis. Explicitly articulating this relationship is a timely reminder for policy-makers and practitioners and seeks to encourage a greater attention to the structure and character of dialogic opportunities over an extended period of time in situations of developing conflict.

The international community's lack of recognition of the complexity of the conflict, reluctant engagement and frequent exclusionary practices during the 1990s, were not only a cause of the conflict which broke out in 1998, but also significantly narrowed the scope for more moderate solutions; fewer Kosovars, for example, were prepared to accept anything less than full independence from 1998 onwards than might have been the case earlier.[8] A relevant counterfactual question to ask in this context is whether the KLA would still have moved into military positions vacated by the Serbs under the terms of the Holbrooke agreement, thereby contributing to a spiral of violence and retribution by the Serbs, had they been included where appropriate in the political negotiations? The limited focus on the period of crisis from 1998–99 which occupies most analyses of the conflict prevents us from seeing wider patterns of poor engagement, neglect, and exclusion by the international community.

Communicative ethics: closing the circle

Constructivism in IR is concerned with 'understanding and explaining the norms that operate in the international realm and the constitution of that realm by these norms'.[9] While it offers an explanation of the 'is', it does not engage sufficiently with an evaluation of the 'ought'. Constructivism, then, lacks the critical interpretive capacity of communicative ethics; it is unable to tell us how we might *better* engage in norm formation or how we might identify those who may have been harmed or excluded by existing practices.

While critical theory secures for communicative ethics an emancipatory

Conclusion

focus, due attention must be paid to its limitations. The balance between a desire to avoid totalising theoretical tendencies whilst remaining relevant for international politics characterises contemporary critical theory and has echoed throughout this book. Keen to avoid authoritarian institutional design or a particular normative agenda, the communicative ethics framework seeks to emphasise the need for substantive outcomes to be decided by the participants through fair and reflective procedures which recognise the constitutive relationship between the nature of particular communicative practices and their subsequent legitimacy.

Recalling the universalist and utopian charges laid at Habermas's door in Chapter 4, Reus-Smit has cast doubt on the 'assumed fit between constructivist empirics and communicative ethics in two important respects'. Placing considerable emphasis on Habermas's insistence on the inclusion of '*all affected*' and the principle (U), he argues that the actual communicative processes which 'accompany the production, interpretation, and reproduction of international law differ, perhaps not surprisingly, from the ideal type posited by communicative action theory'. Furthermore, he remarks that communicative ethics theorists would be likely to 'describe such processes as "distorted" forms of communication – corrupted by unrepresentative patterns of participation, penetration of particularistic interests, or strategic bargaining – and conclude that the norms generated will lack legitimacy, affecting their durability and salience, and cannot be considered normatively "valid"'. He concludes by suggesting that the problem with representing these as 'distorted processes' is that they 'often produce rules and norms that international actors deem legitimate and which our own moral intuitions tell us are right, good, or just'.[10] Ultimately, however, Reus-Smit and those who argue like him move too far towards the consideration of Habermas's ideal speech situation as a guide for direct translation into practice.

The framework of communicative ethics developed in this book is intended to rebut the criticism that a position informed by Habermasian critical theory has little purchase on vital contemporary moral and ethical debates and it does so in four key ways. First, recognising the complexity of political interaction which cannot always empirically distinguish between strategic and communicative action acknowledges the criticisms applied to Habermas's distinction. However, at the same time, communicative ethics retains its critical leverage from both the presuppositions of argumentation and the analytical concept of strategic action. Second, adopting the notion of trade-offs between participation on the one hand, and effectiveness or justice on the other, responds to the pragmatic and, at times, strategic requirements of the political sphere. Such trade-offs may be accepted following their justification by actors as necessary in particular cases. This is intended to alleviate the concerns of those for whom the ideal character of Habermas's theory renders it unsuited for application to international politics. Third, the identification of a temporal dimension to legitimacy that removes our focus solely from the nature of deliberations which take place in moments of crisis not only challenges the construction of political crises by pointing to alternative prior political possibilities, but also contests the reification of necessity as justification in crisis situations. Fourth, and not least of all, communicative ethics removes, as Benhabib suggests, the strong emphasis on (U) and focuses instead on the notion of procedural fairness. Consequently the aim of communicative ethics is not to generate moral norms but to interrogate the intersubjective validity of claims to legitimacy raised by actors in particular contexts. A further implication of conceptualising communicative ethics in this way is that it opens up possibilities for the inclusion of those actors and discourses which are typically marginalised and lack recognition in international politics as a result of their use of affective dimensions of language, their status as an actor or their cultural contexts.

Communicative ethics provides a means of critique for both the political actor and the spectator, to use Arendt's terms, through the lens of reflective judgement. By recognising the relevance of communicative ethics for both actors and spectators, the role of critique is retained while ensuring emancipatory potential for political actors to reflect on, transform, and critique their own practices. As illustrated by the Kosovo case, communicative ethics permits an *ex post* evaluation of the constraints and distortion present within communicative practices. However, the potential for immanent critique also ensures room for reflection and action by participants. The key example here was the repeated call by Contact Group states and others for the initiation of dialogue without pre-conditions between the FRY/Serbs and Kosovars. In reality, analysis revealed the consistent imposition of pre-conditions by the international community and the FRY/Serbia. Conscious recognition of this dissonance might potentially have led to a more reflective stance by the parties regarding the degree of procedural legitimacy (understood in critical communicative terms) under which the dialogue was functioning.

The insights into the conflict in Kosovo offered by the communicative ethics framework developed in this book do go beyond both 'constructivist empirics' and theorising. This is because they are concerned, as Reus-Smit suggests, with the (communicative) ethics of norm formation and justification in relation to the use of force. Communicative ethics holds out the promise at the international level of supplementing the constructivist understanding of how norms shape actors' positions and interactions with an evaluative and critical focus on the legitimacy of the communicative process itself. As a result, the legitimacy of particular decision-making processes is exposed to critical reflection by both participants and spectators.

While acknowledging that states frequently engage in justificatory discourse, communicative ethics offers an awareness of the potential procedures and structures that may distort communication which is crucial to both the task of critique and emancipatory practice. Outlined by the communicative imperatives, such distortion may emerge from a variety of factors, including: the exclusion or marginalisation of particular actors; the excessive agency of some actors, and the lack of social power of others, which in turn affects relative capacity to voice fundamental concerns or contribute to agenda-setting processes; latent strategic action; material and non-material coercion; and the expectations governing acceptable forms of public speech. Even in public spheres governed by democratic norms of deliberation and equality, communicative ethics reveals the operation of relations of power and domination in communicative practice and offers signposts for the acts of reflection necessary for actors to recognise and lift such operative constraints.

The emphasis of communicative ethics is placed on *illegitimacy* rather than legitimacy, *injustice* rather than justice. This is for two reasons. First, one of the charges levelled at Habermas (and other theorists of justice) is that ideals of justice remain too abstract and too far removed from political practice. Instead of aiming for a 'fully just order' it seems appropriate for critical theory to be able to say something about *in*justice precisely because 'the social hopes that should be given priority are those of people who are suffering the brutalizing effects of the worst structural injustices'.[11] We do not, therefore, need to enact an ideal speech situation before we can perceive communicative injustices. In line with reflective judgement which guided the analysis undertaken in Chapter 6, while it helps to have the conditions characterising the ideal speech situation in mind in order to understand the scale of the injustice, it is not necessary to implement it in practice in order to perceive comparative injustices. As Shane O'Neill argues, 'if we want to connect theory and practice effectively, then we should use theory to engage in a process of comparison that allows us to find ways of reducing injustice in (at least) one particular place'.[12] We do not, for example, need to have institutionalised the ideal speech situation in order to understand that the comparative communicative capacities available to the Serbs and the Kosovar Albanians disadvantaged the Kosovars considerably and resulted, for example, in undermining the claim to legitimacy of the Holbrooke agreement.

Second, the orientation towards illegitimacy has an additional bearing on the relationship between theory and practice in terms of guiding emancipatory practice. Discourse ethics cannot, for Habermas, be used 'prescriptively in the direct sense, but indirectly, by becoming part of a critical social theory that can be used to interpret situations'.[13] Within the limits of theory offered by Habermas, it is not possible to outline what 'legitimacy' might ideally look like in the international political sphere. It is, however, somewhat easier to recognise moments of illegitimacy experienced through various forms of harm, injustice or suffering. In sum, the role of discourse ethics sketched out below applies equally to the communicative ethics framework set out in the book:

> it is not the task of a discourse ethics to ground political rights such as participation or freedom of speech – no matter to what extent the pressure to participate grows out of the individual pain engendered by exclusion. Rather, it is up to the state to include individuals in its decision-making processes *if it wishes to remain legitimate.*[14]

The burden of persuasion rests on states, therefore, to show why, if their claims to legitimacy are to be validated, some individuals or groups should be excluded from the conversation on account of particular characteristics. Assenting to the need to historicise and evaluate the legitimacy of particular negotiations and outcomes identified as being at the heart of a communicative ethics, Robyn Eckersley notes that even in 'circumstances where strategic bargaining looms large, the legitimacy of any resulting compromise agreement still turns on the *fairness of the bargaining conditions*'.[15] We cannot know, with any certainty, the motivations which guide states' actions, and therefore cannot determine the degree of strategic or communicative action guiding their interactions. However, as captured by Eckersley's point above, communicative ethics secures an awareness of the ways in which this analytical distinction may inform processes of communicative distortion and impact upon the validity of claims to legitimacy.

The capacity of communicative ethics to 'read' or interrogate claims to legitimacy has important bearings on the potential for critique and transformation within international politics. Given the normative, sociological and praxeological dimensions of inclusion and exclusion which are central to a critical theory of IR, the critical capacity – or ethic of suspicion – of communicative ethics not only provides a means to hold actors accountable for the practices of inclusion and exclusion they adopt but it also contributes to the process whereby emancipatory practices might be identified by state and non-state actors. Nowhere is this more important in international politics than when states make decisions to go to war.

NOTES

1 S. Bryn, 'Engaging the "Other": The Nansen Dialogue Network in the Balkans': www.peoplebuildingpeace.org/thestories/print.php?id=127&typ=theme (accessed 1 December 2010).
2 A similar point is made by D. Allin, 'NATO's Balkan Interventions', *Adelphi Paper 347*, (New York: Oxford University Press, 2002), 51.
3 Wheeler, 'Operationalising the Responsibility to Protect'; Wheeler, 'The Humanitarian Responsibilities of Sovereignty'; ICISS, *The Responsibility to Protect*; Bellamy, *Responsibility to Protect*.
4 Linklater, 'The Good International Citizen and the Crisis in Kosovo'.

5 Ibid., 490; ICISS, *The Responsibility to Protect*, 51–4.
6 ICISS, *Responsibility to Protect*, xiii.
7 M. Walzer, *Arguing About War* (New Haven: Yale University Press, 2004), 54. See also K. Booth, 'Ten Flaws of Just Wars', in Booth (ed.), *The Kosovo Tragedy*, 316–17. This is not the view of last resort iterated in the ICISS report or in Wheeler's *Saving Strangers*, both of which adopt a more pragmatic emphasis on all *credible* non-violent options being exhausted.
8 See Caplan, 'International Diplomacy', 746.
9 Shapcott, 'Critical Theory', 333.
10 Reus-Smit, 'Society, power, and ethics', 286–7.
11 O'Neill, 'Struggles Against Injustice', 130.
12 Ibid., 130.
13 Blaug, *Democracy: Real and Ideal*, 53, citing Habermas.
14 Ibid., 121. Original emphasis. See Benhabib, *Situating the Self*.
15 Eckersley, 'Soft Law, Hard politics', 93. Original emphasis.

Bibliography

Books and articles

Abizadeh, A., 'In Defence of the Universalisation Principle in Discourse Ethics', *The Philosophical Forum*, 36:2 (2005), 193–211

Adler, E., 'Seizing the Middle Ground: Constructivism in World Politics', *European Journal of International Relations*, 3:3 (1997), 319–63

Adorno, T. and M. Horkheimer, *Dialectic of Enlightenment* (London: Verso, 1979)

Aguera, M., 'Air Power Paradox: NATO's "Misuse" of Military Force in Kosovo and its Consequences', *Small Wars and Insurgencies*, 12:3 (2001), 115–28

Albert, M., O. Kessler and S. Stetter, 'On Order and Conflict: International Relations and the "Communicative Turn"', *Review of International Studies*, 34, Special Issue (2008), 43–67

Albright, M. and B. Woodward, *Madam Secretary – A Memoir* (London: Macmillan, 2003)

Alexy, R., *A Theory of Legal Argumentation* (trans. Ruth Adler and Neil MacCormick) (Oxford: Clarendon Press, 1989)

Alexy, R., 'A Theory of Practical Discourse', in S. Benhabib and F. Dallmayr (eds), *The Communicative Ethics Controversy* (Cambridge, MA: MIT Press, 1990)

Allin, D., 'Nato's Balkan Interventions', *Adelphi Paper 347* (New York: Oxford University Press, 2002)

Amnesty International, *Kosovo: The Evidence* (London: Amnesty International, 1999)

Apel, K.-O., 'On the Relationship Between Ethics, International Law and Politico-Military Strategy in Our Time: A Philosophical Retrospective on the Kosovo Conflict', *European Journal of Social Theory*, 4:1 (2001), 29–40

Archibugi, D., *Debating Cosmopolitics* (London: Verso, 2003)

Ashley, R. K., 'Political Realism and Human Interests', *International Studies Quarterly*, 25:2 (1981), 204–36

Ashley, R. K., 'The Poverty of Neorealism', in R. O. Keohane (ed.), *Neorealism and its Critics* (New York: Columbia University Press, 1986)

Bain, W., 'The Pluralist-Solidarist Debate', in R. Denemark (ed.), *International Studies Compendium Project*, vol. IX (Oxford: Blackwell Publishing, 2009)

Bibliography

Baynes, K., *The Normative Grounds of Social Criticism: Kant, Rawls, Habermas* (Albany: State University of New York Press, 1992)

Becker, R., 'The Rambouillet Accord: A Declaration of War Disguised as a Peace Agreement', International Action Center (4 May 1999)

Beetham, D., *Auditing Democracy in Britain* (London: The Charter 88 Trust, 1993)

Beiner, R. (ed.), 'Hannah Arendt on Judging', in H. Arendt, *Lectures on Kant's Political Philosophy* (Sussex: The Harvester Press Limited, 1982)

Bellamy, A. J., 'Human Wrongs in Kosovo 1974–99', *International Journal of Human Rights*, 4:3 (2000), 105–26

Bellamy, A. J., 'Lessons Unlearned: Why Coercive Diplomacy Failed at Rambouillet', *International Peacekeeping*, 7:2 (2000), 95–114

Bellamy, A. J., 'Kosovo: After the War, the War of Words', *International Journal of Human Rights*, 5:3 (2001), 97–110

Bellamy, A. J., 'Pragmatic Solidarism and the Dilemmas of Humanitarian Intervention', *Millennium: Journal of International Studies*, 31:3 (2002), 473–97

Bellamy, A. J., *Kosovo and International Society* (Basingstoke: Palgrave Macmillan, 2002)

Bellamy, A. J., 'Responsibility to Protect or Trojan Horse? The Crisis in Darfur and Humanitarian Intervention after Iraq', *Ethics and International Affairs*, 19:2 (2005), 31–54

Bellamy, A. J., 'Kosovo and the Advent of Sovereignty as Responsibility', *Journal of Intervention and Statebuilding*, 3:2 (2009), 163–84

Bellamy, A. J., *Responsibility to Protect* (Cambridge: Polity Press, 2009)

Bellamy, A. J., 'The Responsibility to Protect – Five Years On', *Ethics and International Affairs*, 24:2 (2010), 143–69

Benhabib, S., *Critique, Norm and Utopia* (New York: Colombia University Press, 1986)

Benhabib, S., *Situating the Self* (Cambridge: Polity Press, 1992)

Benhabib, S., 'Deliberative Rationality and Models of Democratic Legitimacy', *Constellations: An International Journal of Critical and Democratic Theory*, 1:1 (1994), 26–52

Benhabib, S., *The Rights of Others: Aliens, Residents and Citizens* (Cambridge: Cambridge University Press, 2004)

Benhabib, S., *Another Cosmopolitanism* (Oxford: Oxford University Press, 2006)

Benhabib, S. and F. Dallmayr (eds), *The Communicative Ethics Controversy* (Cambridge, MA: MIT Press, 1990)

Berger, P. and T. Luckmann, *The Social Construction of Reality: A Treatise in the Sociology of Knowledge* (New York: Penguin Putnam Inc., 1966)

Bernstein, J., *Recovering Ethical Life: Jurgen Habermas and the future of Critical Theory* (New York: Routledge, 1995)

Bernstein, R. J., 'The Constellation of Hermeneutics, Critical Theory and Deconstruction', in R. J. Dostal, *The Cambridge Companion to Gadamer* (Cambridge: Cambridge University Press, 2002)

Bieber, F. and Ž. Daskalovski (eds), *Understanding the War in Kosovo* (London: Frank Cass, 2003)

Bjola, C. 'Legitimating the Use of Force in International Politics: A Communicative Action Perspective', *European Journal of International Relations*, 11:2 (2005), 266–303

Bjola, C., 'Legitimacy and the Use of Force: Bridging the Analytical-Normative Divide', *Review of International Studies*, 34:4 (2008), 627–44

Bjola, C., *Legitimising the Use of Force in International Politics: Kosovo, Iraq and the Ethics of Intervention* (Abingdon: Routledge, 2009)

Blagojević, M., 'War on Kosovo: A Victory for the Media?', in F. Bieber and Ž. Daskalovski (eds), *Understanding the War in Kosovo* (London: Frank Cass, 2003)

Blair, T., Speech by the British Prime Minister to the Economic Club of Chicago, 22 April 1999: www.pbs.org/newshour/bb/international/jan-june99/blair_doctrine4-23.html (accessed 8 December 2011)

Blaug, R., 'The Distortion of the Face to Face: Communicative Reason and Social Work Practice', *British Journal of Social Work*, 25:4 (1995), 423–39

Blaug, R., *Democracy, Real and Ideal: Discourse Ethics and Radical Politics* (Albany: State University of New York Press, 1999)

Blaug, R., 'Between Fear and Disappointment: Critical, Empirical and Political Uses of Habermas', *Political Studies*, 45:1 (1999), 100–17

Blaug, R., 'Citizenship and Political Judgment: Between Discourse Ethics and Phronesis', *Res Publica*, 6:2 (2000), 179–98

Blokker, N. and N. Schrijver (eds), *The Security Council and the Use of Force* (Leiden: Martinus Nijhoff Publishers, 2005)

Blumi, I., 'A Story of Mitigated Ambitions: Kosova's Tortuous Path to Its Postwar Future', *Alternatives: Turkish Journal of International Relations*, 1:4 (2002), 30–52

Bohman, J., *New Philosophy of Social Science* (Cambridge: Polity Press, 1991)

Bohman, J., 'Formal Pragmatics as a Critical Theory', in L. E. Hahn (ed.), *Perspectives on Habermas* (Illinois: Open Court Publishing Company, 2000)

Boon, V., 'Jürgen Habermas and Islamic Fundamentalism: On the Limits of Discourse Ethics', *Journal of Global Ethics*, 6:2 (2010), 153–66

Boon, V. and N. Head, 'Critical Theory and the Language of Violence: Exploring the Issues', *Journal of Global Ethics*, 6:2 (2010), 79–87

Booth, K., 'NATO's Republic: Warnings from Kosovo', *Civil Wars*, 2:3 (1999), 89–95

Booth, K. (ed.), *The Kosovo Tragedy: The Human Rights Dimension* (London: Frank Cass Publishers, 2001)

Boréus, K. 'Discursive Discrimination: A Typology', *European Journal of Social Theory*, 9:3 (2006), 405–24

Brassett, J. and W. Smith, 'Deliberation and Global Civil Society: Agency, Arena, Affect', *Review of International Studies*, 36:2 (2010), 413–30

Brown, C., 'Turtles All the Way Down: Anti-Foundationalism, Critical Theory and International Relations', *Millennium: Journal of International Studies*, 23:2 (1994), 213–36

Brown, C., 'From Humanized War to Humanitarian Intervention: Carl Schmitt's Critique of the Just War Tradition', in L. Odysseos and F. Petito (eds), *The International Political Thought of Carl Schmitt* (Abingdon: Routledge, 2007)

Bryn, S., 'Engaging the "Other": The Nansen Dialogue Network in the Balkans': www.peoplebuildingpeace.org/thestories/print.php?id=127&typ=theme (accessed 1 December 2010)

Bukanovsky, M., *Legitimacy and Power Politics* (New Jersey: Princeton University Press, 2002)

Bull, H., 'The Grotian Conception of International Society', in H. Butterfield and M. Wight, *Diplomatic Investigations: Essays in the Theory of International Politics* (London: Allen & Unwin, 1966)
Bull, H., *The Anarchical Society* (Basingstoke: Palgrave, 2002)
Bulley, D., 'Negotiating Ethics: Campbell, Ontopology and Hospitality', *Review of International Studies*, 32:4 (2006), 645–63
Bulley, D., *Ethics as Foreign Policy: Britain, the EU and the Other* (Abingdon: Routledge, 2009)
Buzan, B. and L. Hansen, *The Evolution of International Security Studies* (Cambridge: Cambridge University Press, 2009)
Calhoun, C. (ed.), *Habermas and the Public Sphere* (Cambridge, MA: MIT Press, 1992)
Campbell, D., 'Why Fight: Humanitarianism, Principles and Post-Structuralism', *Millennium: Journal of International Studies*, 27:3 (1998), 497–521
Campbell, D., *National Deconstruction: Violence, Identity, and Justice in Bosnia* (Minneapolis: University of Minnesota Press, 1998)
Caplan, R. 'International Diplomacy and the Crisis in Kosovo', *International Affairs*, 74:4 (1998), 745–61
Carpenter, T. G. (ed.), *NATO's Empty Victory* (Washington: Cato Institute, 2000)
Carr, E. H., *The Twenty Years' Crisis 1919–1939* (London: Macmillan and Co. Ltd, 1939)
Cassese, A., 'A Follow-Up: Forcible Humanitarian Countermeasures and *Opinio Necessitatis*', *European Journal of International Law*, 10:4 (1999), 791–9
Chandler, D., *From Kosovo to Kabul: Human Rights and International Intervention* (London: Pluto Press, 2002)
Chandler, D., 'The Paradox of the "Responsibility to Protect"', *Cooperation and Conflict*, 45:1 (2010), 128–34
Charlesworth, H. and J.-M. Coicaud (eds), *The Faultlines of International Legitmacy* (Cambridge: Cambridge University Press, 2010)
Charney, J., 'Anticipatory Humanitarian Intervention in Kosovo', *American Journal of International Law*, 93:4 (1999), 834–41
Chatterjee, D. K. and D. E. Scheid (eds), *Ethics and Foreign Intervention* (Cambridge: Cambridge University Press, 2003)
Checkel, J. T., 'The Constructivist Turn in International Relations Theory', *World Politics*, 50 (1998), 324–48
Chesterman, S., *Just War or Just Peace? Humanitarian Intervention and International Law* (Oxford: Oxford University Press, 2001)
Chesterman, S., 'Legality Versus Legitimacy: Humanitarian Intervention, the Security Council, and the Rule of Law', *Security Dialogue*, 33:3 (2002), 293–307
Chilton, S. and Cuzzo, M., 'Habermas's Theory of Communicative Action as a Theoretical Framework for Mediation Practice', *Conflict Resolution Quarterly*, 22:3 (2005), 325–48
Chinkin, C., 'Kosovo: A "Good" or "Bad" War?', *American Journal of International Law*, 93:4 (1999) 841–7
Chinkin, C., 'The State That Acts Alone: Bully, Good Samaritan or Iconoclast?', *European Journal of International Law*, 11:1 (2000), 31–41
Chomsky, N., *The New Military Humanism: Lessons from Kosovo* (London: Pluto Press, 1999)

Bibliography

Clark, H., *Civil Resistance in Kosovo* (London: Pluto Press, 2000)
Clark, I., *Legitimacy in International Society* (Oxford: Oxford University Press, 2005)
Clark, I., *International Legitimacy and World Society* (Oxford: Oxford University Press, 2007)
Clark, I. and C. Reus-Smit (eds), Special Issue: 'Resolving International Crises of Legitimacy', *International Politics*, 44:2–3 (2007)
Claude, I., 'Collective Legitimation as a Political Function of the United Nations', *International Organization*, 20:3 (1966), 367–79
Coates, A. J., *The Ethics of War* (Manchester: Manchester University Press, 1997)
Cooke, M., *Language and Reason: A Study of Habermas's Pragmatics* (Cambridge, MA: MIT Press, 1994)
Cox, R., 'Social Forces, States and World Order', *Millennium*, 10:2 (1981), 126–55
Crawford, N., *Argument and Change in World Politics: Ethics, Decolonization, and Humanitarian Intervention* (Cambridge: Cambridge University Press, 2002)
Daalder, I. and M. O'Hanlon, *Winning Ugly: NATO's War to Save Kosovo* (Washington, DC: The Brookings Institute Press, 2000)
Dahl, R. *Democracy and Its Critics* (New Haven: Yale University Press, 1989)
Dallmayr, F. 'Conversation Across Boundaries: Political Theory and Global Diversity', *Millennium: Journal of International Studies*, 30:2 (2001), 341–7
Dauphinee, E., 'Rambouillet: A Critical (Re)Assessment', in F. Bieber and Z. Daskalovski (eds), *Understanding the War in Kosovo* (London: Frank Cass, 2003)
Deitelhoff, N. and H. Müller, 'Theoretical Paradise – Empirically Lost? Arguing with Habermas', *Review of International Studies*, 31:1 (2005), 167–79
Devetak, R., 'Between Kant and Pufendorf: Humanitarian Intervention, Statist Anticosmopolitanism and Critical International Theory', in N. J. Rengger and B. Thirkell-White (eds), *Critical International Relations Theory After 25 Years* (Cambridge: Cambridge University Press, 2007)
Dews, P. (ed.), *Habermas: A Critical Reader* (Oxford: Blackwell Publishers, 1999)
Diez, T. and J. Steans, 'A Useful Dialogue? Habermas and International Relations', *Review of International Studies*, 31:1 (2005), 127–40
Dryzek, J., 'Discursive Designs: Critical Theory and Political Institutions', *American Journal of Political Science*, 31:3 (1987), 656–79
Dryzek, J., *Discursive Democracy: Politics, Policy and Political Science* (Cambridge: Cambrigde University Press, 1990)
Dryzek, J. S., 'Critical Theory as a Research Program', in S. K. White (ed.), *The Cambridge Companion to Habermas* (Cambridge: Cambridge University Press, 1995)
Dryzek, J., 'Handle With Care: The Deadly Hermeneutics of Deliberative Instrumentation', *Acta Politica*, 40:2 (2005), 197–211
Dryzek, J., *Deliberative Global Politics: Discourse and Democracy in a Divided World* (Cambridge: Polity Press, 2006)
Dunne, T., *Inventing International Society: A History of the English School* (London: Macmillan, 1998)
Dunne, T., 'New Thinking on International Society', *British Journal of Politics and International Relations*, 3:2 (2001), 223–44
Dunne, T., 'Sociological Investigations: Instrumental, Legitimist and Coercive Interpretations of International Society', *Millennium*, 30:1 (2001) 67–91

Bibliography

Dunne, T. and Wheeler, N. J. (eds), *Human Rights in Global Politics* (Cambridge: Cambridge University Press, 1999)

Dupuy, P.-M., 'The Place and Role of Unilateralism in Contemporary International Law', *European Journal of International Law*, 11:1 (2000), 19–29

Eckersley, R., 'Soft Law, Hard Politics, and the Climate Change Treaty', in C. Reus-Smit (ed.), *The Politics of International Law* (Cambridge: Cambridge University Press, 2004)

Eckersley, R., *The Green State: Rethinking Democracy and Sovereignty* (Cambridge, MA: MIT Press, 2004)

Eckersley, R., 'The Ethics of Critical Theory', in C. Reus-Smit and D. Snidal, *Oxford Handbook of International Relations* (Oxford: Oxford University Press, 2010)

The Economist, 'Welcome to Balkania: Kosovo' (7 September 1996)

Elshtain, J. B., 'Antigone's Daughters Reconsidered: Continuing Reflections on Women, Politics and Power', in S. K. White (ed.), *Lifeworld and Politics: Between Modernity and Postmodernity* (Notre Dame: University of Notre Dame Press, 1989)

Elshtain, J. B., 'Really Existing Communities', from the Forum on 'The Transformation of Political Community', *Review of International Studies*, 25:1 (1999), 141–6

Elster, J. (ed.), *Deliberative Democracy* (Chicago: University of Chicago Press, 1998)

Evans, G., *Making Australian Foreign Policy* (Melbourne: Australian Fabian Society, 1989)

Evans, G., 'Crimes Against Humanity: Overcoming Indifference', *Journal of Genocide Research*, 8:3 (2006), 325–39

Evans, G., *The Responsibility to Protect: Ending Mass Atrocity Crimes Once and For All* (Washington, DC: Brookings Institution Press, 2008)

Falk, R., 'Kosovo, World Order, and the Future of International Law', *American Journal of International Law*, 93:4 (1999), 847–57

Falk, R., '"Humanitarian Wars", Realist Geopolitics and Genocidal Practices: Saving the Kosovars', in K. Booth (ed.), *The Kosovo Tragedy: The Human Rights Dimension* (London: Frank Cass Publishers, 2001)

Falk, R., 'Legality and Legitimacy: The Quest for Principled Flexibility and Restraint', *Review of International Studies*, 31, Special Issue (2005), 33–50

Farer, T., 'Humanitarian Intervention Before and After 9/11: Legality and Legitimacy', in J. L. Holzgrefe and R. Keohane (eds), *Humanitarian Intervention: Ethical, Legal and Political Dilemmas* (Cambridge: Cambridge University Press, 2003)

Fay, B., *Social Theory and Political Practice* (London: George Allen & Unwin Ltd, 1975)

Fay, B., 'How People Change Themselves: The Relationship between Critical Theory and Its Audience', in T. Ball (ed.), *Political Theory and Praxis: New Perspectives* (Minneapolis: University of Minnesota Press, 1977)

Ferrara, A., *Justice and Judgement* (London: Sage Publications, 1999)

Ferrara, A., 'Two Notions of Humanity and the Judgement Argument for Human Rights', *Political Theory*, 31:3 (2003), 392–420

Ferrara, A., '"Political" Cosmopolitanism and Judgement', *European Journal of Social Theory*, 10:1 (2007), 53–66

Fierke, K. M., *Changing Games, Changing Strategies: Critical Investigations in Security* (Manchester: Manchester University Press, 1998)

Bibliography

Fierke, K. M., 'Constructing an Ethical Foreign Policy: Analysis and Practice from Below', in K. E. Smith and M. Light (eds), *Ethics and Foreign Policy* (Cambridge: Cambridge University Press, 2001)

Fierke, K. M., *Diplomatic Interventions: Conflict and Change in a Globalizing World* (Hampshire: Palgrave, 2005)

Fierke, K. M. and K. E. Jørgensen (eds), *Constructing International Relations: The Next Generation* (New York: M. E. Sharpe, 2001)

Fine, R., 'Taking the "Ism" out of Cosmopolitanism: An Essay in Reconstruction', *European Journal of Social Theory*, 6:4 (2003), 451–70

Fine, R., 'Cosmopolitanism and Violence: Difficulties of Judgement', *British Journal of Sociology*, 57:1 (2006) 49–67

Fine, R., 'Judgement and the Reification of the Faculties: A Reconstructive Reading of Arendt's Life of the Mind', *Philosophy and Social Criticism*, 34:1–2 (2008), 157–76

Fine, R., 'Political Argument and the Legitimacy of International Law: A Case of Distorted Modernization', in C. Thornhill and C. Ashenden (eds), *Legality and Legitimacy: Normative and Sociological Approaches* (Baden-Baden: Nomos, 2010)

Finlayson, J. G., 'Debate: What are "Universalizable Interests"?', *The Journal of Political Philosophy*, 8:4 (2000), 456–69

Fishkin, J., *The Dialogue of Justice: Toward A Self-Reflective Society* (New Haven: Yale University Press, 1992)

Fishkin, J. and R. Luskin, 'Experimenting with a Democratic Ideal: Deliberative Polling and Public Opinion', *Acta Politica*, 40:3 (2005), 284–98

Forester, J. (ed.), *Critical Theory and Public Life* (Cambridge, MA: MIT Press, 1985)

Franck, T., *The Power of Legitimacy Among Nations* (Oxford: Oxford University Press, 1990)

Franck, T., *Recourse to Force: State Action Against Threats and Armed Attacks* (Cambridge: Cambridge University Press, 2002)

Franck, T., 'Interpretation and Change in the Law of Humanitarian Intervention', in J. L. Holzgrefe and R. Keohane (eds), *Humanitarian Intervention: Ethical, Legal and Political Dilemmas* (Cambridge: Cambridge University Press, 2003)

Fraser, N., 'What's Critical about Critical Theory? The Case of Habermas and Gender', *New German Critique*, 35, Special Issue 1 (1985), 97–131

Fraser, N., 'Rethinking the Public Sphere: A Contribution to the Critique of Actually Existing Democracy', in C. Calhoun (ed.), *Habermas and the Public Sphere* (Cambridge, MA: MIT Press, 1992)

Frost, M., 'Putting the World to Rights: *Britain's Ethical Foreign Policy*', *Cambridge Review of International Affairs*, 12:2 (1999), 80–9

Gadamer, H.-G., *Truth and Method*, 2nd edn (New York: Continuum, 1991)

Garsten, B., 'The Elusiveness of Arendtian Judgement', *Social Research*, 74:4 (2007), 1071–108

George, J., *Discourses of Global Politics: A Critical (Re)Introduction to International Relations* (Boulder, CO: Lynne Rienner, 1994)

Gilligan, C., *In a Different Voice: Psychological Theory and Women's Development* (Cambridge, MA: Harvard University Press, 1982)

Goff, P. (ed.), *The Kosovo News and Propaganda War* (Vienna: International Press Institute, 1999)

Goldsmith, A., 'Is There Any Backbone to this Fish? Interpretive Communities, Social Criticism, and Transgressive Legal Practice', *Law and Social Inquiry*, 23:2 (1998), 373–428

Gow, J., 'Kosovo After the Holbrooke-Milosevic Agreement. What Now?', *The International Spectator*, 33:4 (1998), 17–22

Gowan, P., 'The NATO Powers and the Balkan Tragedy', *New Left Review*, 234, March/April (1999), 83–105

Grey, C., *International Law and the Use of Force* (Oxford: Oxford University Press, 2000)

Grobe, C., 'The Power of Words: Argumentative Persuasion in International Negotiations', *European Journal of International Relations*, 16:1 (2010), 16–29

Grotius, H., *The Rights of War and Peace*, Book III (ed. by Richard Tuck) (Indiana: Liberty Fund, 2005)

Guicherd, C., 'International Law and the War in Kosovo', *Survival*, 41:2 (1999), 19–34

Günther, K., *The Sense of Appropriateness: Application Discourses in Morality and Law* (New York: State University of New York, 1993)

Haacke, J., 'Theory and Praxis in International Relations: Self-Reflection, Rational Argumentation', *Millennium: Journal of International Studies*, 25:2 (1996) 255–89

Haacke, J., 'The Frankfurt School and International Relations: On the Centrality of Recognition', *Review of International Studies*, 31:1 (2005), 181–94

Habermas, J., *Knowledge and Human Interests* (Boston: Beacon Press, 1972)

Habermas, J., *Theory and Practice* (London: Heinemann Educational Books, 1974)

Habermas, J., 'Hannah Arendt's Communications Concept of Power', in L. Hinchman and S. Hinchman (eds), *Hannah Arendt: Critical Essays* (New York: State University of New York, 1977)

Habermas, J., *The Theory of Communicative Action, Vol. 1: Reason and the Rationalisation of Society* (Cambridge: Polity Press, 1984)

Habermas, J., *The Theory of Communicative Action, Vol. 2: The Critique of Functionalist Reason* (Cambridge: Polity Press, 1987)

Habermas, J. *Moral Consciousness and Communicative Action* (Cambridge: Polity Press, 1990)

Habermas, J., *Justification and Application: Remarks on Discourse Ethics* (Cambridge, MA: MIT Press, 1993)

Habermas, J., *The Inclusion of the Other* (ed. by C. Cronin and P. De Grieff) (Cambridge, MA: MIT Press, 1998)

Habermas, J., 'Bestiality and Humanity: A War on the Border Between Law and Morality', *Constellations*, 6:3 (1999), 263–72

Habermas, J., 'Some Clarifications of the Concept of Communicative Rationality', in M. Cooke (ed.), *On the Pragmatics of Communication* (Cambridge, MA: MIT Press, 2000)

Habermas, J., 'Political Communication in Media Society: Does Democracy Still Enjoy an Epistemic Dimension? The Impact of Normative Theory on Empirical Research', *Communication Theory*, 16:4 (2006), 411–26

Habermas, J., *Europe: The Faltering Project* (trans. C. Cronin) (Cambridge: Polity Press, 2009)

Habermas, J. and P. Dews, *Habermas: Autonomy and Solidarity*, 2nd edn (London: Verso, 1992)

Hammond, P. 'Reporting "Humanitarian" Warfare: Propaganda, Moralism and NATO's Kosovo War', *Journalism Studies*, 1:3 (2000), 365–86

Hammond, P. and Herman, E. (eds), *Degraded Capability: The Media and the Kosovo Crisis* (London: Pluto Press, 2000)

Haxhiu, B., 'Kosova: A Place Where the Dead Speak', in W. Buckley (ed.), *Kosovo: Contending Voices on Balkan Interventions* (Cambridge: Wm. B. Erdmans Publishing Co., 2000)

Head, N., 'Bringing Reflective Judgement into International Relations: Exploring the Rwandan Genocide', *Journal of Global Ethics*, 6:2 (2010), 191–204

Hehir, A., *Humanitarian Intervention: An Introduction* (London: Palgrave Macmillan, 2010)

Heinze, E. A., *Waging Humanitarian War* (Albany: SUNY, 2009)

Held, D., *Introduction to Critical Theory: Horkheimer to Habermas* (Berkeley: University of California Press, 1980)

Held, D., *Models of Democracy*, 2nd edn (Cambridge: Polity Press, 1996)

Held, D. and D. Archibugi (eds), *Cosmopolitan Democracy* (Cambridge: Polity Press, 1995)

Heller, A., 'The Discourse Ethics of Habermas: Critique and Appraisal', *Thesis Eleven*, 10/11 (1985), 5–17

Henkin, L., 'Kosovo and the Law of Humanitarian Intervention', *American Journal of International Law*, 93:4 (1999), 824–8

Herring, E., 'From Rambouillet to the Kosovo Accords: NATO's War against Serbia and Its Aftermath', in K. Booth (ed.), *The Kosovo Tragedy: The Human Rights Dimension* (London: Frank Cass Publishers, 2001)

Hobson, J. M., 'Is Critical Theory Always for the White West and for Western Imperialism? Beyond Westphilian Towards a Post-racist Critical IR', in N. J. Rengger and B. Thirkell-White (eds), *Critical International Relations Theory After 25 Years* (Cambridge: Cambridge University Press, 2007)

Hoffman, M., 'Critical Theory and the Inter-Paradigm Debate', *Millennium: Journal of International Studies*, 16:2 (1987), 231–49

Hoffman, M., 'Conversations on Critical International Relations Theory', *Millennium: Journal of International Studies*, 17:1 (1988), 91–5

Hoffman, M. 'Third-Party Mediation and Conflict Resolution in the Post-Cold War World', in J. Baylis and N. Rengger (eds), *Dilemmas of World Politics: International Issues in a Changing World* (Oxford: Clarendon Press, 1992)

Holbrooke, R., *To End a War* (New York: Random House, 1998)

Holbrooke, R., 'Just and Unjust Wars: A Diplomat's Perspective', *Social Reseach*, 69:4 (2002), 915–24

Hollis, M. and S. Smith, *Explaining and Understanding International Relations* (Oxford: Clarendon, 1990)

Holub, R., *Jürgen Habermas: Critic in the Public Sphere* (London: Routledge, 1991)

Holzgrefe, J. L. and R. Keohane (eds), *Humanitarian Intervention: Ethical, Legal and Political Dilemmas* (Cambridge: Cambridge University Press, 2003)

Honneth, A., *The Critique of Power* (trans. Kenneth Baynes) (Cambridge, MA: MIT Press, 1991)

Honneth, A., *The Struggle for Recognition: The Moral Grammar of Social Conflicts* (trans.

Joel Anderson) (Cambridge: Polity Press, 1995)
Hopgood, S., 'Reading the Small Print in Global Civil Society: The Inexorable Hegemony of the Liberal Self', *Millennium: Journal of International Studies*, 29:1 (2000), 1–25
Horkheimer, M., 'The Present Situation of Social Philosophy and the Tasks of an Institute for Social Research' (1931): www.marxists.org/reference/archive/horkheimer/1931/present-situation.htm (accessed 8 December 2011)
Hoy, D. and T. McCarthy, *Critical Theory* (Oxford: Blackwell Publishers, 1994)
Hurd, I., 'Legitimacy and Authority in International Politics', *International Organization*, 53:2 (1999), 379–408
Hurd, I., 'Legitimacy, Power, and the Symbolic Life of the Security Council', *Global Governance*, 8:1 (2002), 35–51
Hurd, I., *After Anarchy: Legitimacy and Power in the United Nations Security Council* (Princeton: Princeton University Press, 2007)
Hurd, I., 'Constructivism', in C. Reus-Smit and D. Snidal (eds), *Oxford Handbook of International Relations* (Oxford: Oxford University Press, 2010)
Hurrell, A., 'Legitimacy and the Use of Force: Can the Circle be Squared?', *Review of International Studies*, 31, Special Issue (2005), 15–32
Hurrelmann, A., S. Schneider and J. Steffek (eds), *Legitimacy in an Age of Global Politics* (Basingstoke: Palgrave Macmillan, 2007)
Husanović, J. '"Post-Conflict Kosovo": An Anatomy Lesson in the Ethics/Politics of Human Rights', in K. Booth (ed.), *The Kosovo Tragedy: The Human Rights Dimension* (London: Frank Cass Publishers, 2001)
Hutchings, K., 'Speaking and Hearing: Habermasian Discourse Ethics, Feminism and IR', *Review of International Studies*, 31:1 (2005), 155–65
Hutchings, K., 'Happy Anniversary! Time and Critique in International Relations Theory', in N. J. Rengger and B. Thirkell-White (eds), *Critical International Relations Theory After 25 Years* (Cambridge: Cambridge University Press, 2007)
Ignatieff, M., *Virtual War: Kosovo and Beyond* (London: Vintage, 2000)
Ignatieff, M., 'Human Rights, Power and the State', in S. Chesterman, M. Ignatieff and R. Thakur (eds), *Making States Work* (Tokyo: United Nations University Press, 2005)
Independent International Commission on Kosovo, *The Kosovo Report* (Oxford: Oxford University Press, 2000)
International Commission on Intervention and State Sovereignty, *The Responsibility to Protect* (Canada: International Development Research Centre, 2001)
International Crisis Group, 'Kosovo Spring', Report No. 32 (March 1998)
International Crisis Group, 'Kosovo's Long Hot Summer: Briefing on Military, Humanitarian and Political Developments in Kosovo', Report No. 41 (September 1998)
International Crisis Group, *Intermediate Sovereignty as a Basis for Resolving the Kosovo Crisis*, Report No. 46 (November 1998)
International Crisis Group, *Unifying the Kosovar Factions: The Way Forward*, Report No. 58 (March 1999)
International Helsinki Foundation for Human Rights, *From Autonomy to Colonization: Human Rights in Kosovo 1989–1993* (Vienna: IHF, November 1993)

Jackson, R., *The Global Covenant: Human Conduct in a World of States* (Oxford: Oxford University Press, 2000)
Janssen, D. and R. Kies, 'Online Forums and Deliberative Democracy', *Acta Politica*, 40:3 (2005), 317–35
Jay, M., *The Dialectical Imagination* (Berkeley: University of California Press, 1996)
Johnson, J. T., *Morality and Contemporary Warfare* (New Haven: Yale University Press, 1999)
Johnstone, I., 'Treaty Interpretation: The Authority of Interpretive Communities', *Michigan Journal of International Law*, 12:2 (1991), 371–419
Johnstone, I. 'Security Council Deliberations: The Power of the Better Argument', *European Journal of International Law*, 14:3 (2003), 437–80
Johnstone, I., 'Discursive Power in the UN Security Council', *Journal of International Law and International Relations*, 2:1 (2005–6), 73–94
Johnstone, I., 'The Security Council as Legislature', in B. Cronin and I. Hurd (eds), *The UN Security Council and the Politics of International Authority* (Abingdon: Routledge, 2008)
Johnstone, I., 'Legal Deliberation and Argumentation in International Decision Making', in H. Charlesworth and J.-M. Coicaud (eds), *The Faultlines of International Legitimacy* (Cambridge: Cambridge University Press, 2010)
Jordaan, E. 'Dialogic Cosmopolitanism and Global Justice', *International Studies Review*, 11:4 (2009), 736–48
Judah, T., *Kosovo: War and Revenge* (New Haven: Yale University Press, 2002)
Kaldor, M., *New and Old Wars* (Cambridge: Polity Press, 2001)
Kaplan, R., *Balkan Ghosts: A Journey Through History* (New York: Vintage Books, 1993)
Kissinger, H., 'Doing Injury to History', *Newsweek Magazine* (5 April 1999)
Kostovicova, D., 'Albanian Schooling in Kosovo 1992–1998: "Liberty Imprisoned"', in M. Waller, K. Drezov and B. Gokay (eds), *Kosovo: The Politics of Delusion* (London: Frank Cass, 2001)
Kostovicova, D., *Kosovo: The Politics of Identity and Space* (London: Routledge, 2005)
Krasner, S. D., *Sovereignty: Organized Hypocrisy* (Princeton: Princeton University Press, 1999)
Kratochwil, F., *Rules, Norms, Decisions: On the Conditions of Practical and Legal Reasoning in International Relations and Domestic Affairs* (Cambridge: Cambridge University Press, 1989)
Kratochwil, F., 'Constructivism as an Approach', in K. M. Fierke and K. E. Jørgensen (eds), *Constructing International Relations: The Next Generation* (New York: M. E. Sharpe, 2001)
Krisch, N., 'Legality, Morality, and the Dilemma of Humanitarian Intervention after Kosovo', *European Journal of International Law*, 13:1 (2002), 323–35
Kupchan, C. A. and C. A. Kupchan, 'The Promise of Collective Security', *International Security*, 20:1 (1995), 52–61
Lawler, P., 'The Good State: In Praise of "classical" Internationalism', *Review of International Studies*, 31:3 (2005), 427–49
Layne, C., 'Blunder in the Balkans: The Clinton Administration's Bungled War against Serbia', *Policy Analysis*, 345 (20 May 1999), 1–19

Lebow, R. N., 'What's So Different about a Counterfactual?', *World Politics*, 52:4 (2000), 550–85
Lebow, R. N., *Forbidden Fruit: Counterfacutals and International Relations* (Princeton: Princeton University Press, 2010)
Linklater, A., *Men and Citizens in International Relations*, 2nd edn (London: Macmillan, 1990)
Linklater, A., 'The Question of the Next Stage in International Relations Theory: A Critical-Theoretical Point of View', *Millennium: Journal of International Studies*, 21:1 (1992), 77–98
Linklater, A., 'What is a Good International Citizen?', in P. Keal (ed.), *Ethics and Foreign Policy* (Sydney: Allen and Unwin, 1992)
Linklater, A., 'Citizenship and Sovereignty in the Post-Westphalian State', *European Journal of International Relations*, 2:1 (1996), 77–103
Linklater, A., *The Transformation of Political Community: Ethical Foundations of the Post-Westphalian Era* (Cambridge: Polity Press, 1998)
Linklater, A., 'The Good International Citizen and the Crisis in Kosovo', in A. Schnabel and R. Thakur (eds), *Kosovo and the Challenge of Humanitarian Intervention: Selective Indignation, Collective Action, and International Citizenship* (Tokyo: United Nations University Press, 2000)
Linklater, A., 'Dialogic Politics and the Civilising Process', *Review of International Studies*, 31:1 (2005), 141–54
Linklater, A., *Critical Theory and World Politics* (Abingdon: Routledge, 2007)
Linklater, A., *The Problem of Harm in World Politics: Theoretical Investigations* (Cambridge: Cambridge University Press, 2011)
Linklater, A. and H. Suganami, *The English School of International Relations: A Contemporary Reassessment* (Cambridge: Cambridge University Press, 2006)
Lloyd Jones, D., *Cosmopolitan Mediation? Conflict Resolution and the Oslo Accords* (Manchester: Manchester University Press, 1999)
Lose, L. G., 'Communicative Action and the World of Diplomacy', in K. M. Fierke and K. E. Jørgensen (eds), *Constructing International Relations: The Next Generation* (New York: M. E. Sharpe, 2001)
Luck, E. C., 'Sovereignty, Choice, and the Responsibility to Protect', *Global Responsibility to Protect*, 1:1 (2009), 10–21
Lynch, M., 'The Dialogue of Civilisations and International Public Spheres', *Millennium*, 29:2 (2000), 307–30
Lynch, M., 'Why Engage? China and the Logic of Communicative Engagement', *European Journal of International Relations*, 8:2 (2002), 187–230
Malcolm, N., *Kosovo: A Short History* (London: Pan Books, 2002)
Mamdani, M., 'Responsibility to Protect or Right to Punish?', *Journal of Intervention and Statebuilding*, 4:1 (2010), 53–67
Mandelbaum, M., 'A Perfect Failure: NATO's War against Yugoslavia', *Foreign Affairs*, 78:3 (1999), 2–8
Manin, B., 'On Legitimacy and Political Deliberation', *Political Theory*, 15:3 (1987), 338–68
Matheson, M., 'Justification for the NATO Air Campaign in Kosovo', *American Society of International Law Proceedings*, 94 (2000)

Bibliography

McCarthy, T., *The Critical Theory of Jürgen Habermas* (Cambridge, MA: MIT Press, 1978)

McCarthy, T., *Ideals and Illusions* (Cambridge, MA: MIT Press, 1991)

Mccgwire, M., 'Why Did we Bomb Belgrade?', *International Affairs*, 76:1 (2000), 1–23

Mclean, M., *Pedagogy and the University: Critical Theory and Practice* (London: Continuum, 2006)

Mertus, J., *Kosovo: How Myths and Truths Started a War* (London: University of California Press, 1999)

Mertus, J., 'Reconsidering the Legality of Humanitarian Intervention: Lessons from Kosovo', *William and Mary Law Review*, 41:5 (2000), 1743–4

Miller, R., 'Respectable Oppressors, Hypocritical Liberators: Morality, Intervention, and Reality', in D. K. Chatterjee and D. E. Scheid (eds), *Ethics and Foreign Intervention* (Cambridge: Cambridge University Press, 2003)

Mitzen, J., 'Reading Habermas in Anarchy: Multilateral Diplomacy and Global Public Spheres', *American Political Science Review*, 99:3 (2005), 401–17

Müller, H., 'International Relations as Communicative Action', in K. Fierke and K. E. Jørgensen, *Constructing International Relations: The Next Generation* (New York: M. E. Sharpe, 2001)

Müller, H., 'Arguing, Bargaining and All That: Communicative Action, Rationalist Theory and the Logic of Appropriateness in International Relations', *European Journal of International Relations*, 10:3 (2004), 395–435

Murphy, S., 'Contemporary Practice of the United States Relating to International Law', *American Journal of International Law*, 94:4 (2000), 677–8

Neufeld, M., *The Restructuring of International Relations Theory* (Cambridge: Cambridge University Press, 1995)

Norris, J., *Collision Course: NATO, Russia, and Kosovo* (Westport: Praeger Publishers, 2005)

O'Neill, S., 'Struggles Against Injustice: Contemporary Critical Theory and Political Violence', *Journal of Global Ethics*, 6:2 (2010), 127–39

Onuf, N., *World of Our Making: Rules and Rule in Social Theory and International Relations* (North Carolina: University of North Carolina Press, 1987)

Orford, A., *Reading Humanitarian Intervention* (Cambridge: Cambridge University Press, 2003)

Orford, A., *International Authority and the Responsibility to Protect* (Cambridge, Cambridge University Press, 2011)

Outhwaite, W., *Habermas: A Critical Introduction* (Cambridge: Polity Press, 1994)

Pajnik, M., 'Feminist Reflections on Habermas's Communicative Action', *European Journal of Social Theory*, 9:3 (2006), 385–404

Passerin d'Entrèves, M., *The Political Philosophy of Hannah Arendt* (London: Routledge, 1994)

Passerin d'Entrèves, M., 'Arendt's Theory of Judgement', in D. Villa (ed.), *The Cambridge Companion to Hannah Arendt* (Cambridge: Cambridge University Press, 2000)

Pattison, J., *Humanitarian Intervention and the Responsibility to Protect* (Oxford: Oxford University Press, 2010)

Pavković, A., 'Kosovo/Kosova: A Land of Conflicting Myths', in M. Waller, K. Drezov

and B. Gőkay (eds), *Kosovo: The Politics of Delusion* (London: Frank Cass, 2001)
Payrow Shabani, O., *Democracy, Power, and Legitimacy: The Critical Theory of Jürgen Habermas* (Toronto: University of Toronto Press, 2003)
Pellet, A., 'Brief Remarks on the Unilateral Use of Force', *European Journal of International Law*, 11:2 (2000), 385–92
Perritt Jr, H. H., *Kosovo Liberation Army: The Inside Story of an Insurgency* (Chicago: University of Illinois Press, 2008)
Pettifer, J., 'The Kosovo Liberation Army: The Myth of Origin', in M. Waller, K. Drezov and B. Gőkay (eds), *Kosovo: The Politics of Delusion* (London: Frank Cass, 2001)
Pettifer, J. and M. Vickers, *The Albanian Question: Reshaping the Balkans* (London: I. B. Tauris, 2007)
Pilger, J., 'Revealed: The Amazing Nato Plan, Tabled at Rambouillet, To Occupy Yugoslavia', *New Statesman* (17 May 1999)
Pilger, J., 'What Really Happened at Rambouillet? And What Else is Being Kept Under Wraps by our Selective Media?' *New Statesman* (31 May 1999)
Podrimja, A., *A Split Stone: An Anthology of Albanian Poets for Kosova* (Prishtina: DÇJ Rozafa, 2006)
Power, S., *A Problem from Hell: America and the Age of Genocide* (New York: Basic Books, 2002)
Price, R., 'The Ethics of Constructivism', in C. Reus-Smit and D. Snidal (eds), *Oxford Handbook of International Relations* (Oxford: Oxford University Press, 2010)
Price, R. and C. Reus-Smit, 'Dangerous Liaisons? Critical International Theory and Constructivism', *European Journal of International Relations*, 4:3 (1998), 259–94
Ramsbotham, O., *Transforming Violent Conflict: Radical Disagreement, Dialogue and Survival* (Abingdon: Routledge, 2010)
Rasmussen, D., *Reading Habermas* (Oxford: Blackwell, 1990)
Rehg, W., *Insight and Solidarity: The Discourse Ethics of Jürgen Habermas* (California: University of California Press, 1997)
Rengger, N. J., 'Going Critical? A Response to Hoffman', *Millennium*, 17:1 (1988), 81–9
Rengger, N. J., 'The Fearful Sphere of International Relations', *Review of International Studies*, 16:4 (1990), 361–8
Rengger, N. J., 'The Judgement of War: On the Idea of Legitimate Force in World Politics', *Review of International Studies*, 31, Special Issue (2005), 143–62
Rengger, N. J. and B. Thirkell-White (eds), *Critical International Relations Theory After 25 Years* (Cambridge: Cambridge University Press, 2007)
Reus-Smit, C., 'In Dialogue on the Ethic of Consensus: A Reply to Shapcott', *Pacifica Review*, 12:2 (2000), 305–8
Reus-Smit, C., 'Society, Power, and Ethics', in C. Reus-Smit (ed.), *The Politics of International Law* (Cambridge: Cambridge University Press, 2004)
Reus-Smit, C., 'The Liberal Licence to Use Force', *Review of International Studies*, 31, Special Issue (2005), 71–92
Reus-Smit, C., 'International Crises of Legitimacy', *International Politics*, 44:2/3 (2007), 157–74
Risse, T., 'International Norms and Domestic Change: Arguing and Communicative Behavior in the Human Rights Area', *Politics and Society*, 27:4 (1999), 529–59

Risse, T., 'Let's Argue!: Communicative Action in World Politics', *International Organization*, 54:1 (2000), 1–39

Roberts, A., 'NATO's "Humanitarian War" over Kosovo', *Survival*, 41:3 (1999), 102–23

Robertson, G., 'Kosovo: An Account of the Crisis' (London: Ministry of Defence, 1999)

Robertson, G., 'JISB Interview: Intervention, Statebuilding and Security', *Journal of Intervention and Statebuilding*, 3:2 (2009), 259–75

Robinson, P., 'Ready to Kill but Not to Die', *International Journal*, 54:4 (1999), 671–82

Rogel, C., 'Kosovo: Where It All Began', *International Journal of Politics, Culture and Society*, 17:1 (2003), 167–82

Røhr, H. S. (ed.), *Dialog – Mer Enn Ord* (Lillehammer: Nansenskolen, 2005)

Rothman, J., *From Confrontation to Cooperation: Resolving Ethnic and Regional Conflict* (London: Sage, 1992)

Rugova, I., *La Question du Kosovo, Entretiens realisés par Marie-Françoise Allain et Xavier Galmiche* (Paris: Fayard, 1994)

Russell, P., 'The Exclusion of Kosovo from the Dayton Negotiations', *Journal of Genocide Research*, 11:4 (2009), 487–511

Sarooshi, D., 'The Security Council's Authorization of Regional Arrangements to use Force: The Case of NATO', in V. Lowe, A. Roberts, J. Welsh and D. Zaum (eds), *The United Nations Security Council and War: The Evolution of Thought and Practice since 1945* (Oxford: Oxford University Press, 2008)

Saward, M., 'Enacting Democracy', *Political Studies*, 51 (2003), 161–79

Schneider, S., F. Nullmeier and A. Hurrelmann, 'Exploring the Communicative Dimension of Legitimacy: Text Analytical Approaches', in A. Hurrelmann *et al.* (eds), *Legitimacy in an Age of Global Politics* (Basingstoke: Palgrave Macmillan, 2007)

Sell, L., *Slobodan Milosevic and the Destruction of Yugoslavia* (Durham, NC: Duke University Press, 2002)

Shapcott, R., 'Solidarism and After: Global Governance, International Society and the Normative "Turn" in International Relations', *Pacifica Review*, 12:2 (2000), 147–65

Shapcott, R., *Justice, Community and Dialogue* (Cambridge: Cambridge University Press, 2001)

Shapcott, R., 'Cosmopolitan Conversations: Justice Dialogue and the Cosmopolitan Project', *Global Society*, 16:3 (2002), 221–43

Shapcott, R., 'Critical Theory', in C. Reus-Smit and D. Snidal (eds), *Oxford Handbook of International Relations* (Oxford: Oxford University Press, 2008)

Simma, B., 'NATO, the UN and the Use of Force: Legal Aspects', *European Journal of International Law*, 10:1 (1999) 1–22

Skinner, Q., 'Language and Political Change', in T. Ball, J. Farr and R. L. Hanson (eds), *Political Innovation and Conceptual Change* (Cambridge: Cambridge University Press, 1989)

Skinner, Q., *Visions of Politics, Volume 1: Regarding Method* (Cambridge: Cambridge University Press, 2002)

Smith, K. E. and M. Light (eds), *Ethics and Foreign Policy* (Cambridge: Cambridge University Press, 2001)

Smith, N. H., *Strong Hermeneutics: Contingency and Moral Identity* (New York: Routledge, 1997)
Smith, S., K. Booth and M. Zalewski (eds), *International Theory: Positivism and Beyond* (Cambridge: Cambridge University Press, 1996)
Smith, W., 'Anticipating a Cosmopolitan Future: The Case of Humanitarian Military Intervention', *International Politics*, 44:1 (2007), 72–89
Stavrianakis, A., 'A Tale of Two Ethnicities? An Analysis of Approaches to "Ethnic Conflict": The Case of Kosovo', *Global Politics Network*, Fall (2002), 1–41
Steffek, J., 'The Legitimation of International Governance: A Discourse Approach', *European Journal of International Relations*, 9:2 (2003), 249–75
Steffek, J., 'Legitimacy in International Relations: From State Compliance to Citizen Consensus', in A. Hurrelman *et al.* (eds), *Legitimacy in an Age of Global Politics* (Basingstoke: Palgrave Macmillan, 2007)
Strydom, P., 'The Ontogenetic Fallacy: The Immanent Critique of Habermas' Developmental Logical Theory of Evolution', *Theory, Culture and Society*, 9:3 (1992), 65–92
Taylor, C., 'The Politics of Recognition', in C. Taylor and A. Gutman (eds), *Multiculturalism* (Princeton: Princeton University Press, 1994)
Terrett, S., *The Dissolution of Yugoslavia and the Badinter Arbitration Commission* (Aldershot: Ashgate, 2000)
Tesón, F. R., 'Collective Humanitarian Intervention', *Michigan Journal of International Law*, 17:2 (1996), 323–72
Tetlock, P. E. and A. Belkin (eds), *Counterfactual Thought Experiments in World Politics: Logical, Methodological and Psychological Perspectives* (Princeton: Princeton University Press, 1996)
Thakur, R., 'Outlook: Intervention, Sovereignty and the Responsibility to Protect: Experiences from ICISS', *Security Dialogue*, 33:3 (2002), 323–40
Thakur, R., 'Intervention, Sovereignty and the Responsibility to Protect: Experiences from ICISS', *Security Dialogue*, 33:3 (2002), 323–40
Thaqi, H., 'Kosova', in W. Buckley (ed.), *Kosovo: Contending Voices on Balkan Interventions* (Cambridge: Wm. B. Erdmans Publishing Co., 2000)
Thussu, D. K., 'Legitimizing "Humanitarian Intervention"? CNN, NATO and the Kosovo crisis', *European Journal of Communication*, 15:3 (2000), 345–61
Toros, H., *Terrorism, Talking and Transformation*, PhD thesis (Aberystwyth University: 2009)
Touval, S., 'Coercive Mediation on the Road to Dayton', *International Negotiation*, 1:3 (1996), 547–70
Transnational Foundation for Peace and Future Research, *UNTANS – Conflict-Mitigation for Kosovo. A UN Temporary Authority for a Negotiated Settlement* (1996)
Troebst, S., *Conflict in Kosovo: Failure of Prevention? An Analytical Documentation 1992–1998* (Flensburg: European Centre for Minority Issues, Working Paper No. 1, 1998)
Vatikiotis, M., 'Let's Talk to Religious Radicals, Too', *International Herald Tribune*, Singapore, 1996
Vickers, M., *Between Serb and Albanian: A History of Kosovo* (London: C. Hurst & Co., 1998)

Vik, I., *Dialogue in Practice: Nansen-dialogue Network and Activities in the West Balkans*, Helsinki Committee for Human Rights in Bosnia and Herzegovina (2005)

Vincent, R. J., *Human Rights and International Relations* (Cambridge: Cambridge University Press, 1986)

Walker, H., 'The Case of Kosovo', *Civil Wars*, 7:1 (2005) 28–70

Walker, R. B. J., *Inside/Outside: International Relations as Political Theory* (Cambridge: Cambridge University Press, 1993)

Waltz, K. *Man, the State and War* (New York: Columbia University Press, 2001)

Walzer, M., 'Spheres of Affection', in M. Nussbaum, *For Love of Country?* (Boston, MA: Beacon Press, 2002)

Walzer, M., *Arguing about War* (New Haven: Yale University Press, 2004)

Walzer, M., *Just and Unjust Wars* (USA: Basic Books, 2006)

Weber, M., 'The Critical Social Theory of the Frankfurt School, and the "Social Turn" in IR', *Review of International Relations*, 31:1 (2005), 195–209

Wedgwood, R., 'NATO's Campaign in Yugoslavia', *American Journal of International Law*, 93:4 (1999), 828–34

Weller, M., 'The International Response to the Dissolution of the Socialist Federal Republic of Yugoslavia', *American Journal of International Law*, 86:3 (1992), 569–607

Weller, M., *The Crisis in Kosovo 1989–1999: From Dissolution of Yugoslavia to Rambouillet and the Outbreak of Hostilities*, vol. 1 (Cambridge: Documents & Analysis Publishing Ltd, 1999)

Weller, M., 'The Rambouillet Conference on Kosovo', *International Affairs*, 75:2 (1999), 211–51

Weller, M., 'The Self-determination Trap', *Ethnopolitics* 4:1 (2005), 3–28

Wellmer, A. 'Practical Philosophy and the Theory of Society: On the Problem of the Normative Foundations of a Critical Social Science', in S. Benhabib and F. Dallmayr (eds), *The Communicative Ethics Controversy* (Cambridge, MA: MIT Press, 1990)

Wellmer, A., *The Persistence of Modernity* (Cambridge, MA: MIT Press, 1991)

Welsh, J. M., 'From Right to Responsibility: Humanitarian Intervention and International Society', *Global Governance*, 8:4 (2002), 503–21

Wendt, A., *Social Theory of International Politics* (Cambridge: Cambridge University Press, 1999)

Wheeler, N. J., 'Pluralist or Solidarist Conceptions of International Society: Bull and Vincent on Humanitarian Intervention', *Millennium Journal of International Studies*, 21:3 (1992), 463–87

Wheeler, N. J., *Saving Strangers: Humanitarian Intervention in International Society* (Oxford: Oxford University Press, 2000)

Wheeler, N. J., 'Humanitarian Intervention After Kosovo: Emergent Norm, Moral Duty or the Coming Anarchy', *International Affairs*, 77:1 (2001), 113–28

Wheeler, N. J., 'Legitimating Humanitarian Intervention: Principles and Procedures', *Melbourne Journal of International Law*, 2:2 (2001), 550–67

Wheeler, N. J., 'The Humanitarian Responsibilities of Sovereignty: Explaining the Development of a New Norm of Military Intervention for Humanitarian Purposes in International Society', in J. Welsh (ed.), *Humanitarian Intervention and*

International Relations (Oxford: Oxford University Press, 2004)
Wheeler, N. J., 'The Kosovo Bombing Campaign', in C. Reus-Smit (ed.), *The Politics of International Law* (Cambridge: Cambridge University Press, 2004)
Wheeler, N. J., 'Operationalising the Responsibility to Protect: The Continuing Debate over where Authority Should be Located for the Use of Force', NUPI Report, No. 3 (2008)
Wheeler, N. J., 'Saving Strangers: A Personal Reflection', Lecture delivered in Rio de Janeiro, 10 December 2010
Wheeler, N. J. and T. Dunne, 'Hedley Bull's Pluralism of the Intellect and Solidarism of the Will', *International Affairs*, 72: 1 (1996), 91–107
Wheeler, N. J. and T. Dunne, 'Good International Citizenship: A Third Way for British Foreign Policy', *International Affairs*, 74:4 (1998), 847–70
White, S., 'Reason and Authority in Habermas: A Critique of the Critics', *The American Political Science Review*, 74:4 (1980), 1007–17
White, S. K., *The Recent Work of Jürgen Habermas: Reason, Justice and Modernity* (Cambridge: Cambridge University Press, 1988)
White, S. K., *Political Theory and Postmodernsim* (Cambridge: Cambridge University Press, 1991)
Wight, M., 'International Legitimacy', *International Relations* 4:1 (1972), 1–28
Wight, M., *International Theory: The Three Traditions* (London: Leicester University Press, 1991)
Willcox, D., *Propaganda, the Press and Conflict: The Gulf War and Kosovo* (New York: Routledge, 2005)
Wittgenstein, L., *Philosophical Investigations* (Oxford: Basil Blackwell, 1958)
Wolff, R., *In Defense of Anarchism* (New York: Harper & Row Publishers, 1970)
Wolin, S., 'Fugitive Democracy', *Constellations*, 1:1 (1994), 11–25
Wyn Jones, R., 'On Emancipation: Necessity, Capacity, and Concrete Utopias', in K. Booth (ed.), *Critical Security Studies and World Politics* (Boulder: Lynne Rienner Publishers, 2005)
Young, I. M., 'Communication and the Other: Beyond Deliberative Democracy', in S. Benhabib (ed.), *Democracy and Difference: Contesting the Boundaries of the Political* (Princeton: Princeton University Press, 1996)
Youngs, T., 'Kosovo: The Diplomatic and Military Options', House of Commons Research Paper 98/93 (27 October 1998)
Zehfuss, M., *Constructivism in International Relations: The Politics of Reality* (Cambridge: Cambridge University Press, 2002)
Zolo, D., 'A Cosmopolitan Philosophy of International Law? A Realist Approach', *Ratio Juris*, 12:4 (1999), 429–44
Zolo, D., *Invoking Humanity: War, Law and Global Order* (London: Continuum, 2002)

Bibliography

UN Security Council documents

UN Charter: www.un.org/aboutun/charter/

S/1998/223, Letter from the Deputy Permanent Representative of the United Kingdom of Great Britain and Northern Ireland to the United Nations addressed to the President of the Security Council, 11 March 1998

S/1998/229, Letter from the Chargé d'affaires a.i. of the Permanent Mission of Yugoslavia to the United Nations addressed to the Secretary-General, 12 March 1998

S/1998/234, Letter from the Permanent Representative of Bulgaria to the United Nations addressed to the Secretary-General, 13 March 1998

S/1998/240, Letter from the Chargé d'affaires a.i. of the Permanent Mission of Yugoslavia to the United Nations addressed to the Secretary-General, 16 March 1998

S/1998/246, Letter from the Permanent Representative of Poland to the United Nations addressed to the President of the Security Council, 17 March 1998

S/1998/250, Letter from the Chargé d'affaires a.i. of the Permanent Mission of Yugoslavia to the United Nations addressed to the Secretary-General, 18 March 1998

S/1998/272, Letter from the Permanent Representative of the United States of America to the United Nations addressed to the President of the Security Council, 27 March 1998

S/1998/285, Letter from the Chargé d'affaires a.i. of the Permanent Mission of Yugoslavia to the United Nations addressed to the President of the Security Council, 30 March 1998

S/PV.3868, Transcript of the 3868th Meeting of the Security Council, 31 March 1998

S/RES/1160, Resolution 1160 (1998) adopted 31 March 1998

S/1998/313, Letter from the Secretary-General addressed to the President of the Security Council, 8 April 1998

S/1998/361, Report of the Secretary-General prepared pursuant to Security Council Resolution 1160, 30 April 1998

S/1998/401, Letter from the Permanent Representative of the Former Yugoslav Republic of Macedonia to the United Nations addressed to the Secretary-General, 15 May 1998

S/1998/454, Report of the Secretary-General on the United Nations Preventive Deployment Force pursuant to Security Council Resolution 1142, 1 June 1998

S/1998/470, Report of the Secretary-General prepared pursuant to Resolution 1160 of the Security Council, 4 June 1998

S/1998/567, Letter from the Permanent Representative of the United Kingdom of Great Britain and Northern Ireland to the United Nations addressed to the Secretary-General, 24 June 1998

S/1998/608, Report of the Secretary-General prepared pursuant to Resolution 1160 of the Security Council, 2 July 1998

S/1998/627, Letter from the Permanent Representative of the former Yugoslav Republic of Macedonia to the UN addressed to the Secretary-General, 9 July 1998

S/1998/644, Report of the Secretary-General on the United Nations Preventive

Bibliography

Deployment Force, 14 July 1998

S/1998/657, Letter from the Acting Permanent Representative of Germany to the United Nations addressed to the Secretary-General, 16 July 1998

S/PV.3911, Transcript of the 3911th Meeting of the Security Council, 21 July 1998

S/RES/1186, Resolution 1186 (1998) adopted 21 July 1998

S/1998/712, Report of the Secretary-General prepared pursuant to Security Council Resolution 1160, 5 August 1998

S/1998/757, Letter from the Chargé d'affaires a.i. of the Permanent Mission of Yugoslavia to the United Nations addressed to the Secretary-General, 13 August 1998

S/PV.3918, Transcript of the 3918th Meeting of the Security Council, 24 August 1998

S/1998/834, Report of the Secretary-General prepared pursuant to Resolution 1160 of the Security Council, 4 September 1998

S/PV.3930, Transcript of the 3930th Meeting of the Security Council, 23 September 1998

S/RES/1199, Resolution 1199 (1998) adopted 23 September 1998

S/1998/912, Report of the Secretary-General prepared pursuant to Resolutions 1160 and 1199 of the Security Council, 3 October 1998

S/1998/953, Letter from the Chargé d'affaires a.i. of the Permanent Mission of Yugoslavia to the United Nations addressed to the President of the Security Council, 14 October 1998

S/1998/959, Letter from the Permanent Representative of Poland to the United Nations addressed to the President of the Security Council, 16 October 1998

S/1998/962, Letter from the Chargé d'affaires a.i. of the Permanent Mission of Yugoslavia to the United Nations addressed to the President of the Security Council, 16 October 1998

S/1998/963, Letter from the Permanent Representative of Canada to the United Nations addressed to the President of the Security Council, 16 October 1998

S/1998/966, Letter from the Secretary-General to the President of the Security Council, 14 October 1998

S/1998/978, Letter from the Permanent Representative of Poland to the United Nations addressed to the Secretary-General, 19 October 1998

S/1998/991, Letter from the Chargé d'affaires a.i. of the Mission of the United States of America to the United Nations addressed to the President of the Security Council, 22 October 1998

S/1998/993, Letter from the Chargé d'affaires a.i. of the Permanent Mission of Yugoslavia to the United Nations addressed to the President of the Security Council, 23 October 1998

S/1998/1068, Report of the Secretary-General prepared pursuant to resolutions 1160, 1199 and 1203 of the Security Council, 12 November 1998

S/PV.3937, Transcript of the 3937th Meeting of the Security Council, 24 October 1998

S/RES/1203, Resolution 1203 (1998) adopted 24 October 1998

General Assembly Resolution 53/164, Situation of Human Rights in Kosovo, 9 December 1998

Bibliography

S/1999/50, Letter from the Permanent Representative of Albania to the United Nations addressed to the President of the Security Council, 16 January 1999

S/1999/51, Letter from the Chargé d'affaires a.i. of the Permanent Mission of Yugoslavia to the United Nations addressed to the Secretary-General, 17 January 1999

S/1999/52, Letter from the Permanent Representative of Albania to the United Nations addressed to the Secretary-General, 18 January 1999

S/PRST/1999/2, Statement by the President of the Security Council, 19 January 1999

S/PV.3967, Transcript of the 3967th Meeting of the Security Council, 19 January 1999

S/1999/77, Letter from the Representatives of the Russian Federation and the United States of America to the United Nations addressed to the Secretary-General, 26 January 1999

S/1999/96, Letter from the Permanent Representative of the United Kingdom of Great Britain and Northern Ireland to the United Nations addressed to the President of the Security Council, 29 January 1999

S/PV.3974, Transcript of the 3974th Meeting of the Security Council, 29 January 1999

S/PRST/1999/5, Statement by the President of the Security Council, 29 January 1999

S/1999/107, Letter from the Chargé d'affaires a.i. of the Permanent Mission of Yugoslavia to the United Nations addressed to the President of the Security Council, 1 February 1999

S/1999/216, Report of the Chairman of UN Committee pursuant to Resolution 1160, 26 February 1999

S/1999/292, Letter from the Chargé d'affaires a.i. of the Permanent Mission of Yugoslavia to the United Nations addressed to the President of the Security Council, 17 March 1999

S/1999/293, Report of the Secretary-General prepared pursuant to Resolutions 1160, 1199 and 1203 of the Security Council, 17 March 1999

S/1999/320, Letter from the Permanent Representative of the Russian Federation to the United Nations addressed to the President of the Security Council, 24 March 1999

S/1999/322, Letter from the Chargé d'affaires a.i. of the Permanent Mission of Yugoslavia to the United Nations addressed to the President of the Security Council, 24 March 1999

S/1999/323, Letter from the Permanent Representative of Belarus to the United Nations addressed to the President of the Security Council, 24 March 1999

S/1999/327, Letter from the Chargé d'affaires a.i. of the Permanent Mission of Yugoslavia to the United Nations addressed to the President of the Security Council, 24 March 1999

S/PV.3988, Transcript of the 3988th Meeting of the Security Council, 24 March 1999

S/1999/332, Letter from the Permanent Representative of Belarus to the United Nations addressed to the Secretary-General, 24 March 1999

S/1999/331, Letter from the Permanent Representative of Tajikistan to the United Nations addressed to the Secretary-General, 25 March 1999

Bibliography

S/1999/335, Letter from the Permanent Representative of Ukraine to the United Nations addressed to the Secretary-General, 25 March 1999

S/1999/336, Letter from the Permanent Representative of Ukraine to the United Nations addressed to the Secretary-General, 25 March 1999

S/1999/338, Letter from the Secretary-General addressed to the President of the Security Council, 25 March 1999

S/1999/328, Draft resolution tabled by Belarus, India and Russian Federation, 26 March 1999

S/PV.3989, Transcript of the 3989th meeting of the Security Council, 26 March 1999

S/1999/516, Letter from the Permanent Representative of Germany to the United Nations addressed to the President of the Security Council, 6 May 1999

S/1999/523, Letter from the Permanent Representative of China to the United Nations addressed to the President of the Security Council, 7 May 1999

S/PV.4000, Transcript of the 4000th Meeting of the Security Council, 8 May 1999

S/1999/529, Letter from the Chargé d'affaires a.i. of the Permanent Mission of Yugoslavia to the United Nations addressed to the President of the Security Council, 9 May 1999

S/1999/530, Letter from the Permanent Representative of South Africa to the United Nations addressed to the President of the Security Council, 10 May 1999

S/1999/541, Letter from the Permanent Representative of the Sudan to the United Nations addressed to the President of the Security Council, 12 May 1999

S/1999/542, Letter from the Permanent Representative of Turkey to the United Nations addressed to the President of the Security Council, 12 May 1999

S/1999/552, Letter from the Permanent Representative of Qatar to the United Nations addressed to the President of the Security Council, 12 May 1999

S/PV.4001, Transcript of the 4001st Meeting of the Security Council, 14 May 1999

S/PRST/1999/12, Statement by the President of the Security Council, 14 May 1999

S/PV.4003, Transcript of the 4003rd Meeting of the Security Council, 14 May 1999

S/RES/1239, Resolution 1239 (1999), adopted 14 May 1999

S/1999/631, Letter from the Chargé d'affaires a.i. of the Permanent Mission of Yugoslavia to the United Nations addressed to the President of the Security Council, 1 June 1999

S/1999/650, Letter from the Chargé d'affaires a.i. of the Permanent Mission of Germany to the United Nations addressed to the Secretary-General, 2 June 1999

S/1999/646, Letter from the Chargé d'affaires a.i. of the Permanent Mission of Yugoslavia to the United Nations addressed to the Secretary-General, 5 June 1999

S/1999/647, Letter from the Chargé d'affaires a.i. of the Permanent Mission of Yugoslavia to the United Nations addressed to the President of the Security Council, 5 June 1999

S/1999/648, Letter from the Permanent Representative of France to the United Nations addressed to the Secretary-General, 7 June 1999

S/1999/649, Letter from the Permanent Representative of Germany to the United Nations addressed to the President of the Security Council, 7 June 1999

S/1999/655, Letter from the Chargé d'affaires a.i. of the Permanent Mission of Yugoslavia to the United Nations addressed to the President of the Security Council, 7 June 1999

S/1999/662, Letter from the Secretary-General addressed to the President of the Security Council, 9 June 1999
S/1999/663, Letter from the Secretary-General addressed to the President of the Security Council, 19 June 1999
S/PV.4011, Transcript of the 4011th Meeting of the Security Council, 10 June, 1999
S/RES/1244, Resolution 1244 (1999), adopted 10 June 1999
S/1999/779, Report of the Secretary-General on the United Nations Interim Administration Mission in Kosovo, 12 July 1999
S/1999/987, Report of the Secretary-General on the United Nations Interim Administration Mission in Kosovo, 26 October 1999
S/PV.4061, Official Communiqué of the 4061st Meeting of the Security Council, 5 November 1999 (meeting held in private, therefore no transcript)
General Assembly, A/RES/60/1, World Summit Outcome Document, 24 October 2005

The Hill Process documents

(Source unless otherwise stated: Weller, M., *The Crisis in Kosovo 1989–1999: From Dissolution of Yugoslavia to Rambouillet and the Outbreak of Hostilities*, vol. 1 (Cambridge: Documents & Analysis Publishing Ltd, 1999, Chapter 14)

FRY: Serbian government invites ethnic Albanians to Dialogue, 14 March 1998
FRY: Yugoslav President Milosevic calls for referendum, 2 April 1998
Serbian President Milutinovic issues statement on President Milosevic's letter, 2 April 1998
Serbian government proposes calling of a referendum, 2 April 1998
FRY: Letter of Serbian Vice-President to President of the Democratic Alliance of Kosovo, 26 April 1998
FRY: Ethnic Albanian Representatives fail to appear at talks once more, 28 April 1998
FRY: Serbian Vice-Premier Markovic invites minorities to talks on 12 May 1998
Statement on the talks of FRY President Milosevic with Dr Ibrahim Rugova and his Delegation, 15 April 1998
FRY on talks in Pristina, including statement by Albanian side read by B. Salja, 22 May 1998
Press release of the Minister of the Interior of the Republic of Serbia, 5 June 1998
First [Hill] Draft Agreement for a Settlement of the Crisis in Kosovo, 1 October 1998
Kosovo Statement on Fundamental Principles for a Settlement, 3 November 1998
Statement by Milan Milutinovic, President of Serb Republic, 18 November 1998
Concluding remarks by the President of the Republic of Serbia, Pristina, 18 November 1998
Joint Proposal on Political Framework of Self-Governance in Kosovo and Metohija, Belgrade, 20 November 1998
Declaration in Support of Joint Proposal for Agreement, Belgrade, 25 November 1998
Kosova Press Release: Hill draft plan should be further improved, 1 December 1998
Third Hill Draft Proposal for a Settlement of the Crisis in Kosovo, 2 December 1998

Bibliography

Kosova Press Release: UCK won't settle for anything less than full independence, 5 December 1998
Kosova Press Release: Demaci rejects Hill's Plan, 8 December 1998
Kosova Press Release: Kosovo Parliament's commissions discuss draft plan, 11 December 1998
Final Hill proposal, 27 January 1999

List of Rambouillet documents, 1999

(Source unless otherwise stated: Weller, M., *The Crisis in Kosovo 1989–1999: From Dissolution of Yugoslavia to Rambouillet and the Outbreak of Hostilities*, vol. 1 (Cambridge: Documents & Analysis Publishing Ltd, 1999, Chapter 15)

Joint Statement by Secretary of State Albright and Russian Foreign Minister Ivanov, Moscow, 26 January 1999
Statement to the Press by Dr Javier Solana, NATO Secretary-General, Brussels, 28 January 1999
Statement by UN Secretary-General to NAC, NATO HQ, Brussels, 29 January 1999
US Secretary of State Albright, Statement on NATO Final Warning on Kosovo, Washington, DC, 30 January 1999
Response of Kosova to Views Adopted by the Contact Group, 30 January 1999
Address by Mr Jacques Chirac, President of the Republic, Rambouillet, 6 February 1999
Opening Remarks by Robin Cook, UK Secretary of State, Rambouillet, 6 February 1999
Interim Agreement for Peace and Self-Government in Kosovo, Initial Draft, 6 February 1999
Statement of both delegations on a bomb explosion in Pristina, 7 February 1999
Press Briefing by the three Negotiators, Rambouillet, 9 February 1999
Secretary of State Albright, Briefing following Contact Group meeting, 14 February 1999
Press Briefing by Spokesman for Contact Group Negotiators, Rambouillet, 16 February 1999
Joint Press Briefing given by Messrs Vedrine and Cook, Paris, 17 February 1999
Letter from Delegation of Kosova to Contact Group Negotiators, Rambouillet, 17 February 1999
Interim Agreement for Peace and Self-Government in Kosovo, 2nd Draft, 18 February 1999
Press Briefing by the Contact Group Negotiators, 18 February 1999
Kosova Delegation Statement on New Proposal for a Settlement, 18 February 1999
Draft Chapter 5, Implementation I, 19 February 1999
President Clinton and President Chirac, Joint Press Conference, Washington, DC, 19 February 1999
James Rubin, US Press Briefing, Rambouillet, 20 February 1999
Secretary of State Albright, Press Conference on Kosovo, France, 20 February 1999

Bibliography

Department of State Spokesman Briefing on Kosovo peace talks, Rambouillet, 20 February 1999
James Rubin, Press Briefing on the Kosovo peace talks, Rambouillet, 21 February 1999
Draft for Chapter 8, Article 1 (3), 22 February 1999, 05.25 hrs, and proposed draft side-letter
Joint Press Conference by the Two Co-Chairmen, Rambouillet, 23 February 1999
Press Conference, Rambouillet, 23 February 1999
Letter from the FRY/Serb Delegation to the Negotiators, 23 February 1999
James Rubin, Interview, Rambouillet, 23 February 1999
Interim Agreement for Peace and Self-Government in Kosovo, 23 February 1999
Co-Chairmen's conclusions on the Rambouillet Accords, 23 February 1999
Joint Press Conference by the two co-Chairmen, Rambouillet, 23 February 1999
Secretary of State Albright, Press Conference, Rambouillet, 23 February 1999

Paris Conference, March 1999

(Source unless otherwise stated: Weller, M., *The Crisis in Kosovo 1989–1999: From Dissolution of Yugoslavia to Rambouillet and the Outbreak of Hostilities*, vol. 1 (Cambridge: Documents & Analysis Publishing Ltd, 1999, Chapter 16)

Cook–Vedrine Statement on Kosovo, 5 March 1999
US Envoy Senator Dole and Amb. Hill, Press Conference, US Embassy, London, 6 March 1999
Press Statement by James Rubin, US Spokesman, 10 March 1999
Letter from Hashim Thaci, Chairman of the Presidency of the Kosova Delegation, 15 March 1999
FRY Revised Draft Agreement, 15 March 1999
Letter from the three Negotiators to Head of Republic of Serbia Delegation, 16 March 1999
Declaration submitted by Kosovo to Negotiators upon Signature of the Rambouillet Accords, 18 March 1999
Kosovo Statement on Formal Signing of Interim Agreement for Peace and Self-government, 18 March 1999
Department of State Daily Press Briefing, Washington, DC, 18 March 1999
Secretary of State Albright, Remarks on Developments in Kosovo, Washington, DC, 18 March 1999
Statement by the Co-Chairs of the Contact Group, France, 19 March 1999
President Clinton, Excerpt from Press Conference, Washington, DC, 19 March 1999
Ambassador Holbrooke, Interview on ABC's Nightline, 24 March 1999
Statement made by UN Secretary-General on NATO military action against Yugoslavia, 24 March 1999

Bibliography

UK Government documents

(Source unless otherwise stated: Weller, M., *The Crisis in Kosovo 1989–1999: From Dissolution of Yugoslavia to Rambouillet and the Outbreak of Hostilities*, vol. 1 (Cambridge: Documents & Analysis Publishing Ltd, 1999)

Statement by the Prime Minister, Tony Blair, in the House of Commons, Tuesday, 23 March 1999
'Robin Cook's speech on the government's ethical foreign policy', Monday, May 12 1997, Guardian Unlimited: www.guardian.co.uk/ethical/article/0,2763,192031,00.html (accessed 8 December 2011)
Cook, Robin: 'Foreign policy and human rights', Foreign Affairs Committee, 6 January 1998: www.publications.parliament.uk/pa/cm199899/cmselect/cmfaff/100/8010605.htm 255 (accessed 1 June 2011)
Select Committee on Foreign Affairs, Minutes of Evidence, 6 January 1998, Examination of witnesses, the Rt Hon Robin Cook MP: www.publications.parliament.uk/pa/cm199899/cmselect/cmfaff/100/8010605.htm (accessed 8 December 2011)
Memorandum by the Foreign and Commonwealth Office (Foreign Policy and Human Rights, January 1998): www.publications.parliament.uk/pa/cm199900/cmselect/cmfaff/28/9111803.htm (accessed 8 December 2011)
Edited transcript of Press Conference by Prime Minister Tony Blair, Berlin, 24 March 1999
UK Parliamentary Testimony on the Threat or Use of Force, November 1998 and January 1999

Contact Group documents

(Source unless otherwise stated: Weller, M., *The Crisis in Kosovo 1989–1999: From Dissolution of Yugoslavia to Rambouillet and the Outbreak of Hostilities*, vol. 1 (Cambridge: Documents & Analysis Publishing Ltd, 1999)

Statement of the Contact Group Foreign Ministers, New York, 24 September 1997
Contact Group Statement on Kosovo, 8 January 1998
Statement by the Contact Group on Kosovo, Moscow, 25 February 1998
Statement by the Contact Group, London, 9 March 1998
Joint Statement of Foreign Ministers of Countries of Southeastern Europe, Bonn, 25 March 1998
Contact Group and the Foreign Ministers of Canada and Japan, Statement, London, 12 June 1998
Contact Group Statement, Bonn, 8 July 1998
Chairman's Conclusions, Contact Group meeting on Kosovo in London, 2 October 1998
Contact Group Discussion on Kosovo, Statement by UK Foreign Secretary, 8 October 1998
Contact Group Statement, London, 29 January 1999

Bibliography

Contact Group Non-negotiable Principles/Basic Elements, 30 January 1999
Chairman's Conclusions, Contact Group Meeting, Paris, 14 February 1999
Statement by Madeleine Albright at the Contact Group Ministerial on Kosovo, London, 9 March 1998: http://secretary.state.gov/www/statements/1998/980309.html (accessed 8 December 2011)
Conclusions of the Contact Group, Rambouillet, 20 February 1999

NATO documents

(Source unless otherwise stated: Weller, M., *The Crisis in Kosovo 1989–1999: From Dissolution of Yugoslavia to Rambouillet and the Outbreak of Hostilities*, vol. 1 (Cambridge: Documents & Analysis Publishing Ltd, 1999)

NAC Statement on the situation in Kosovo, 5 March 1998
NAC statement on the situation in Kosovo, 30 April 1998
Statement of Ministerial Meeting, NAC, 28 May 1998
Statement issued at the meeting of the NAC in Defence Ministers session, 11 June 1998
Statement by NATO Secretary-General on Exercise 'Determined Falcon', 13 June 1998
Statement by NATO Secretary-General following ACTWARN Decision, Vilamoura, 24 September 1998
NATO statements and approval of the Activation Warning, 24 September 1998
Statement to the Press by NATO Secretary-General, Dr Javier Solana, 29 January 1999
Statement to the Press by NATO Secretary-General, Dr Javier Solana, 30 January 1999
Statement by the NAC on Kosovo, 30 January 1999
NATO–Russia Permanent Joint Council Meeting at Ambassadorial level, NATO HQ, 17 February 1999
Statement by the NATO Secretary-General on behalf of the NAC, 19 February 1999
Statement by the Secretary-General of NATO on the outcome of the Rambouillet talks, 23 February 1999
NATO–Russia Permanent Joint Council Meeting at Ambassadorial Level, 17 March 1999
Statement by the NAC on the situation in Kosovo, 22 March 1999
Press Statement by Dr Javier Solana, Secretary-General of NATO, 23 March 1999
NATO Press Release: Political and Military Objectives of Action with Regard to Kosovo, 23 March 1999
Press Statement by the NATO Secretary-General following the commencement of air operations, 24 March 1999
Statement by Secretary General following decision on the ACTORD, 13 October 1998
NATO/FRY Kosovo Verification Mission Agreement, FRY, 15 October 1998
Press points by NATO Secretary-General, 15 October 1998
NATO Statement on Kosovo following NAC meeting, 16 October 1998
Record of NATO–Serbia/FRY meeting, 25 October 1998
Statement by NATO Secretary-General following NAC meeting, 27 October 1998
NAC Press Statement, 19 November 1998
Letter dated 27 October 1998 from the Secretary-General of NATO addressed to the UN Secretary-General

Bibliography

Miscellaneous communications

(Source unless otherwise stated: Weller, M., *The Crisis in Kosovo 1989–1999: From Dissolution of Yugoslavia to Rambouillet and the Outbreak of Hostilities*, vol. 1, (Cambridge: Documents & Analysis Publishing Ltd, 1999)

Letter from Dr Rugova to Lord Carrington, Peace Conference on Yugoslavia, 22 December 1991
Letter from Lord Carrington, Chairman, Conference on Yugoslavia to Dr I. Rugova, 17 August 1992
Kosovo Memorandum to the International Conference on the Former Yugoslavia, 26 August 1992
Opinion No. 1 of the Arbitration Commission on the former Yugoslavia, 11 January 1992
Cook, R. 'Mission Statement', 12 May 1997: www.guardian.co.uk/indonesia/Story/0,2763,190889,00.html (accessed 24 November 2010)
US Representative to OSCE, Statement at Extraordinary OSCE PC Meeting, Vienna, 18 January 1998
OSCE Permanent Council Decision No. 218, 11 March 1998
President Clinton, Address to the Nation, Washington, DC, 24 March 1999
Remarks by US President on Kosovo, 8 October 1998
Statement by Secretary of State Albright on Kosovo, 8 October 1998
Serbian government endorses accord reached by President Milosevic, Belgrade, 13 October 1998
OSCE–FRY Verification Mission Agreement, 16 October 1998
Letter from the FRY to the UN Secretary-General, 23 October 1998
Albright's remarks on Kosovo, 27 October 1998
Press Conference by Richard Holbrooke and William Walker, 28 October 1998
Press Conference by Richard Holbrooke and William Walker, 29 October 1998
Kosovo statement on Fundamental Principles for a Settlement, 3 November 1998

Index

Note: 'n' after a page reference indicates the number of a note on that page.

Ahtisaari, Martti 163
Albright, Madeleine 66–7, 161–2, 167, 175, 182
Alexy, Robert 134, 138
alternative peace proposals 59–60
Apel, Karl-Otto vii
Arendt, Hannah 11, 134, 148–51
  on Eichmann 150
  see also reflective judgement
'argumentative self-entrapment' 83–4
  see also Risse

Badinter Arbitration Commission 45, 55–6, 178, 191
Balkans 46, 49, 51, 160, 167, 176, 178, 180, 191
Battle of Kosovo Polje 46, 48
Bellamy, Alex J. 4, 32, 41n58, 56
Benhabib, Seyla 111, 118–19, 125, 138, 148, 150, 198
Bjola, Corneliu 77, 84, 89–93, 192
Blair, Tony 62–3, 67, 174–5
Blaug, Ricardo 139, 145–7, 148, 150
Boréus, Kristina 137, 143
Bull, Hedley 25

Campbell, David 8, 49–50
Carr, E. H. 145

Carrington, Peter (Lord) 57
cheap talk 82
Chernomyrdin, Viktor 163
China 26, 62–5, 67–9, 92, 166, 170–1, 173, 193, 196
Clark, Howard 50, 52, 54–5
Clark, Ian 35
Claude, Inis 2
Clinton, Bill 67, 86
communicative distortion 10, 31, 78, 80, 91, 105, 107, 109, 111, 113, 121, 124–5, 134, 150–1, 161, 166, 170, 172, 174, 177, 181, 190–1, 197–8, 199, 200
  constraints 89, 146, 151–2, 164, 168, 180–1, 183–4, 194–5
  pathologies 13
communicative imperatives 3, 10–11, 13, 95, 119, 126, 134–5, 139–40, 144–7, 150–2, 157, 178–9, 183–4, 190–2, 199
  coercion 10, 13, 31, 33, 36, 66, 69, 94, 115, 119, 136–41, 143, 157, 165–8, 173, 175, 180, 191, 194, 195, 199
  coherence 93, 135, 141, 175–8, 191
  as critique 7, 11, 27–8, 37, 105, 109, 125, 133–6, 150–1, 194,

198–9, 200
diversity 135–6, 139–40, 173
exclusion 4–5, 10, 13, 21, 36, 45, 51, 54–6, 58, 69, 70, 91, 95, 112, 115, 136–7, 143, 147, 157–9, 161–4, 172–3, 179, 183–4, 191, 196, 199–200
as fairness 31, 89, 112, 119, 128n44, 146, 148, 163, 197–8, 200
inclusion 4, 21, 51, 56–7, 69, 89, 94–5, 115, 125, 135–7, 146, 158–61, 163, 165, 198, 200
limitations of 151, 184, 197, 199
as normative 2–3, 9, 11, 13, 33, 36, 105–6, 108, 125, 133, 135, 138, 191–2
recognition 13, 122, 125, 135–6, 143–4, 157, 160, 181–2, 196, 198
reflexivity 13, 89, 93, 135, 142, 145–6, 161, 170, 178–80, 191
'communicative turn' 2, 8, 9, 79, 109, 184
positivism, critique of 8, 78, 80, 106, 146
constructivism 2, 9, 11–12, 27, 33, 77–84, 95, 124, 172, 184, 190, 196, 197–8
Contact Group 63, 91–3, 158–61, 164–9, 176, 180
Cook, Robin 44, 63, 161, 166
Cooke, Maeve 108
cosmopolitanism 5, 8, 109, 115–16, 123, 125, 144
 see also Linklater
counterfactual 37n5, 54, 183, 196
Cox, Robert 26, 79–80
Crawford, Neta 28, 30
critical theory 2, 8–11, 27, 33, 77–81, 85, 93–4, 106, 115, 117, 119, 133, 144–6, 178, 184, 196–7,

199–200
Cŭbrilović, Vaso 46

Daalder, Ivo 170
Dayton Accords 4, 45, 57–61
deliberative democracy 106, 121, 136
deliberative legitimacy 84, 89, 90, 91, 93, 192
 see also Bjola
Democratic League of Kosovo (LDK) 45, 52–5, 58–60, 62
Drenica 61, 179
Dunne, Tim 25–7

Eckersley, Robyn 10, 200
Elshtain, Jean Bethke 121
emancipation 78, 80, 105–6, 117, 124, 133, 145–6
empathy 148–9
English School 3, 24–5, 27, 192
ethnic cleansing 5, 28–9, 67, 175, 181, 193
European Community Conference on Yugoslavia 55–6, 191
Evans, Gareth 23

Falk, Richard 35, 69
fallibility 122, 134, 142, 146
Fay, Brian 145–6
Federal Republic of Yugoslavia (FRY) 36, 56, 58, 62–5, 67, 69, 91, 159, 182, 164–7, 169, 170, 172 176–8, 181–2, 191, 196, 198
feminism 77, 79, 119, 120, 124–5, 136
Fierke, K. M. 12, 54, 83, 105
Fishkin, James 137
Forester, John 84, 107, 112–13
Franck, Thomas 141
Frankfurt School 8, 10, 77, 79–80, 94, 106, 108

Index

G-8 163
Gadamer, Hans-Georg 122–3
Gelbard, Robert 181
Gilligan, Carol 114, 120
good international citizenship 3, 21–7, 36, 144, 192–5

Habermas, Jürgen
  communicative action 3, 10, 12–13, 33, 77, 79, 81–2, 84, 87–9, 93–4, 106, 108–10, 115, 125, 134, 138–9, 161, 164, 171–3, 195, 200
  communicative competence 109, 124
  communicative rationality 10, 88, 105, 108, 121
  discourse ethics 8–9, 11, 33, 84, 93, 95, 105–6, 108–9, 111–13, 115–16, 118–19, 120–5, 134, 136, 147, 149, 151, 199, 200
  ideal speech situation 84, 105–6, 109, 111–12, 119, 121, 139, 184, 197, 199
  lifeworld 87, 90, 105, 107–9, 120
  limitations of theory 9, 11, 113–14, 122, 145–6, 151, 184, 197
  on Kosovo 5–7, 35
  post-conventional morality 116–17, 123
  presuppositions of argumentation 12, 87, 105, 108–9, 111, 118, 124–5, 134, 138, 148, 197
  principle of Discourse (D) 109, 111, 118, 149
  principle of Universalization (U) 109, 111, 118–20, 123, 125, 140, 148–9, 197–9
  public sphere 77, 90, 108, 120, 136, 140, 149
  strategic action 12–13, 78–9, 82, 93, 105, 108, 138, 142, 152, 162, 164, 171–2, 192, 197, 199
  system 105, 107–8, 120
hermeneutics 122–4, 140, 175
Hill, Christopher 64–5, 162, 166, 180
Holbrooke
  Agreement 45, 64, 66, 93, 162, 166–7, 179, 196, 199
  Holbrooke, Richard 57–8, 64, 161–2
  negotiations 13, 157, 183, 191
Honneth, Axel 143
Hopgood, Stephen 116
humanitarian intervention
  dilemma of 1, 5–6, 22, 55, 180
  justification 1–3, 5, 7–10, 13, 22–3, 27–31, 35, 37, 45, 67–9, 81–3, 86, 89, 124, 157, 173–4, 178, 180
  pluralism 3, 23–6, 34–5, 39n28, 45, 56, 68, 92, 115, 165, 174, 191–3
  solidarism 3, 23–6, 28, 30–1, 34–5, 39n31, 45, 68, 86, 115, 165, 169, 174, 191–3
Hurrell, Andrew 33

Independent International Commission on Kosovo (IICK) 21, 23, 28–9, 35–6, 190
indeterminacy 11, 56, 86, 150
instrumental rationality 78, 82, 106–8, 113
International Commission on Intervention and State Sovereignty (ICISS) 1, 3, 28, 193–4
International Conference on Former Yugoslavia 45
interpretive community 86–9, 124, 139
intersubjective 1, 2, 8–9, 11–12, 31, 81–2, 86–7, 108–10, 112, 114,

233

119, 125, 136, 141, 144–6, 148, 158, 164, 184, 198

Jackson, Robert 24, 51, 68
Johnstone, Ian 77, 81, 84–90, 94, 108, 192
Judah, Tim 47, 53, 57–8, 161, 177
judgement 32, 86, 124, 143, 147–8, 196
  determinant 147–8
  political 2, 11, 31, 151, 179
  reflective 11, 114, 134, 148–51, 198–9
  see also Arendt
just war tradition 28, 29, 31, 194
  jus ad bellum 1, 194
  just cause 29
  last resort 1, 2, 4, 13, 29–30, 45, 51, 62, 68–9, 91, 93, 138–40, 158, 168, 171–3, 180, 194–6
  proportionality 30
  right authority 29, 40n51, 194
  right intention 29
justification 27–8, 31–3, 36, 93, 109–11, 114, 125, 133–4, 136, 138, 140, 158, 170–1, 179, 183, 198
  and application 37, 93, 114, 125, 134, 141, 145, 147, 150
  legal 1, 3, 22, 27, 81, 84–6, 88, 175
  moral 1, 22, 27, 35, 133, 174–5

Kadaré, Ismail 182
Kant, Immanuel 109–10, 136, 147–9, 158
  categorical imperative 109, 158
Kohlberg, Lawrence 116, 120
Kosovo
  constitutional status of 45–9, 51–3, 55–7, 59, 61, 64, 162, 165–6, 176–8, 183
  deliberative process 90–1, 125–6, 166
  ethnic identity (history and as cause of conflict) 4, 10, 45, 47–50, 69, 166, 176
  Martinović, Djordje 47
  non-violent resistance 4, 14, 45, 49–54, 57, 59–62, 69, 93, 175, 180, 184, 191–2, 195–6
  parallel state 50, 53–5, 59–61
  politics of 45–9, 52, 57–9, 160, 185n16
Kosovo Liberation Army (KLA) 47, 51, 59, 61–3, 66, 91, 158–9, 160, 162, 164, 167, 169, 170, 177, 181–2, 191, 196
Kratochwil, Friedrich 82

language of manoeuvre 12, 83, 129
  see also Fierke; strategic action
legitimacy
  communicative ethics as a principle of 151
  critical communicative dimension 2–4, 13, 21–2, 27–8, 31, 33–4, 40n51, 44, 147, 190, 194
  illegitimacy 2, 33, 36, 121, 125, 129n55, 142, 145, 157–8, 168, 183–4, 199
  immanent claims to 3, 80, 84, 93–4, 106, 157, 165, 191, 198
  legal 2, 5–7, 13, 21–3, 26–7, 30–1, 33–6, 45, 81, 83, 85–6, 89, 93, 113, 175, 196
  moral 2–4, 6–7, 13, 21, 23–4, 26–7, 31, 33–6, 45, 89, 93, 107, 113, 140, 151, 174–5, 180, 183–4, 190, 193, 196
  as procedural 2, 7, 11, 30–1, 33, 35, 37, 68, 84, 90, 105–6, 109, 112, 119, 125, 134, 142, 146, 150, 159, 166, 168,

178–9, 184, 191–2, 194–5, 197–9
  as substantive 35
  temporal dimension 4, 13, 44, 93–4, 157, 178, 192, 195–6, 198
  see also justification
Linklater, Andrew 10, 23, 25, 27, 39n28, 39n31, 79–80, 94, 115–6, 144, 193
  see also good international citizenship
London Conference 57

Milošević, Slobodan 48, 51–2, 57, 59, 63–5, 67, 162–3, 167, 171, 182, 185n16
missing dialogues 51, 70, 195
moral norms 6–7, 93, 109, 114, 125, 134, 149, 198
Müller, Harald 94

NATO 1, 21, 62–4, 66–8, 163, 167, 173, 175, 190
  Activation Order 65
  Operation Determined Falcon 63

O'Hanlon, Michael 170
O'Neill, Shane 199
Orford, Anne 4
OSCE 55, 65, 160, 164, 178
  Kosovo Verification Mission 65–6

post-structuralism 8–9, 79, 109
praxeological dimension 9, 95, 116, 200
preconditions 62, 91, 93, 115, 164–6, 168, 178, 183, 198
Price, Richard 94–5

Račak 66
Rambouillet negotiations 13, 66, 69, 157, 160, 162–3, 166–70, 172–3, 175, 179, 183
  military implementation agreement 169–70
rationalism 27, 33–4, 78, 79, 82, 120
realism 8–9, 12, 31, 34–5, 49, 61, 78–9, 82, 89, 109, 145
relationship between communicative and strategic rationalities 12, 79, 82, 88–9, 108, 139, 171–2, 195, 197, 200
responsibility to protect 3, 21–2, 24, 28–9, 31–2, 36, 192–5
  Darfur 32
Reus-Smit, Christian 81, 94–5, 197–8
Risse, Thomas 83–4, 87, 94
Rubin, James 167, 169
Rugova, Ibrahim 52–5, 57–9, 62, 160–1, 169, 177, 179
Russia 6, 22, 26, 62, 63–5, 67–9, 85–6, 89, 91–2, 161, 163, 166–7, 171–3, 193, 195–6

Saward, Michael 140
Sell, Louis 55, 63
Shapcott, Richard 116–17
Skinner, Quentin 83, 88, 139
Socialist Federal Republic of Yugoslavia (SFRY) 55, 159
Suganami, Hidemi 25, 39n28, 39n31

Talbott, Strobe 163
theory of communicative action 2, 5, 7–8, 11, 13, 33, 78, 94, 107, 112–13, 115, 124, 147, 197
  see also Habermas
threshold criteria for humanitarian intervention 29–30, 62, 171, 173, 193
trade-offs 142, 146, 150, 161, 179, 197

United Nations Charter 22–3, 62, 65, 67, 85, 159, 178, 193
United Nations Security Council
  authorisation 22–3, 28, 63, 65, 178, 193, 195
  Resolutions
    1160 62–3, 65, 89, 159, 164
    1199 63, 65, 89
    1203 65, 89, 162, 179
    Russian draft resolution 67–8, 171–2, 178, 195
  veto 6, 22, 27, 63–4, 158, 161, 163, 193–4
universal pragmatics 10, 13
uti possidetis 55–6

validity claims 11, 90, 93, 110–11, 113, 133, 139, 141, 150–1, 158, 165, 171, 175, 177, 183

Walzer, Michael 195
Weller, Marc 57, 167–9
Wellmer, Albrecht 144
Wheeler, Nicholas J. 25–31, 40n51
White, Stephen K. 9
Wight, Martin 21, 32
Wolin, Sheldon 89

Young, Iris M. 120–1

Zolo, Danilo 7

EU authorised representative for GPSR:
Easy Access System Europe, Mustamäe tee 50,
10621 Tallinn, Estonia
gpsr.requests@easproject.com

www.ingramcontent.com/pod-product-compliance
Ingram Content Group UK Ltd.
Pitfield, Milton Keynes, MK11 3LW, UK
UKHW021848140426
52171PUK00022B/1652